SCATTERED HOMES – BROKEN HEARTS

By

VICKY NORMAN

EDITED

By

JOY DAVID

COVER ILLUSTRATIONS

By

SHIRLEY HOLE

D1344527

ACKNOWLEDGEMENTS

The Author tenders sincere thanks to everyone too numerous to mention who gave useful information. I am indebted to Author Joy David who edited this book and made available her wealth of experience and graciously introduced me to the contacts needed making this publication possible. I must also thank Trudie Hodge whose unfailing support has been invaluable. Grateful thanks to my very special friends Jewel and Raymond Vittle who have given me support throughout the production of this book and for their belief in me. Real friendship is a very precious thing.

ISBN 0-9540974-1-6
JDC Publications
Copyright Vicky Norman 2002

Printers: Bendles Print Limited of Torquay.

INTRODUCTION

This book is in memory of all past and present Scattered Homes and Stoke House children who suffered many heartaches when finding themselves unwanted, abandoned or orphaned, and placed in foster care or institutions for financial expediency. Wherever you live, or whatever you do, know that you are not forgotten and that you have been the generation, who endured loss of parents and family life, coupled with the horrific war years. Let your true stories prove a revelation in preventing children of the future being neglected and cruelly treated, and most of all to arouse public awareness of the need to keep brother and sister together and to treat all foster children with love. The Author extends an apology to anyone inadvertently offended and to inform all readers that every effort has been made to obtain copyright from the correct sources. Should any reader question copyright please accept this as a genuine mistake.

JUST A THOUGHT

LOOK TO THIS DAY, FOR IT IS LIFE-THE VERY LIFE OF LIFE.
FOR YESTERDAY IS BUT A DREAM AND TOMORROW IS ONLY A VISION.
BUT TODAY-WELL LIVED-MAKES EVERY YESTERDAY
A DREAM OF HAPPINESS AND EVERY TOMORROW A VISION OF HOPE. (ANON)

I dedicate this book to my dear Grandfather and Grandmother: Mr Albert Edward Foster and Mrs Harriet (Nell) Helen Beatrice Foster (nee Parsonage) and my Aunt and Uncle (second Mum and Dad) Albert Edward Foster and Mrs Muriel Emily Elizabeth Foster (nee Burch).

The Winds of Love blow softly on my face as I whisper your names...

CONTENTS.

FOREWORD

Some six months ago Vicky Norman approached me to help her in getting **Scattered Homes – Broken Hearts** published. Quite frankly I did not want the task but having met this very determined, dedicated lady, it was simpler to give in – and I am glad I did!

I grew up in Plymouth in the 1930's and 1940's and had not an inkling of the suffering, the misery, the hopelessness and despair that was being experienced by so many of the city's children. Vicky Norman was one of these children, orphaned at the age of two. It is her careful research, her seeking out of information and the organisation of two reunions for these children, now, like her, mainly in their seventies and eighties, which has resulted in a remarkable book after four year's of determined hard work, undaunted by the many set backs she has suffered at the hands of Government departments.

The book is full of heartache, full of expectation, full of memories. As you read it you feel the sorrow of these children, the desire for love and for tangible affection. You read of the horror of the Plymouth Blitz; Vicky herself was buried alive during one raid. Its moments of tragedy are lifted by entertaining accounts of the sort of toys, the games played and the various comics of that era together with the indomitable spirit that has carried these children throughout their lives.

I cannot imagine any reader not being moved by the contents of 'Scattered Homes-Broken Hearts' and oddly enough entertained at the same time.

Joy David
January 2002

CHAPTER ONE

THE QUEST & REUNIONS

And has the truth brought no New Hope at all?
Heart that you're weeping yet for Paradise?
(Rupert Brooke: 1905-1908)

I am just a very ordinary person, so how can I explain my reason for writing this book? It has come about because of a continuing nightmare that I cannot get rid of, a subconscious heartache that is beyond logical reasoning. Behind the nightmare is the quest of finding out the truth, which had been denied me and the hurt, which has haunted me for sixty years. Why do I still wake after the same dream? I awake sobbing with real tears rolling down my cheeks at the age of eight at the New Inn in Clovelly, North Devon, in 1941. My heart is heavy and there is a feeling of rejection. How can I clarify this nonsense with a clear answer, the truth is I cannot, and my only help will be in finding the truth. There is an old saying: "Truth will Out!" Little did I know what I had let myself in for. It is said there is one book in each of us that can be written, however, any reader thinking of writing one, beware! For the road is long and the cost expensive.

After the search for my own personal records, which proved partially successful, I began the search for my childhood friends. My quest took me back to Clovelly, North Devon to meet one of the villagers, Sheila Ellis, who has spent her whole life in Clovelly and whose family were closely associated with the children at the New Inn 1941-1945. Another meeting was with Harry Clement (BEM) who was a London Evacuee sent to Clovelly in 1940, he never forgot his childhood and after serving in the Army and the Police Force he moved back to the village he loved on his retirement. Both he and Sheila Ellis encouraged me in my search for contacts. I organised two reunions; one that was held in Plymouth in 1997, which local dignitaries attended, and a very special group of former old school friends came from Clovelly. The other reunion in 1998 was held at Clovelly, North Devon.

Our wartime Teacher came from Bristol and ex-evacuees travelled from many parts of the country to attend the nostalgic reunion. Former school friends and Clovelly villagers gave us a wonderful reception. The local press and television that had supported us with our enquiries to obtain answers covered the reunion. The authorities were very apprehensive and there was a deep disquiet as I persisted in asking for information that had been withheld for many years. It was then that I realised there were many people out there who had been in the same position as myself, who still did not know the truth about their lives as children and now in their twilight years wanted to know their roots. Genealogy research is becoming more and more popular as awareness of family history gains importance. The research was long and the task arduous trying to breach stringent bureaucratic rules. Department clerks simply said "All the records were destroyed in the war" or " They are no longer held." On pointing out that a seventy-five year ban had been placed on our records and that legal regulations would not allow the records to be destroyed prior to their release date, meant that the authorities were obliged to have an in depth search. Interdepartmental meetings were held and access to some public record registers was restricted. I formed an opinion that a book was needed to highlight the many years of secret heartache the ex-scattered homes former residents had endured.

Then once in a while I would approach someone who was keen on family history, or were themselves interested in my quest for answers. Experienced researchers in the records office gave me avenues to explore and guided me, on how and where, to search for evidence. Because of these caring people, who had pointed me in the right direction, I obtained the first clues and from my research evidence began to emerge. Bleary-eyed and tired but with determined resolve; I searched the Record Offices, Libraries, and Museums and wrote many letters and pursued the authorities for answers. I pounded the streets and knocked on doors. Friends began to question my sanity and some acquaintances who would often speak to me suddenly drifted away into obscurity when I refused to quit, and there were of course the 'Pretend' and 'Fine weather' friends who vanished when difficulties arose, thankfully my genuine friends remained fully supportive. Soon I became a thorn in everyone's side as I refused to be deterred or brushed off with veiled answers. Emotions were high and without question difficult to suppress.

I asked myself, "Should I go on?" "How many more people would be hurt?" "Could I ever find out the truth?" Again I questioned my reasoning, "Do I have the courage of my conviction to continue with the book, or do I call it a day as a lost cause?"

Then came the anonymous phone calls and letters from people anxious to tell me about the abuse and cruelty which had been covered up for so many years. Later came the letters of encouragement from the ex-children of Stoke House and Scattered Homes, and through the letterbox their stories started to arrive at my home. Many wished to prevent the next generation of foster children from suffering the same indifference about their records and facing many years of heartache and mystery. Those who have taken the opportunity to give their names and present their stories triggered many emotive feelings, but it proved that even after so many years they still wanted to know the truth. When questioning the local population of Stoke, Plymouth, about Stoke House, it was unbelievable that many had never heard of it's existence or said "Ah Yes! Stoke House - there are many tales to tell about that place!

Seeking the true stories led to many visits and searching for the lost generation was a real challenge. Sometimes it was successful and sometimes it was fruitless. Opinions were divided. Remarks that would be made were: The truth should be known! Why the secrecy? I want to know if I have brothers or sisters! What is my heritage? Where did I come from? Others commented, I will help in anyway I can! It is not fair keeping our records for seventy-five years! What are the authorities hiding? Conversely, comments were let sleeping dogs lie! You could be opening a can of worms! Sweep it under the mat and forget it! I do not want to know it is too painful - I want to forget! One or two stated; Too many bridges to cross - I am still ashamed of my background! I do not want my sons and daughters to know! It will open up old wounds! You are wrong to seek answers; too many people will be hurt! My answer was simple: What of our feelings? We the victims of past social hierarchy decisions who had the right to know! Of course it opened up old wounds, the inner scars of wounded hearts can never be healed, but knowing the truth could help in reasoning and understanding with logic the loss of a normal childhood.

For many years I have wondered about my own very mixed fortunes as a child and what really happened to my sisters. When I had been taken into care I did not see them again and was not to know that two of my sisters died whilst I lived with my foster parents. The agony of finding out two sisters had lived in the same city as me, yet never spending any time together was most distressing. Constantly frustrated at my questions from other family members throughout the years being passed over as "That is water under the bridge" or "I don't remember". There were other sayings of avoiding awkward questions such as "I don't know for sure" or "Well it does not matter now!" How wrong, because it did matter to me! Ironically it is sometimes revealed that certain members of a child's family are covering up periods of guilt! Children should be told the truth to enable them to put it in the right perspective of life. The utter blind alley approach to block the citizens from having their own records by putting long years of closed access on them, such as one hundred or seventy-five years is not acceptable. When other bodies were asked to search for the records, for example, the Salvation Army, the information was unavailable as it was deemed classified.

People in position of authority in the 1930's/1940's did not give a clear and fair assessment of the child in their care, and many citizens asking for their records today have had missing pieces of the jig saw puzzle of their lives withheld. Certain information important to them was deleted from their record when visited by the departmental visitor, they were not fully co-operative with all the information when visiting the recipient and although counselled by an experienced social worker it still left many of us with unanswered questions.

In contacting the people and writing these stories of former children, who had experienced life in the Scattered Homes and Stoke House environment, meant that it raised controversial issues which still held very painful memories for them, and little did I know what an emotive subject it would be, the strain of writing this book has been an emotional nightmare but one that has to be told. Some of the stories written are of the ex-residents own accounts, and in some instances sons and daughters have insisted on knowing the truth and encouraged them to write their stories. Others only now, have found out that their genealogy family tree is not what they had assumed, and try to hide it from their own children still ashamed of the stigma which had surrounded their lives, reluctant to talk about it and deeply distressed at even the mention of scattered homes. Others have begun the search for missing siblings.

One fact has emerged from the production of this book and that is the feeling of anger and rejection. Some still re-act strongly to the authorities of that era, stating clearly that they were not favourably impressed and hating the system still for what it did to their young lives. Remember in a children's home there is no escape, children were treated almost like prisoners and the psychological scars are impossible to heal. Some of the former residents have made a pilgrimage back to Clovelly, that little North Devon village where they were evacuated in 1941, which became a haven from the tyranny of the Scattered Homes and Stoke House. The reunion eased their troubled minds and they reminisced about the good times they had enjoyed in Clovelly that had made their lives more bearable.

The quest did result in locating the records which still do exist and evidence emerged confirming their storage points at Exeter and Plymouth in Devon, and at Kew in London. Most satisfying of all was locating the original Stoke House Deeds, which are still held by the Plymouth City Council, however, I had to knock on many doors before the official representatives finally relented. The Government Act granting the citizens the right to know opened the way to finding some of the answers. Credit must go to the Plymouth Authorities who once "Awakened" by the obvious emotive subject, and knowing the people seeking answers was supported by the local press and television, were suddenly confronted with the "Awareness" of awkward questions. They made the progressive decision to form a group of researchers to cope with the demand and influx of our enquiries, which must have involved an extra heavy load of work in their already overworked service. They were dismayed at the disparaging derogatory remarks notated on the various reports on some of the children from the scattered homes circa 1930's/1940's and found some of the remarks distasteful. Plymouth Social Services have set up several small sections of personnel to deal with the flood of enquiries from Scattered Homes, Stoke House, Nazareth House, Adoptions, Doctor Barnados and many other institutions. The way is now clear to obtain the truth.

The Clovelly group at the Reunion Masonic Hall Manadon Plymouth 1997. From the Left. Mrs Margaret Braund (nee Tridgell), Miss Sheila Ellis, Mr Harry Clement (BEM), Mr John Ellis & Mrs Bessie May (nee Perkin). Photo courtesy of Mr & Mrs R Vittle Plymouth.

In July 1997 my friends took me to Hugglepit Farm Clovelly to meet Harry Clement (BEM) who was a former London evacuee during the war years and had settled in Clovelly on his retirement from the Police Force. My search had begun for the New Inn children. Here am I with Harry obtaining my copy of his Book "No time to kiss Goodbye" depicting the stories of the London Evacuees. Photo courtesy of Mr & Mrs R Vittle Plymouth.

Deputy Lady Mayoress Vivian Pengelly and Miss Veronica Norman at the Manadon Masonic Hall Plymouth 1997 at the first reunion.

Mrs Ethel Finnerty (nee Gerry) one of the original Stoke House Orphans who had travelled from Benfleet Essex to attend the 1997 reunion at Plymouth. Photo courtesy Mr Raymond Vittle Plymouth.

CHAPTER TWO

SCATTERED HOMES

Light a candle to start a new dawn!

During the 1920's and the early 1930's there were many houses in Plymouth known as Scattered Homes where children who had been abandoned, orphaned, unwanted, or cruelly treated by their own parents, had been taken by the authorities into care. Some children had been subjected to physical, emotional or sexual abuse. There were children whose relatives were so poor they could not keep them and others who were victims of neglect. Sadly some children were still to experience the same problems in the Scattered Homes depending on whom they met and where they were placed. Scattered Homes children had no secure loving and supportive family backgrounds.

These Scattered Homes were for the very poorest and the public perception of these left much to be desired. The children placed in these homes have deep-seated emotional scars with which they have lived with all their lives. Even now as senior citizens, they will cry when they talk of their experience, some withdraw into a shell and pretend it did not happen, subconsciously it is still there. Others try to control a deep inner anger, and still talk with bitterness of the treatment they received, there are those who were ashamed of it being known that they came from the Scattered Homes and of their background. However, there were happy times too, as some foster mothers were real gems and one or two ex-residents speak of them with high regard, unfortunately few and far between. For years many Scattered Homes children pretended and told everyone in their lives that they came from a middle class well to do family.

Summertime tea party. Taken outside the children's wing Ford House circa 1938. Copyright courtesy of Doctor Robert Crowte MBA Ph.D. Worcestershire. (Joan Henderson's son)

Bath Time! Ford House late 1930's. Photo from Author's collection by kind permission Doctor Robert Crowte MBA Ph.D. Worcs. (Nurse Joan Henderson's son.)

Orphan children in Scattered Homes were loveless, and governed by regulations regimented by set institution rules that dehumanised any personal visionary attribute the child may have had. The crassness of the decision by the authorities to keep siblings apart destroyed forever the closeness and union that brothers and sisters should have had. Some children were lucky, depending in which Scattered Home they were placed, for some had very nice foster carers, others suffered dreadfully, both physically and emotionally. These Scattered Homes were usually small houses in various districts of Devonport and Plymouth where eight to fifteen children were placed under the care of a foster mother appointed by the authorities. In the late 1930's they were listed in local directories as Plymouth Incorporation Scattered Homes, and the Superintendent was Miss M.I.Holden. They were indeed in sharp contrast to other recognised orphanages in Plymouth, which were considered far superior to the Scattered Homes. Ford House Plymouth was a workhouse for adults and children. Children brought into care under the auspices of the Scattered Homes would be sent to Ford House for assessment and the childrens' wing was always full to capacity during the nineteen thirties. Such were the number of orphaned and illegitimate children that sheer numbers sometimes overwhelmed the authorities.

Other notable homes were the Devonport Royal Dockyard Orphanage, which was for children who had lost a parent who had served in some capacity in naval service. It was well provided for and financed by the services and various charities. The home was founded in 1849 following the cholera epidemic in that year which had ravaged Stoke, Devonport and Plymouth and was located originally at Morice Square but later re-sited at Salisbury Terrace, Tavistock Road. It was a lovely building, well maintained by members of the committee, who came from different departments in the Dockyard, they were all volunteers who gave their time without payment. Because of war damage in 1944 the Orphanage, (Mrs Varney, Matron) was transferred to Ashsprington, Totnes, but lack of space forced it to move again in 1947 to Mary Tavy, Devon. In 1951 the former Dockyard building known as 'Brightside' became a Residential Home for men run by the Plymouth City Council. That too has closed, and in later years used as a hall of residence for students of Plymouth University.

There was also the Royal United Services Orphan Home for Girls, formerly called the Royal British Female Orphan Asylum, which was situated in a large building opposite Stoke Terrace, Stoke, Devonport, and in 1938 the Matron was Miss M Partridge. The home had always been well supported by residents of Stoke Village and Morice Town. The foundation stone had been laid in 1845 and on completion homed two hundred girls, always immaculately dressed in blue-and-white uniforms and bonnets. The girls were well treated and many speak of happy times. In the 1950's this home was to be found in Newquay, Cornwall, and the former home at Stoke became the Royal Sailors Rest.

Lady Astor campaigning for votes in the 1900's. The children's champion. Photo with permission courtesy of the Plymouth City Museum.

Another home was the Astor Institute at Mount Gould Road, and in 1938 Miss D. Grime was Warden. Doctor Barnardo's home was at Welby, Tavistock Road, Peverell, Plymouth, and the Reverend Eric.V.McKeeman was the Local Superintendent in the late 1930's. It is interesting to note that in February 1962 Plymouth was selected as an experiment for a new Doctor Barnado's home at Springfield Green, Pennycross, Plymouth. The first to be built on a housing estate in the hope that it would allow the children to grow up in a family environment. Reminiscent of the scattered homes in the 1920-1930's, I wonder how they fared?

More orphanages in Plymouth were Saint Margaret's Home for Girls, (Preventive and Rescue) which was at 17, Portland Villas, in 1938 a Miss G Shaw was Lady Superintendent at this home. Nazareth House, (Sisters of

Nazareth) Convent was located at Durnford Street, Stonehouse. Another home was Saint Gregory's, run by the Church of England Waifs and Strays Society, it was sited at Highbury, Tavistock Road, Peverell, and a Miss O. Barrow was Matron in the late 1930's. At the same time Stoke House, number 39A, appeared under local directories as the Devonport Guardians Childrens'

Nazareth House circa 1930's/1940's. Some Stoke House children were assessed there. Photo with permission from the archive of Plymouth City Museum.

Home, Miss M Holden, Matron. Devon and Cornwall Female Orphanage in Lockyer Street, was another Scattered Home and in 1939 the Matron was Miss Durston. There was a very old building called Hampton House in Ebrington Street which was used as a female penitentiary and home for twenty-five girls, having been established in 1883. In the 1930's it had a laundry contract to supplement its upkeep and the inmates had to work very hard.

The public knew little in the 1920's and early 1930's of the Scattered Homes in Plymouth. Children who asked questions were told "children should been seen and not heard!" With no statutory welfare services and numerous examples of appalling poverty and privation in the 1900's meant that the workhouse and Church of England Waifs and Strays Society was overwhelmed with unwanted children. Care of children was the responsibility of the Guardians of the Poor who were directly elected by the ratepayers. The Scattered Homes came under the control of the Devonport Guardians of the Poor, who usually met at St Aubyn Street, Devonport. It was partially supported by charities which comprised a consortium of well to do business gentlemen and philanthropists who met all costs until 1926/1927 when the homes were taken over by the Plymouth City Council and subsequently supported by the Public Assistance Board. The Scattered Homes then came under the umbrella of Stoke House, which was designated the Orphanage Headquarters. In the early years of the 1930's the childrens' home at Stoke House was kept away from public view allowing bureaucracy to cover up incidents. For example, there is conclusive evidence of sexual abuse to girls and proof that imprisonment was given to the offender in 1931. However, it was kept quiet from the public as the court case was conducted 'In Camera.'

Religion was not considered when the children were taken into care as the children were of all denominations; each Scattered Home had a designated foster mother who cared for up to fifteen children. Boarding out policy of placing an individual child into a family environment was employed by the Welfare Authorities in the 1930's/1940's, as they found it difficult to cope with so many children entering the care system. It was deemed prudent to ease the excessive numbers in care in the middle thirties by fostering some children in private homes with financial assistance. However, when war was declared most of the children were brought back from the Scattered Homes and foster homes to Stoke House. With the onset of the Second World War some children aged under five were sent to the Nethway House Residential Nursery at Kingswear near Dartmouth. However, once they had reached the age of five they were returned to Plymouth, or evacuated to the area where the institution was based.

13 Hill Park Crescent taken during Council renovation work to convert to flats for rent in the 1950's. Photo with permission from the archive of Plymouth City Museum.

Some of the experiences of these now senior citizens of ex-Scattered Homes are highlighted by various reminiscences of former inmates. Children can be cruel when they carry a dislike for an adult as noted in some of the nicknames that were attached to some of the foster carers. Names like, 'Beakie' because of a big nose, 'Creeps' who would sneak up the stairs at night hoping to catch a child talking and the 'Terrier' as no child would dare cross her because she was known to be extremely strict. Here are some of the points that are so vivid in their minds and these are some of the memories they recall. There was Miss Wyatt who would follow the children secretly to see or hear what they were doing or saying, she was very strict and the children were quite scared of her. Miss Foster (a relief Matron) was

16

well liked and she took charge of the children when staff had a day off. Miss Foster was later to become a permanent member of the staff of Stoke House and was also evacuated to the New Inn, Clovelly. Miss Henderson and Miss Bull (both these ladies were well liked) were in charge of numbers 9, 13 and 36 Hill Park Crescent, Greenbank, Plymouth. If a child was lucky enough to be put into the care of these ladies they fared reasonably well. Miss Durban was in charge of 20 Channel View 1920's to the 1930's. Miss Ilford of 2 Gifford Terrace (same era) and Miss Reid was at 36 Hill Park Crescent until 1934 when Miss Male became foster mother who in turn was relieved by Miss Bull in 1936. Mrs Saunders was matron of 80 Mount Gould Road, until 1934 when her services were no longer required.

Four boys ran away on a particular Sunday in September during the 1930's, which was to have a chain reaction that led to a review of the Scattered Homes. The four boys were George Stuart, Frank Bond, Lesley Travers and Norman Dukes. They ran along Salisbury Road, and thinking they were sighted ran away in panic as far as they could. Frank Bond had hammer-toes so could not run very fast. Norman Dukes and Frank Bond climbed into Beaumont Park and hid but were soon caught, and the other two, George Stuart and Lesley Travers managed to escape again. Improvising and eating raw vegetables they scavenged along the way, they succeeded in reaching Maker Camp, Cornwall. They broke into the huts to sleep on the iron beds and survived for nearly a week before they were picked up on their way back to Maker Camp after a trip to the beach at Cawsand to scrounge food from day trippers. When finally caught, by an official from Plymouth, they were asked why they had run away from the Scattered Home and told the officer their reason and of their treatment which had led to the decision to abscond. Subsequently, they were asked to report their experiences to the committee at the Guildhall, which eventually led to the dismissal of a foster parent found to be unworthy of looking after vulnerable children.

Other Matrons were Miss Cox, who relieved Mrs Saunders, on a temporary basis. One gentleman who had been at the Scattered Home, at 80 Mount Gould Road remembered the boys coming home from school to find they had a new Matron, Miss Hayes. She was a lovely lady, who was very kind to us and took us to swim at Jennycliff. Another man recalled Mrs Perryman who was Matron at the Scattered Home at Old Laira Road, Laira. There was a relief matron Mrs Crooks and she would circulate various Scattered Homes to cover holiday periods. Highlight of the year for the Scattered Homes children were the holidays at Maker Camp, although camping equipment was crude the fun the children had more than compensated. There were lovely walks and the study of wild flowers, thrilling visits to Whitsand Bay, Cawsand and Kingsand, and swimming in the sea. The freedom to run in open spaces and the games they played remained imprinted in their minds for all time. Children of Scattered Homes were allowed pocket money (if you got it!) under twelve years of age, one penny a week, over twelve years of age (provided good behaviour was achieved) three pennies per week. In Christmas 1937 every child who was in a childrens' home was granted 1/6 in cash spending money for Christmas week.

In 1931 Miss Ethel Mannin the well-known novelist had an article on the welfare of children in the Western Evening Herald, a Plymouth newspaper. Her descriptive analysis's symbolises exactly the problems children faced, and for the children under the regime of the Scattered Homes and Stoke House it rang very true. What a revelation it would have been if the Public Assistance Board and the welfare bodies of that era responsible for the unwanted, orphaned and abandoned children in homes, and the foster child, had read and acted on its presentation. It was a very striking article and a strong indictment of interfering adults and argued that children should have the right to develop their own lives. Extracts from her article would be considered controversial today, as any opinion of childrens' care would.

These are some of the quotes from that article that I think are relevant. "The child has an even greater need for freedom, for in freedom there is room for growth, in frustration nothing but conflict and the ground work for neurosis." "Consider how little freedom the majority of children get from the time they are born. They are required to live according to adult rules and regulations from the moment they come into the world, they must eat and sleep and play not when they want to, but when they are required to." She continues, "Never for a single moment are they allowed to be themselves. There is a legend, which dies hard that childhood is the happiest time of life. People who say that are people who do not remember what it felt like to be a child." "My plea for the freedom of the child is a plea for recognition that the child also has rights. The freedom of the child means only that, granting to the child the freedom of adults; freedom to be itself." "Childhood ought to be happy, but seldom is, because grown-ups do not allow it to be; they have a fixed idea that education and moral training are good for the child. Adults, in general, have this fixed idea that discipline is good for the child; they cannot see that it does the child incalculable harm, that it is the death of spontaneity, honesty and trust; that it destroys the individuality of the child." Miss Mannin refers to A S Neill's theory and quotes: "I believe with A S Neill that the child is born good, but that we make the child bad by trying to teach him or her to be moral, and I believe with him that there is no such thing as the naughty child, only happy children and unhappy children. What is commonly called the naughty child is merely the child at war with itself, with grown-ups and with life."

When war was declared most children were recalled to Stoke House, a few children were adopted and some had reached the age of fourteen and were put into service or apprenticed. When Stoke House was bombed all the children were temporarily held at an emergency rest centre at Montpelier School, Peverell, Plymouth. Three days later they were once more bombed out and after suffering endless distress were eventually evacuated to Clovelly, North Devon. The children remained there until 1945 unless individually boarded out or adopted beforehand. On their return the children were billeted at Astor Hall, Stoke.

Mutley House Plymouth renamed Parklands when opened as children's home in 1957. The new policy of a Housemother and a closer union with the children were to enhance their lifestyle toward family orientation. Photo print taken shortly before it was pulled down. From Authors private collection.

Mrs Nunn was appointed as Matron and later smaller homes as family units were created to give the children a better quality of life and thankfully the name Scattered Homes is lost in the annals of time. In 1957 Mutley House opened as a childrens' home and it was called Parklands. Number 9 Hill Park Crescent is now converted into five separate flats rented out as private lets from the Executive Lets Agency. Number 13 Hill Park Crescent is a Safe House for drug rehabilitation residents and the flats are the property of a Housing Association. Number 36 Hill Park Crescent is now owned privately after being converted into two separate houses. So with the passage of time ends the era of Scattered Homes but it does not ease the heartache of children who were to form the body of citizens now known as the Lost Generation.

The Scattered Homes consisted of the following addresses in Devonport and Plymouth.

2, Gifford Terrace, Mutley, Fifteen Boys, Closed November 1937.

2, Old Laira Road, Lipson, Boys only.

5, Saltram Villas, Fifteen Girls, Closed June 1933.

132, Old Laira Road, Laira, Boys.

20, Channel View, Efford. Fourteen Girls. Miss Durban/Mrs Sarah Dervin 1920's/1930's. Closed December 1938. Later became a Remand Home.

9, Hill Park Crescent, Greenbank, Miss Alice Bull Superintendent. Children attended Mount Street School.

13, Hill Park Crescent, Greenbank, for fourteen Girls, formerly the Central Home. Children attended Mount Street School.

36, Hill Park Crescent, Greenbank. Miss Male Foster Mother 1938, later Miss Bull. Children attended Mount Street School. The home was closed in late 1930's and taken over by the police for living quarters.

65, North Down Crescent.

15, Lipson Hill, Lipson.

80 Mount Gould Road, Mount Gould, Plymouth. Fifteen Boys. Mrs E. Elford Foster Mother 1938. Closed March 1940, later it was to become a Doctor's residence.

2, Woodside for Boys, purchased in 1905.

Boys attended Salisbury Road School.

Plymleigh home for Boys, Laira.

Devon & Cornwall Female Orphanage Lockyer Street Plymouth 1934. Note the blanked out windows to avoid paying window tax. Photo courtesy of Westcountry Publications.

The fire damaged Devon & Cornwall Female Orphanage Lockyer Street after the raid on 21st March 1941. Photo courtesy of Westcountry Publications.

Refurbishing of the kitchen interior 1950 13 Hill Park Crescent. (Note the old style gas cooker) Photo from the archive of Plymouth City Museum.

CHAPTER THREE

THE LOST GENERATION

This above all: To thine own self be true.
(Hamlet. William Shakespeare).

Some of the former Scattered Homes and Stoke House residents are still searching to this day for their missing kin, or the circumstances surrounding their separations from family members. When brothers and sisters were separated, placed in homes or fostered, they were restricted in communicating with them again, and some mothers and fathers or other close relatives whose circumstances had changed, who had perhaps tried to recover their children, were given wrong information in an effort to avoid awkward questions being asked. Government policies made it difficult for childrens' officers to fully communicate with relatives of children in their care, and they were reluctant in revealing the truth to sibling's questions if subsidies for children in care would be affected. Relatives acting as foster carers were governed by strict guidelines by a Public Assistance and Welfare ruling, which if not adhered to would involve their allowances being cut or taken away. This resulted often in sibling sisters and brothers losing touch with other.

Pressure from Christian Sects and internal squabbles between different religious organisations caused many unnecessary separations. A cruel and unforgiving decision and a scathing indictment on the welfare state of the 1930's/1940's era, whose rigid policy applied this rule leaving the children with lasting lifetime heartache into their twilight years! Finding missing relatives result in emotional reunions and some are still searching to this day for their kinfolk and those who have lost relatives have carried an ache in their heart for many years. The loss of family union was devastating, and where siblings were separated and have managed to trace their lost kin it has led to many emotional and distressing reunions. In some instances no reunion at all, as death, and the years, and lifestyles have proven too great a barrier to cross. Look at everything they lost! Their personal identity, their family life, some abused both sexually and physically, others emotionally disturbed.

Although some ex Scattered Homes and Stoke House people have been given their records, the welfare authorities were unable to discover vital information that could fill in the missing links for others. Links that could tell the complete truth of their childhood, they still find it difficult to answer our enquiries for information on our brothers and sisters. It has to be appreciated that they have set rules that restrict certain information being released. The question must be asked however, who instigates these rules and on what basis is the enforcement used? Surely it is morally wrong? Since when has the strong evidence of social workers in the area of morality assumed the status of an imperative? Some siblings of scattered homes folk are still living who could be hurt if the truth was known. Their lives could be totally disrupted and certainly, some genealogy enthusiasts would have to re-write their family trees. Although we have the new act "Your right to Know–Freedom of Information Act" that in itself is restricted by the Data Protection Act, here the old saying proves right, "One door opens and another closes". The Social Services in Plymouth have responded to the search for our records and have gone to great lengths to try and heal the anger and hurt we have felt. They have inherited a legacy, which has been quite an eye opener to the present day counsellors, and social workers, who have been astounded in the application of child care in the 1930's/1940's. We have had counselling from individual social workers and the department itself has been upset at some of the derogatory labelling of children in that era which earmarked them for life! Under the old system, Registers of Institutions were kept noting the Name, Forename, Age, Date of Birth, Date of Admission, Discharge, and cost of Maintenance. How differently children are viewed today by the local authorities, a vast improvement on the Children and Young Persons Act 1931/1933. Perhaps they have learnt from past experiences. The terrible backlash the present Social Services have in dealing with the search for records from various childrens' homes, including the Scattered Homes, Stoke House, Nazareth House and Doctor Barnados, has left them with a legacy of distressed and broken hearted citizens.

Adoptions were to involve a lost generation in the search for missing siblings after the release of the government's white paper, which gave them the freedom to do so. The Government White Paper "Your right to know - Freedom of Information Act" was published by The Stationery Office Limited in December 1997 and was a piece of history in the making, because for the first time the public had the right to see the files of government ministries and local councils. A reform that was long overdue, as Britain was the only country in Europe without a Freedom of Information Act, for people like me this culture of secrecy had created a living nightmare. Large groups of silent grieving mothers and fathers who lost their children and those searching for lost brothers and sisters know that they have been living a lie. The lost generation requires services and an enormous amount of understanding to help them to come to terms with the hidden truth. Government funding is needed toward the costs to help Social Services trapped by restrictions designed to stop what should be the lost generation's right to be told the truth. There should be an independent judicial enquiry into the scandal, which separated so many children from their families and made it hard for them to come to terms with life. What happened in the 1930's/1940's was disgraceful and the moral obligations owed to the lost generation should be acknowledged. Many times the war has been used as an excuse for indiscretions during the 1940's. The failure to right the wrongs of the past is shameful and one day the policies exercised by those government departments may be challenged. Asking for official apologies prove fruitless. Why is it so difficult for the government departments to say sorry? If we cannot actually face that, we cannot face our past! Why can't we look it in the face, deal with it! How can we deal with today and tomorrow? There is still to come - the lost generation of forgotten children of the 1950's/1960's who were sent to Australia. Their kinfolk not even informed of their whereabouts so they too would be seeking answers! This book is meant to be evocative. So let it be a reminder of what life was like for the poor children of the 1930's/1940's. It is our history-we lived it!

I'se lonely 'cose you're not here.

WELL I'LL SWEAR —
I AIN'T GOT NOTHING,
AIN'T HAD NOTHING,
DON'T WANT NOTHING,
'CEPT YOU

I AIN'T SEEN NOBODY,
AIN'T HAD NOBODY,
AIN'T LOVED NOBODY,
THAT'S TRUE.

BUT IF YOU'LL LOVE ME,
I'LL LOVE YOU,
IF YOU WANT MONEY
I WON'T DO,
'CAUSE I AIN'T GOT NOTHING
NEVER HAD NOTHING
DON'T WANT NOTHING
'CEPT YOU.

CHAPTER FOUR

THE HISTORY OF STOKE HOUSE

To solve the mystery of Stoke House the history of Stoke had to be explored to justify its existence. Stoke takes its name from Stock a Saxon word for Dairy Farm, and before the Norman conquest it was held by Brismar who was an Anglo-Saxon. He called it Stoches, and eventually it transferred to a Norman Lord, Robert De Albamarla, transcribed as Damerel. It was also known as Stockes De Albemare and through the years the name changed, and in some very early maps it is shown as Stoke Dameret. In later years the manor became known as Stoke Damerel. The D'Albemarle's held Stoke until about 1290, the Domesday Survey book clearly names the Manor of Stoke as belonging to the Damerel family, on their demise it passed to the Courtneys. In the reign of Edward the Second the land in the parish belonged to the Kemiells (Kemyells), and the Branscombes, from whom it passed to the families of Britt and Sir Thomas Wise. Geoffrey St. Aubyn of Clowance had married Elizabeth, daughter and heiress of Peter Kemyell of Clowance, in the mid 1300's. When he died in 1400 it is interesting to note that this is how the estate came into the St Aubyn family, and as there are two farms called Upper and Lower Kemyell which still belong to Lord St. Levan the Kemyells must have been very big land owners.

The Wise family acquired Stoke by 1428 but they continued to live at Sydenham House, Marystowe, near Lifton, Devon, letting the Manor House of Stoke remain as a farm. One important piece of history that took place in 1525, was when the Wise family relinquished their rights on the northern bank of Stonehouse Creek to the new owner of Stonehouse, Sir Piers Edgecumbe to build a tidal mill at Millbridge. This bridge opened up a new route from Stonehouse, up to Molesworth Road and down the hill to a ford over the Keyham Creek, which in time gave its name to the modern district of Ford. This in turn could have been a key factor in later years in the siting of "Travers House" a derivation from the name "Travellers" as the transport of the day were horse drawn carriages. They would stop en route as a staging post at the coach-house at Stoke on their way through to Ford.

In 1667 Sir William Morice, Baronet, purchased the Manor of Stoke Damerel with its appurtenances, for the sum of eleven thousand and six hundred pounds. Sir William Morice was Secretary of State to Charles the Second when he bought Mount Wise Manor. His grandson Sir Nicholas Morice had a son William and two daughters. The eldest daughter, Catherine, married Sir John St. Aubyn the third baronet in 1725 because he was a Member of Parliament and won a considerable reputation for helping tin miners in Cornwall in bad times. The St Aubyns originated from France in the wake of the Norman Conquest. Catherine's sister Barbara married Sir John Molesworth of Pencarrow. Catherine was co-heiress of Stoke Damerel (on which now stands Devonport Dockyard, Morice Town and Stoke) with her brother William, so that the St Aubyn family inherited Stoke Damerel as part of Catherine's dowry. In 1749 with no male heir of Sir Nicholas Morice to claim the title, the Stoke Damerel estate passed under his will to his nephew the twenty-three year old Sir John St Aubyn, Baronet of Clowance, Cornwall. Sir John St. Aubyn's grandson, Sir John St. Aubyn, the fifth Baronet, did not marry his mistress Juliana Vinnicombe until after all their children were born, so that they were illegitimate and the Baronetcy was held in abeyance. His seventh son Edward (born 1799 died 1872) eventually succeeded to St. Michael's Mount and the Stoke Damerel estate in Devonport. He was created a baronet by Queen Victoria in 1866 so family honour was restored. Considered a capable man he concentrated all his energies on the management of the family properties in Devonport and never lived at Saint Michael's Mount. Edward's son John, who was a Member of Parliament, later became the first Lord St. Levan. Sir Edward St. Aubyn then left the management of the Devonport properties to his son, also called Edward, who was not so efficient and not well liked. Two of his daughters were burnt to death when getting ready for a Ball in Devonport. They had put their candle on the floor of the water closet and as one daughter's dress caught fire the sister tried to extinguish the flames only to be set on fire herself, a tragic end for two young women.

In 1700-1783 many houses had been erected at Stoke for gentlemen of wealth which enhanced the quality of the area and brought much needed income into the parish, the population was either rich or poor. Virtually all the properties and houses, (with the exception of Government and Public buildings) in the Manor and Parish of Stoke Damerel, including Devonport and Swilly, came into the possession of the St Aubyn family and the land belonged to the Lord St Levan. In 1839 the nephew, Reverend J Molesworth inherited the estate and later John Townshend St Aubyn second Baronet, born 1857, became Lord St Levan and was a Companion of the Victorian Order. St Aubyn's family name is known under the title of Baron St Levan. The present Lord St Levan is Sir John Francis Arthur St Aubyn, DSC. DL. Fourth Baron St Levan of Saint Michael's Mount, Marizion, County Cornwall, he is also the fifth Baronet. He was born in 1919 and served with honour in the Second World War, and, as a Lieutenant in the Royal Naval Volunteer Reserve, won the Distinguished Service Cross for gallantry in 1944. He was appointed High Sheriff of Cornwall in 1974 and Deputy Lieutenant of Cornwall 1977-1992; he served as Vice Lord Lieutenant in 1992-1994. Sir John is highly respected and is very popular with the Cornish citizens, he is known far and wide as a champion of the ordinary people. Lord St Levan's nephew, Nicholas, is managing director of the Fitzroy Joinery Works in Devonport, Plymouth, which has recently expanded by taking over a joinery works in Bodmin, Cornwall. He was, until he lost his seat in the last election, member of Parliament for Guildford.

With the peace of 1815, (after the Napoleonic Wars 1795-1815) there was a demand for dwellings to meet the needs of professional men and prosperous tradesmen. Plymouth had been used as an assembly point for the fleet since the thirteenth century. Officers of the Navy and Army were seeking homes, and the influx of Dockyard Officials warranted the need for further buildings. The suburb of Higher Stoke began to take shape during the early years of the nineteenth century. Stoke Terrace had been built about 1815, Navy Row (now Albert Road) had been developed by 1820 and Home Park in 1822, all these streets became closely associated with a prosperous community. Plymouth Dock was renamed Devonport in 1824. In 1832 the Reform Bill united Stonehouse and Devonport in one constituency. By 1850 the village of higher Stoke had developed on to the Devonport to Tavistock turnpike and as such was a new suburb of Devonport, with the amalgamation of the Three Towns in 1914, Devonport (which was the youngest) Stonehouse (which was the smallest) and Plymouth (which was the largest) meant that Stoke from that union would forever be classified as part of Devonport. Stoke was by far the most important member of the triad, as its appearance in the Domesday Book is confirmed under its name Stoke

Damerel. Plymouth was situated on the shores of the Hamoaze (formerly called Ham-Ouse because of its muddy tributary) and Plymouth Sound, between the estuaries of the River Tamar and the River Plym, and it was the largest maritime town in England. Royal Charter created the Borough of Plymouth a City in October 1928.

Stoke House and Stoke Cottage, formerly known as Travers House and Stoke Villa, (insert map here) in the parish of Stoke Damerel, Higher Stoke, was plot number thirteen of thirteen lands belonging to the Lord St Levan, in the parish of Stoke Damerel, in the Hundred of Roborough, in the Deanery of Tamerton (originally Tambretona) and the Diocese of Exeter. The house was considered to be a very high-class residence, which had beautiful vistas of the surrounding landscape with commanding views of Mount Edgcumbe, Plymouth Sound and the Breakwater. The land it occupied was extensive, bounded on the East by a road leading to Ford, on the North by a field called Underhill, on the West partly by ground in the possession of the Board of Ordnance and partly on a field called Bromley Meadow. The Ordnance location could be either the Ordnance Ground which, later became Devonport Park, or Mount Pleasant Blockhouse colloquially known as the "Pattypan." The building of the ditches known by historians as "The Lines" were granted in 1758-1766. The Mount Pleasant Blockhouse was built in 1778-1780, it was erected in the reign of George the second, and was intended originally as a fortification presumably having been granted a Royal Licence. As it was the highest point of land in the area, some local historians believe that Mount Pleasant was possibly an ancient hill fort that had been built in the Bronze or Iron Age.

In September 1926 the Plymouth City Council bought the Mount Pleasant redoubt consisting of 8.8 acres of land from the War Department. The war office had considered auctioning the land if the Plymouth City Council did not accept the offer of sale, as previously it had been on a yearly rental from the War Department. Facing south, Stoke House and Stoke Cottage were situated at the top of Ford Hill and Tavistock Road, and were surrounded by walls. There were two driveways and inside the iron gates were stables, a coach-house, cow-house, laundry, and various outhouses. The beautiful enclosed lawn and garden in a sylvan setting contained three acres of land with planted borders, trees, shrubs, and a fish pond, arranged so that picturesque walks were available, and there was a fruit and kitchen garden coupled with a greenhouse stocked with vines. The House comprised of appropriate dining, drawing and breakfast rooms, six principal bedrooms, and several rooms for servants, sculleries and toilets. The building was classified as a very desirable residence and families of the highest respectability always occupied it. On the roof was a glass conservatory that viewed the landscape from all points of the compass.

Near by Stoke House was Bromley Place and Packington Street, (named after one of Lord Nelson's Captains) at the northern end of Stoke House was Northesk Street, (named after William Carnegie, Rear Admiral the Earl of Northesk 1758-1831). The entrance was sited in Tavistock Road, (later to be renamed Devonport Road) just off the pavement facing the Argyle Cycle Shop and the Pear Tree Public House. Objections by the residents in 1968 meant that the section between Ford Hill and Milehouse Junction was renamed Milehouse Road. The entrance had large wooden gates eight feet high, and these were kept shut. As you walked towards Ford Hill there was a low wall further heightened by hedging, and it was impossible to see any building inside.

In the early 1800's at the very bottom of Ford Hill was a farm and field called Underhill. At the top of Ford Hill near the corner was a barred wrought iron gate which one could peer through and see the driveway of Stoke House. Everything was hidden from the outside by shrubs and trees and the gates were kept locked, remote and unseen to the outside world, almost a replica of a Dickensian scene. Stoke House was surrounded by a wall, parts of which may still been seen running down Ford Hill. The wall ceases just opposite Beresford Street where you can see the cliff face. It continues across the cliff face and vanishes behind the terraced houses in Northesk Street. There is a narrow lane at the corner of these houses, and here Northesk Street runs away to the left on almost a hairpin bend. At the top of Northesk Street the wall emerges at the end of Packington Street and again appears opposite the terraced houses at Bromley Place, this wall is gone now and flats occupy that space, as you walk to the end of Bromley Place, you are again in what was Tavistock Road.

Stoke Cottage would be let separately on occasion to trade merchants or officers of the Royal Navy. There could be confusion on some of the historical records as regards Stoke Cottage, as there were two residences with the same name, the other Stoke Cottage was between Underhill Road and Somerset Place, quite near the Stoke Nursery, and this is clearly shown in the 1895 ordnance survey map. (Insert copy of map here). Properties in Higher Stoke were held under Tenure to the Saint Aubyn Family, which could be let at rack rent from year to year, for short-term periods not exceeding seven years. Alternatively, it would be allocated on lease at a conventionary rent for ninety-nine years, The property known as Stoke House, was leased on a ninety-nine year agreement. Leases for ninety-nine years were determinable at the death of three lives, nominated by the Lessee, subject to an annual Quit Rent, and a Heriot, which doubled after the first demise. In some parts of the manor the right of adding a fourth life, upon the payment of a fine is allowed with a covenant for perpetual renewal. The late Sir John St Aubyn resorted to the leases within the years 1790 and 1800 as an expedient for raising money.

On the demise of Sir John St Aubyn, who had been the exclusive owner of all the houses and land in the manor and parish of Stoke Damerel, including the town of Devonport, Edward St Aubyn, acting as receiver for the late Sir John St Aubyn, with the nominated trusts, issued an Estate Report in 1841 stating that no further leases had been granted of this nature from the year 1800. The trusts under Sir John's will was called for by a considerable body of Tenants and Lessees who had submitted complaints against the tenures by which most of St Aubyn's properties were held. When a leasehold house falls in hand it is usually sold by Auction for three lives at an improved ground rent. The highest sum bid at such auctions forms the fine or consideration for granting the new lease. There were strong objections to the number of years properties were leased, opinions were in favour of reduced tenures of perhaps sixty or thirty years, ninety-nine years was considered unfair. If the house was out of repair, or in either of the principal streets of the town, it was kept in hand and let at a rack rent. All repairs were uniformly imposed upon the tenants, only gentlemen of wealth could afford to live at Stoke House! However, the St Aubyn family did recognise the anomalies the system presented and in later years made alterations to rectify the situation. Since the time before the second World War, with capable managers and a better understanding, there has frequently been restrictive covenants in Tenancy Agreements to prevent any use of a property which might be detrimental to tenants of neighbouring properties and in order to maintain a good standard of management.

At a meeting in 1951 the Plymouth City Council in conjunction with the Social Welfare Committee agreed to release the land that had belonged to Stoke House for other purposes. The war had destroyed so many homes and land was at a premium that the decision was taken to sell 1.77 acres. The housing committee appropriated the ground and new council homes were built on the land, which are now known as Bromley House and Packington Street Flats. There is a new Stoke House, (however, not on the scale of the old mansion) built in a peaceful setting at Derriford, Plymouth, by a relative of Sir Clifford and Lady Tozer, who remembered his many visits to the original Stoke House as a child. After the Second World War, the St Aubyn family built housing estates at Devonport, Manadon and Widey. They also built three blocks of flats in Devonport and the Minister of Housing at the time presented the St. Aubyn family with two Housing Gold Medals. On the opposite side of Packington Street Flats (now Milehouse Road) the old cowhouse still survives, and is now a garage belonging to a private resident. The remnants of the old coach-house and stables can be found in the yard behind The Stoke Inn opposite Dewdneys pasty shop, you can still see the entrance to it between the buildings under the arch. The original wall, which had surrounded Stoke House in Ford Hill, still stands today, and one tree planted many years ago in the grounds facing the Flats stands as a defiant survivor of all that Stoke endured in those tragic years of the Second World War.

CHAPTER FIVE

WHO LIVED IN STOKE HOUSE?

The light of hope shines out in the darkness
and the darkness cannot put it out. Take Courage.
(Fra Giovanni AD 1513)

Without people there would be no history, such is the case with Stoke House. So who were the people who lived there before it became a childrens' home? What did they do? And how much influence did they have with the community? It is clear that very little has been written about the people who worked, loved, married and died there throughout its history. Stoke House was covered by a veil of secrecy and shrouded in mystery for many years, and little was known about the citizens who had lived there. Researching the evidence of former residents required infinite patience, however, once revealed, it gave a fascinating insight into the many distinguished people who had resided there.

In the extracts from old Survey Books of the St Aubyn Estates (Devon) Stoke House was shown as "Travers" plot number thirteen. The first known-recorded lease in December 1751 was to a Gentleman called Francis Moses Thomas with his family Jane and Elizabeth Thomas. He had moved from Cherry Garden Street, (formerly Back Street) Devonport, (both named streets no longer exist) where he had lived from 1745. He was obviously a man of means as he had leased other property in the area, notably Pond Lane, east side, and St Aubyn Street, west side, where his brother resided. It would appear that Moses Thomas was a baker and he had rented "The Bakehouse" in King Street from the St Aubyns in 1748 where he had conducted his very successful business, which had thrived enabling him to lease "Travers." He then let part of the house to a tenant called Richard Bayley (Bailey) a Gentleman, Bayley had moved from Boot Lane, south side, which was near Queen Street, further notations in the records show that the house was being referred to then as "Travers House."

Captain John Thomas Duckworth Esquire took possession of Travers House as it was then listed, in early 1791. His family included his wife, ten-year-old son George Henry Duckworth, and eight-year-old daughter Sarah Ann. In July 1791 he bought a small plot of land adjoining his property to make improvements. He further enhanced the residence when in 1792 he leased, in addition to the house, other property such as stables, a coach house, outhouses, oddments of buildings and the garden from the Quarry Tenement. He completely redesigned the buildings and the alterations he made increased the size of the house to make it look more like a mansion. He strongly favoured the Regency style of the late 1700's and it could be that it was he who added the Doric portico of four columns to the front of the house, which gave it a mansion like appearance. On completion he renamed the house Stoke Villa. He was the son of the Reverend Henry Duckworth of Lancaster. John, however, was born in Leatherhead, Surrey, and did not want to follow in his father's profession, but chose instead the Royal Navy.

He proved to be a brave officer and rose rapidly in the ranks. A Midshipman in 1774, Lieutenant in 1779, Post Captain in 1780, Captain in 1781, this was followed, in 1781 to 1793, by a period of "Out of Commission" but in 1794 he was appointed Commander, and in 1798 rose to the rank of Commodore. By 1799 he was Rear Admiral of the White Squadron and in 1804 Vice Admiral of the Blue Squadron. He was made a Knight Commander-Order of the Bath (KB) in 1801. He became Governor and Commander-in-Chief Newfoundland 1810-1813. Admiral Sir John Thomas Duckworth KB lived at Stoke Villa for several years with his first wife the former Anne Wallis of Drethill who had been the only child of John Wallis of Trentonwoonith, near Camelford, Cornwall. They were married in July 1776 and their son George Henry Duckworth was born in 1780 and their daughter Ann in 1782. Sadly his son George was killed in the war against the French in his country's service as a Colonel at the battle of Albuera, Spain, in 1811.

Admiral Sir John Thomas Duckworth (1748-1817) lost his first wife Anne in 1797. After her death he continued with his naval career and he was also made a freeman of Plymouth in 1810. In the Plymouth Directory, by Rowe 1814, the name Duckworth is listed in the nobility page as still living at Stoke, but he was not at Stoke Villa. Sir John had bought the Manor of Weare-Park, anciently called Heneaton, Hineton or Honiton Siege at Exeter, from William Francis Spicer in 1804; he greatly improved the house before moving in with his wife from his second marriage. He moved out of the Mansion House at Exeter when he took up his appointment at Admiralty House, ensuring that his wife and second son were duly provided for by leaving them secured for life at the Manor. He died in September 1817 whilst still an Admiral serving at Admiralty House, Mount Wise, Plymouth Dock, and was buried with full naval honours. Mount Wise (formerly Keame) was constructed in 1795. Like most famous naval officers his name lives on with a road in the village of Stoke called Duckworth Street named in 1900, which can be found adjoining Packington Street near Mount Pleasant Blockhouse.

In June 1808 Travers House/Stoke Villa was occupied by Mr Proctor Smith and in 1809 was leased to Martin Thomas and his three children John, Elizabeth and Ann Thomas. In January 1818 the Reverend Francis Humbertstone became the resident of Stoke Cottage, as it was listed then, by announcing the re-opening of his classical school. Richard Bromley Esquire who was a purser in the Royal Navy bought the lease of Stoke House (Travers House-Stoke Villa) and the adjoining field Bromley Meadow in 1821. He had done extensive alterations to the house somewhere around 1823, and it is possible that the improvements made were under the superintendence and guidance of the well known architect John Foulston who favoured Grecian Architecture.

Unable to find historical records to prove the truth some knowledgeable locals believe that J. Piers St. Aubyn may have assisted in the alterations to the mansion. Mr Bromley was a lover of fine arts and his house was full of valuable paintings and objet d'arts so popular with the mid victorians. He lived there for a short while, as evidenced by Robert Brindley's Directory (1830) until he and his family moved to Middlesex and the property was again sold. Although Bromley held the lease until 1838 Brindley's directory clearly states that Richard Bromley was living at Travers House.

It would appear he let the house to other tenants as in September 1829 Stoke House and Stoke Cottage were put up for sale by auction with Mrs Bremner removing, it is noted however, that Mrs Bremner was still living there in 1830. The Auctioneer and House Agent was Dennis Henry Hainsselin of 1, St Aubyn Street, Devonport, who was to complete thirty-six years in the trade. Auction of the house was advertised in the then local newspaper the Devonport Telegraph. This paper, the Devonport and Plymouth Telegraph, was a first class advertising medium having been established in 1803; it published on a Saturday from the office at Chapel Street, Devonport. Its political views strongly favoured the Liberals. (The bankrupt owner Mr Richards sold this newspaper in 1850 by auction).

In 1831 Sir Charles Holloway occupied Stoke House, until he moved to Blackburn House in 1837. The Stoke Estate and grounds became the property and residence of William Hancock Esquire; he became Mayor of Devonport in 1839-1840. Stoke Cottage appeared to have two residents, a Major Cockram of the army, and a tea dealer John Palmer. Mrs Elizabeth Bromley on the death of her husband Richard Bromley in 1838 eventually sold the lease of Stoke Villa in February 1840 to William Hole Evens who lived there until the winter of 1844. Stoke House as it was now known, was occupied in December 1844 by Captain George Aldham, RN, until his death in 1846, when both the house and the cottage were put up for sale by public auction at the Royal Hotel by order of the Executors for the Aldham family.

The property then came into the hands of William Vosper a barrister in 1847 and he resided at Stoke House until December 1851 when the lease came into possession of William Frank Fisher. His family lived there from 1857 to 1878 when the property once more changed hands, this time to a corn merchant William Joll and his wife Elizabeth, and on William Joll's demise in 1894 the estate was left to his widow. In early 1895 Mrs Elizabeth Joll had decided to sell the property to Samuel Vosper and eventually he bought the remainder of the lease in 1897 to secure the estate. Formerly of East Stonehouse, Samuel Vosper was a wines and spirits Merchant of Regent's Brewery, Stonehouse, which was linked with the Plymouth Breweries. He served as Chairman of the East Stonehouse Urban District Council from 1896-1899. Eventually on obtaining Stoke House premises complete, lived there from 1895 until his death in 1902. Although the window tax had been abolished in 1851 an agreement was reached between Samuel Vosper and the Earl John St Aubyn, First Baron St Levan of St Michael's Mount, County Cornwall, in 1896, to blank out some of the windows in Stoke House to avoid overlooking the portion of Sir John's land which was still in his possession. Samuel Vosper had purchased the rest of the land for £300 pounds, a princely sum in those days! As the lease for lives had been surrendered, Mr Vosper bought a fixed term lease of fifty years to commence from Christmas 1895. In early 1903 the property was passed to his widow Mrs Jane Vosper.

John Clark Tozer OBE (1860-1923) who became Mayor of Devonport in 1902-1903 then purchased the house and leasehold in June 1904 from William Walter Blight and Robert David Sale who were ironmongers at Stonehouse. John Tozer and his wife Henrietta lived at Stoke House until 1923, and when they died the property passed to their daughter Dorothy Mary Tozer (1893-1979), and their son James Clifford Tozer (1889-1970). Clifford was later to be Lord Mayor of Plymouth in 1930-1931 and eventually honoured with the title Sir Clifford Tozer having received his knighthood in 1939. The Tozer family owned a drapery, outfitting and furnishing store at Fore Street, Devonport, from 1887 and later expanded into Princess Street and Marlborough Street. The premises stretched for three hundred yards incorporating Tavistock Street and both sides of Fore Street until the store was destroyed during the blitz in April 1941. Tozer's built its reputation on the letters SPQR, which stood for "Small Profits-Quick Returns" his store had stretched from Marlborough Street into Granby Street, Devonport. For a while the business operated from various little premises in Marlborough Street and other premises, which had survived the bombing. Eventually the business moved to New George Street, Plymouth, and it was then that the third generation of the Tozer family J.A.G.Tozer later joined.

In June 1926 Mrs H.Tozer and John Townshend Baron St Levan with his trustees sold the leasehold and Stoke House to Myer Fredman Esquire, Justice of the Peace, for the sum of one thousand and nine hundred pounds. The Tozer family moved to Belmont House 1922-1929 and later took up residence in Penlee Gardens. In November 1926, at the request of Myer Fredman, (who now held the Freehold to Stoke House), plans were submitted by the architects Thornley and Rooke to convert Stoke House into a childrens' home. The Guardians of the Poor of the Parish of Devonport purchased the house on 14 January 1927 from Myer Fredman Esq, Argaum Villas, Justice of the Peace, for the sum of four thousand, three hundred pounds. Sold within seven months of his purchase he indeed profited richly pounds. Sold within seven months of his purchase he indeed profited richly from the sale!

Meanwhile, an offer was submitted on behalf of Lord St. Levan to hand over to the Plymouth Corporation for road widening purposes, strips of land adjoining Stoke House abutting on Tavistock Road-Ford Hill and Northesk Street. The Corporation was carrying out improvements to the streets and were faced with building a new boundary wall around Stoke House along with the road alterations, which the Borough Surveyor, in order to complete the work, had estimated the costs to be approximately £7,000. The Special Works Committee of the Plymouth City Council in April 1927, accepted the offer of the land from Lord St. Levan and his trustees to enable them to purchase the freehold of that portion of land for access to the childrens' home and the street improvements. The Right Honourable John Townshend Baron St Levan C.B. C.B.O. and his trustees, sold the land for a sum of one pound only, this was indeed a very generous gift from the trustees and Lord St Levan.

With the introduction of the Local Government Act 1929 and The Poor Law Act 1930 the Public Assistance Board replaced the old Board of Guardians, therefore, the Plymouth City Council inherited Stoke House from the Devonport Guardians of the Poor, and alterations were considered to accept children in conditions of safety. Later in 1933 came the Place of Safety of Young Persons Act. On becoming a childrens' home Stoke House became the Headquarters of the Scattered Homes under the control of the Plymouth City Council and the Public Assistance Board, superseding the former headquarters at 36 Hill Park Crescent, Mutley, Plymouth, which had reverted back as a normal scattered home. Stoke Cottage, one of the outbuildings belonging to Stoke House in 1930, was earmarked for a twelve-month trial period to receive new admissions that were to be transferred to Ford House. Known as the workhouse for the poor and mentally ill, many hearts were broken here, children and adults alike. There is a verse published by A Granville and Son 1812 from the booklet "A view of Plymouth Dock, Plymouth, and the Adjacent Country." The verse is written by "Crabbe."

THE WORKHOUSE

"HERE CHILDREN DWELL, WHO KNOW NO PARENT'S CARE;
PARENTS WHO KNOW NO CHILDREN'S LOVE, DWELL THERE:
HEART-BROKEN MATRONS, ON THEIR JOYLESS BED;
FORSAKEN WIVES, AND MOTHER'S NEVER WED."

True facts well said! Stoke Cottage was then converted temporarily into an Isolation Hospital. In 1931 after a police investigation and a trial held in camera which resulted in a child abuser being sent to prison, Plymouth City Council considered selling some of the land at the rear of Stoke House as a possible building site to reduce garden maintenance and obtain much needed revenue. However, the transaction did not take place and the plan was shelved. In January 1935 Messrs E J Manning & Son were awarded the tender for structural alterations and building additions to Stoke House, as the original plans submitted by the Architects in 1926 were not accepted. By now all the walls of Stoke House had Virginia Creeper growing on them, which did little to alleviate it's cold, stark look.

What a downturn in Stoke House's history, from wealthy well to do families of highest respectability, to a home for orphaned and unwanted children! Stoke House was never to regain its former glory and from this period gradually fell into decline. It was empty for two years (1927-1929) whilst waiting funding to improve the premises for habitation. The local children would often climb over the wall into the garden to scrump apples, plums and pears, and as one dear former senior citizen told me, "My sister and I, Mary and Doris Russan, called it "The Big House." It was always shrouded in mystery and we were scared stiff of the place, but the challenge and thrill of entering the garden was just too tempting to resist!

The Public Assistance and Education Committee were committed to improving the home and later funds were allocated to build a new bathroom and improve drains at Stoke House. There had always been problems with the drainage of the land as in 1795-1796 part of the thirty-seven miles long, Devonport Leat, had been built close to the property. The leat flowed through Stoke Damerel and eventually descended into a small reservoir situated at the top of Scott Road, channelled onward into a culvert under the lane to reappear in the grounds of what is now known as Outlands,

Milehouse. New windows and a verandah were supplied for Stoke Cottage to ensure it could be adapted as an isolation ward if and when needed. In early 1932 the City Surveyor of Plymouth suggested, that the policeman's telephone box which was in Church Street, Stoke, should be moved to a position at the North-East side of the main entrance to Stoke House, this would enable the authorities to keep a more observant eye on the children to afford them security and safety in view of recent anomalies that had occurred at Stoke House. In 1937 permission was given to erect an electricity sub-station in the grounds, subject to an undertaking by the Electrical Engineer that the shed and fruit trees be replaced and made good. As Stoke Cottage was not used in accordance with the plans originally submitted by the 1926 Architects, from 1935 onwards the rooms were used for other purposes, such as a store room for the seamstress, as clothes for the children were made by her, and for safe storage of boots and shoes.

In the 1938 Plymouth Directory, homes with orphaned children were listed as Orphanages, not so Stoke House, it is recorded as The Plymouth Public Assistance Committee's Childrens' Home, Miss M I Holden, Matron, a grim reminder that they were children of the poor! Stoke House housed fifty children, and was to remain the Headquarters of the Scattered Homes until the house was fire bombed and destroyed by Hitler's Luftwaffe on Saint George's day Wednesday 23 April 1941. (Because it was a childrens' home fire- watchers had kept the house monitored from March 1941 under instructions from the Education Authority). Explosive bombs were dropped in Northesk Street and Packington Street. Stoke House was caught in the middle of these two bombs and received a batch of high incendiaries which ignited and severely damaged the building. The final death throes came when on the night of 26 April 1941 Stoke House caught a direct hit by a time bomb, earlier a UXB which had been dealt with by the Bomb Disposal Unit was defused, but the other time bomb did further damage.

Sadly, a building of architectural historical value was lost for all time and was never to be occupied again, remaining derelict for many years, but it did serve as an adventure playground for the boys who lived in the area. The children and staff of Stoke House were rescued from the burning building; the children were passed over the walls by the rescuers. One of the rescuers John Proctor was a firewatcher and lived in Packington Street and it was he who raised the alarm. The children were then temporarily housed for one night in other accommodation, the following day on the 24 April 1941 all the staff and the children walked to Montpelier Junior School, Peverell, which had been turned into an emergency rest home. They had red blankets given to them by firemen, wrapped around their bodies. It must have been a strange sight seeing fifty children walking to the school covered only in those red blankets. Unfortunately, Montpelier Junior & Infants School received four direct hits from parachute land mines on the 28 April 1941 and extensive damage to the school made it unserviceable for use as an emergency rest shelter. Some Stoke House staff and children were buried alive in the damaged area and had to be dug out. On the 30 April 1941 the childrens' home was transferred to The New Inn, Clovelly, North Devon, these children were the first official evacuees from Plymouth. Fifty children were taken by bus and when they arrived at Clovelly had only second hand shoes and clothes, as all their own clothes had been lost in the fire and bomb damage. The villagers were shocked at the sight of their pitiful state, this was a clear sign of how the war was coming closer to their doorstep, and the true story of how they accepted us is found in later chapters.

The Argyle Cycle Company formerly owned by Mr Bill Tracy rented the outbuildings of Stoke House that were still usable. An application was received asking the Plymouth City Council for a tenancy agreement that would allow them the right to use the premises at a rental of £80 per annum, plus rates, and in October 1944 this was granted. In July 1945 the Plymouth City Council made the decision not to rebuild Stoke House. The children on their return from Clovelly to Plymouth would be rehomed at Astor Hall, Stoke, Devonport, Plymouth. This was accepted and the City Architect was asked to draw up plans to convert Astor Hall, to make it acceptable as a childrens' home. During the war and until 1950, the older boys of Somerset Place School used the grounds of Stoke House as allotments, under the supervision of the teacher in charge Mr Dowrick. Notable past traders in the area were A Richards, a coal dealer J. Dawe, and nearby was the Pear Tree public house.

A registered forage store (corn chandler and seed merchant) run by W. Robins was situated on the south side of Tavistock Road in Stoke. Massive double doors opened to allow horse drawn carts to back in for loading and unloading into the loft above. The store always smelt of hay, and numerous sparrows could be seen eating the seed, spilt from the sacks. The chandlers closed in the late 1930's to be replaced by the Argyle Cycle Shop, and the exterior was altered to display a black and chrome shop front coupled with two huge windows and a door in the centre. Apart from bicycles the windows displayed Dinky Toys and model boats to the delight of the children who would spend precious time watching and admiring. One of the store's special features was the model railway, which was always in operation and many a child was late home fascinated by the rolling stock and reluctant to leave.

At the top of Ford Hill was a chemist shop, Attwells, which was there for many years. Another long-term shopkeeper was Mrs Emily Furzeman who kept a general store at number forty-three Tavistock Road (now Devonport Road) in the 1920's/1930's. She sold cold meat, cooked beetroot, sweets, bread and pasties. On her death Ivor Dewdney, renowned for his home made pasties took over the premises in 1943 and his business is still there to this day. Next door was the Plymouth Co-operative Society (CWS) which stretched from Tavistock Road around to Dundas Street. Another large house existing at the time was Belmont House, which was built in 1820 by John Foulston in the Greek Revival style for the wealthy banker John Norman to store his art collection. From 1845 to 1854 the property became the home of Francis Whish Wilson who was a Major General in the Indian Army, he too was awarded the honour of Companion of Bath. In the 1950's it was used by the Youth Hostel Association, now it has been converted into spacious apartments for private residents, thankfully it is listed, as a Grade Two building which should protect its future. Stoke Manor House at Trafalgar Road, was another fine house.

The loss of such beautiful Neo Classical, Grecian Revival, Italianate Houses and Regency Buildings from the village of Stoke rests not only with the German bombing of 1941 but also with our own architects and builders. Rather than repair, or replace those precious heritage buildings, they chose to create a concrete jungle of blocks of flats to house the local population. A sad demise indeed for a very unique district of Plymouth. Of course, on a balanced view, one has to consider the dilemma facing Plymouth City Council to replace hundreds of homes destroyed in the war, and finding the finance to complete the rebuilding of a devastated city. The residents and businesses of Stoke Village, however, are fiercely proud of the history of Stoke, and rightly so, and the citizens today still retain their pride and endeavour to ensure that Stoke Village never loses its heritage. As for Stoke House, it is hoped that this book will be a record of its existence and ensure that it will never be forgotten again!

Stoke House in 1846 was called Stoke Cottage as this advertisement from the Plymouth & Devon Weekly Journal dated 30th July 1846 shows. The House was for sale after the death of Captain George Aldham R.N.

Samuel Vosper's letter to Earl St Aubyn the Lord St Levan written in 1896 securing the lease for fifty years and the agreement to keep some windows blanked out that overlooked Lord St Levan's land. Confirmed also was the building of the new boundary wall. Article courtesy Plymouth & West Devon Record Office. (Copyright approved 387/2/191).

42

CHAPTER SIX

STAFF - STOKE HOUSE

Staff Stoke House Devonport Plymouth 1940 outside enjoying their tea. From the Left. Miss Joan Henderson (Nurse in charge of the Boys) Miss Audrey Penna (Nurse in charge of the girls) Miss Beatrice Thompson (Cook) sitting in front Miss Holly Penna (Assistant and sister to Nurse Penna). Photo courtesy Doctor Robert Crowte MBA PhD Barnt Green Worcestershire. (Joan Henderson's son.)

In 1931-1932 the decision had been taken to completely review all the Staff at Number 39A Tavistock Road, known as Stoke House. Rumours and speculation were rife, it was prudent for public relations to be appeased and the welfare and the educational care of the children reassessed. Many changes were made in 1931-1932 when the cruelty and abuse cases were predominant. With the imprisonment of a Stoke House workman for child abuse after a trial which had been held "In Camera" the Plymouth City Council terminated his appointment at Stoke House. The position the workman had held was to be advertised and applications considered at the next meeting.

Mr Arthur Scott, a family man with two daughters and one son, was appointed as full time Gardener and he proved to be a very kind and nice man, respected by everyone who knew him. His garden was a joy and many of the children who are now in their twilight years still speak highly of him as he was kind to the little mites without love. He remained at Stoke House and Clovelly, North Devon, until his recall into the RAF in 1943. When he was released from the services he returned to the Orphanage which was now situated at Astor Hall, Stoke, to continue his position until his retirement.

Miss Margaret Isabella Holden was designated Matron of Stoke House from September 1931, another of the new appointments actioned by Plymouth City Council and the Welfare Department. On Miss Bull's retirement in November 1938 Miss Holden was given the dual position of Superintendent of the Childrens' Homes (including all Scattered Homes) and Matron of Stoke House at a salary of £150 per annum with emoluments in addition

Taken on a day trip to the seaside 1948. From the Left. Betty Newham (Stoke House girl) Miss Holden (Matron retired) Man unknown, Miss Audrey Penna (retired), Man unknown, Miss Holly Penna (retired). Photo courtesy Mrs Susan Doney Cornwall.

valued at £76.10. However, in April 1939 Miss Holden was admitted to the isolation hospital with what I understand to be a nervous breakdown, and was released later in November 1939. Many senior citizens now in their twilight years have asked the question why was Miss Holden put back in charge of vulnerable children, it had been a dreadful mistake. Many a child of that era remembers receiving insuperable treatment in the years that followed. Former residents of Stoke House recall the beatings Miss Holden handed out, she had a special slipper set aside to mete out the punishment and a little queue of children would wait their turn outside her office to pay for their misdemeanours. Unfortunately, with the commencement of World War Two in September 1939 staff would be at a premium so no action was taken. In July 1945 Miss Holden on return from Clovelly asked for her appointment to continue for another twelve months. However, after the report from the Inspectors visits to Clovelly it was clear another change of social welfare policy was in the pipeline and her request was denied, but she was retained for another month, to allow the new Superintendent Mrs D Reid time to settle into her new appointment at the new childrens' home Astor Hall, Stoke, Devonport, Plymouth.

Miss Audrey Kate Penna (1901-1989) (RIP) (Nurse-Girls) Assistant Matron (Deputy Superintendent).
Audrey Kate Penna was one of four sisters. She was a qualified Childrens' Nurse and was working at Tavistock Hospital, Devon, when she was approached by the Matron to take on the post of Childrens' Nurse at Stoke House Devonport, Plymouth, which was a home for orphaned, unwanted and abandoned children. The authorities had requested someone who loved children. The matron was very persuading and eventually succeeded in arranging the transfer. It was to change her life and she spent the rest of her working days as childrens' nurse, at Stoke House Plymouth and Clovelly North Devon. She was a kind and fair person and most children related to

Nurse Audrey Penna helping to cut the grass in the grounds of Stoke House circa 1930's. Note the large Greenhouse at the back where wealthy families grew their grapes in the past. Photo courtesy Mrs Audrey Ray (nee Stacey) Uxbridge Middlesex. (Niece).

Audrey had her sights set on obtaining the post of Home Matron in time, alas this never happened and she took the disappointment very hard. Another sad event in her life which marred her happiness was when her dear friend policeman Alfred Crosby was killed in the war near the policeman's hut in Stoke in July 1940. Both middle aged they had planned to marry but had decided to wait so as not to jeopardise their pensions. Audrey now contented herself with taking care of the children in the home.

Miss Holly D Penna (1903-1987) (RIP) (Girls).
Although having never worked before and having no qualifications in nursing or child guidance she was appointed as Assistant at Stoke House in November 1934 in succession to Miss Lock. Miss Holly Penna was Nurse Audrey Penna's sister and Audrey had managed to recommend Holly for the post. A clear case of nepotism which was predominant in the nineteen thirties. Miss Holly Penna was to abuse the position of trust for she made life a misery for the children, being an acrimonious person and, to the children in her care, formidable. The children were scared of her and considered her not so much strict, as acting out of petty spite!

Mrs Beatrice L Thompson (RIP) (1898-1944) (Cook)
Mrs Thompson was appointed as Cook, Stoke House in December 1931, she superseded Mrs Coulling who had left in August 1931. Mrs Thompson was

Beatrice Thompson Cook at Stoke House 1931- 1941. Photo courtesy of Mrs Jean Job (nee McFadyen) Plymouth.

absent from duty owing to illness in 1938 and another cook was employed on a temporary basis. On return to her duties as Cook Mrs Thompson was transferred with the Orphanage in 1941 to the New Inn Clovelly, North Devon. In 1942 she fell and fractured her ankle whilst on duty and was taken to Bideford General Hospital. She never returned to the post as cut backs on costs meant that other arrangements were made. Later in 1944 she was taken very ill with cancer and died at the age of forty-six. Cookie, as we used to call her, had a "Jekyll and Hyde" personality, one-minute caring and helping the children with unofficial tidbits another time reporting children for punishment. The children learned to assess her moods before asking or tempting fate in any way. Beattie the cook's sister Mabel was a Nurse and was also an ARP Warden (died 1989 in her seventies) who used to visit Clovelly regularly to see Cook.

Miss B J Henderson (RIP) (1916-1987)

Miss Joan Henderson a fully qualified childrens' nurse was appointed Assistant to Stoke House and Ford House (Boys) on 1st January 1936. She succeeded Assistant Miss V Major, whose appointment was terminated on the 31 December 1935. A very private person, she was well liked and looked after the boys only. She alternated between Stoke House and Ford House; both were closely linked with Scattered Homes as children were sent to Ford House for assessment. Former boys under her care have spoken very highly of her treatment toward them and respected a professional who treated the boys humanely. Born in 1916 she did her nursing training in London, it was thought at Virginia Water and the hospital she worked at was St Helier's Carshalton near Richmond. Miss Henderson kept her post on the evacuation in April 1941 with all the children to the New Inn Clovelly until 1945, when the evacuated children were returned to Plymouth.

A mature Nurse Henderson taken in 1940 in the grounds of Stoke House.

On leaving Clovelly she worked in school nursing and in dental nursing in Plymouth where she met her fiancé at a dance. She found happiness and married late in life at the age of forty to Ronald Crowte in 1956. Her husband was a Technical Engineer at Rolls Royce Bristol. Joan continued to work as an administration clerk till her son Robert was born. Joan was forty-five years old when she gave birth to her son and it led to medical complications for her throughout life resulting in debilitating arthritis. Sadly she suffered a heart attack and passed away in 1987. A kind nurse remembered with affection.

Miss Doris J. Lavis (Domestic Cleaner)

Miss Lavis was appointed in January 1937. Miss Lavis wore glasses and had dark hair, and the girls remember that she always wore a hair net. She wore one of the floral printed cross over aprons, and was a very pleasant person and kind to the children, being sympathetic to their plight. Sybil Webb (nee Bond) remembers the day Miss Lavis approached Miss Holden and asked permission to take Sybil and another girl called Audrey Pester Christmas shopping in town to the ever-popular sixpenny store Woolworths! Miss Holden at first said no but compromised when Miss Lavis agreed to accept full responsibiltiy, this is understandable as the children were in her care. The girls never forgot that day when they were free for just a little while.

Mrs Violet Leyman was another cleaner who worked at Stoke House Orphanage in the early 1930's, she lived in Packington Street, which was close by, and she too is remembered with affection. It seemed as if the lady cleaners could see the effect the rigid regime imposed on the children had and did their level best to help in any way they could without risking the loss of their jobs.

Young Nurse Joan Henderson (left) with a Miss Foster (right) on their appointments as children's nurses Stoke House 1936. Photo courtesy Doctor Robert Crowte MBA PhD Barnt Green Worcestershire. (Miss Henderson's son).

Miss Vera Foster.

Miss Foster was the Assistant Attendant to Miss Henderson the Nurse who helped to look after the boys at Stoke House. She was in her thirties when transferred to Clovelly, circa 1941-1945; she was a short person with very pretty hair. In November 1943 Miss Foster was one of the unlucky staff to be chosen to leave Clovelly to ease the cost of maintenance at the New Inn. She was appointed to the position of Assistant Attendant at Ford House Plymouth a home for poor and female mental cases in May 1944, however, unhappy she resigned in June 1944 and returned to Clovelly as a companion to a lady called Mrs Bates. She was a great friend of Fanny Shackson of Clovelly. After the war she stayed on at Clovelly as a companion to Mrs Bates, and would visit her friend Fanny who lived opposite the Post Office. Many years later she moved to Devonport to live either at Pier Street or Chapel Street.

Miss Ellen Crimp Seamstress.

This lady spent her working years at the Scattered Home at Hill Park Crescent, at Stoke House, and at the New Inn Clovelly. A short person with glasses and grey hair, she was a lovely lady and she above all changed the clothing styles of the children in the homes. On her appointment, seeing the drab clothes the boys and girls wore upset her so much, she decided to arrange for brighter material to be issued and she would make all the clothes for the children in the future and what a transformation. Each week at Hill Park Crescent and later at Stoke House two large bales of printed cloth would arrive at the homes. On occasion she would let the older girls select the print of their choice and made the dresses closer to the fashion at the time. Unfortunately the war years and the rationing did not allow her to continue making fashionable clothes and as clothing was being supplied to the children of the New Inn by various war relief agencies she was relegated to maintaining and repairing what clothes and uniforms the children had.

Miss Alice H Bull.

Miss Bull was appointed Superintendent of all the Scattered Homes (including Stoke House) as from 1-9-31. Miss Holden was appointed Matron of Stoke House on the same date. Miss Bull was held in very high esteem by the girls of 36 Hill Park Crescent, who stated that she was a very nice person, was kind to the children and treated them with respect. When Miss Bull retired on 29-11-38 the children were all transferred to Stoke House and their quality of life was never the same. Stoke House and its reputation was instilled in the girls memories and it is indeed sad that more stringent action was not taken by the authorities to remove the martinets from Stoke House. The children cringed at the names of Miss Holden and Miss Holly Penna. Their tasks in running a childrens' home must have been formidable, but however difficult, and irrespective of financial complications, there is no excuse for physical violence or mental torture.

Miss K Blackford.

Boarded out visitor appointed female assistant relieving officer Grade C2 (F) at a commencing salary of £135 per annum. Miss M Uglow undertook the whole of the boarded out duties at the same salary. On the 11-10-37 Miss K Blackford was appointed Boarded out Visitor Grade 2. Not much is known about this lady, as her roving position did not allow regular contact

Miss S C Hay.
Foster mother at 80 Mount Gould Road resigned 5-3-37 and arrangements were being made for a successor. At the same time Miss Francis Cartwright resigned as Foster Mother at 13 Hill Park Crescent. Miss Francis was a qualified Nurse. A tall person rather austere, she had a quiet and reserved ambience. She was the daughter of a School Headmaster and seemed out of place in the position she was in, however, she is remembered with affection.

Miss E.A.B. Male Grade C2.
Miss Male was appointed as Foster Mother in July 1937 on a temporary basis. Later she was appointed Boarding-Out Visitor and was employed full time in April 1942 in the Education Department on Social Welfare Duties. In September 1943 Miss Male was designated Boarded Out Visitor and female assistant Social Welfare Officer, to resume duties of visiting out relief cases with children, in addition to acting as Boarding-Out Visitor. Miss Male as visiting officer was liked by the children but she had a difficult task in accompanying children to their new boarded out premises; as often children would be upset at this disruption because it meant being put with a foster family they had not met.

Hilda Glover 1931 as a child. She spent the whole of her childhood life in scattered homes and Stoke House and was later employed to work there on reaching the age of fourteen. Photo courtesy of Mr & Mrs R. Meaker Manadon Plymouth. (Sister)

Miss Hilda Glover Kitchen Maid. (RIP) (1924-1997)
Hilda was born in Laira Plymouth in 1924 and spent her childhood life in Scattered Homes and Stoke House. When she reached the age of fourteen she was given a post of kitchen maid and was evacuated with the home to Clovelly, North Devon in April 1941 with all the Stoke House children. There are many instances where children of the Scattered Homes were given posts but always in the most mundane jobs. However, Hilda was very happy in Clovelly and had fond memories of the years spent there and often talked of her experiences with cookie! (Beatrice Thompson) Her husband was pleased to submit information so that Hilda would be remembered in this book and stated that had she lived she would have loved to have met the girls again. When she left the home she found a job at Bonnies Milk Bar and later met Ken Seeby who was a

restaurant car attendant on British Rail; they married in August 1949. They had five sons and later moved to Birmingham when husband Ken was promoted. Sadly Hilda suffered a terrible brain disease and had to go into a nursing home where she later died.

Doctor Sandford. Appointed Medical Officer to Ford House Institution, Stoke House Childrens' home and also the Scattered Homes. Doctor Sandford's Salary was set into three allowances i.e., Ford House £150, Stoke House £50, Scattered Homes £50. Plus travelling expenses. Little is known about Doctor Sandford although he attended all the sick children at Ford Workhouse and at Stoke House.

Taken at Astor Hall 1948 the new Headquarters of the children's home on return from Clovelly 1945. Left Arthur Scott (Gardener) Middle Miss Ellen Crimp (Seamstress) Right Miss Dorothy Saul who had spent the whole of her childhood in Stoke House. Photo courtesy of Mrs Muriel Ellison (nee Gray) Plymouth.

CHAPTER SEVEN

STOKE HOUSE IN THE 1930'S

Class divisions have existed in Britain for centuries and this was even more pronounced in the 1930's when, due to economic problems and the many people who were unemployed, there was a much greater division between rich and poor. Some poor were financially unable to support their families, particularly so if one parent had died. There were many children, like those who were the subject of cruelty cases. Stoke House, number 39 (A) Tavistock Road, Devonport, Plymouth, known as the Poor Law Institution, had many such placements, children who were never to experience luxuries that a child living in a normal family environment would have. The old Poor Law Act took away pride and privacy from poverty-stricken citizens and children were to become aware at a very early age of the social class gap.

Life for a child should be an exhilarating experience and if adults could see the world through the eyes of a child what a wonderful thing it would be! Stoke House staff and children did not mingle with the local people, indeed some citizens would view the children with disdain, and as to the quality of their lives, that continued daily in the same trammelled environment. Children in institutions were programmed, and the regime was strict. Children were not allowed to show any emotion and they were never consulted as to their feelings. Children of the poor were not told anything in the 1930's/1940's and were considered second class citizens. Staff and children alike lived as hermits and were unseen. It was indeed sad that the local citizens did not include the children of Stoke House in their activities. On occasion someone would accidentally leave the huge iron gates ajar and one could peek through. That person would risk a disapproving look from a member of staff.

In 1931 there had been sweeping changes of staff at Stoke House and the Scattered Homes as cruelty and abuse was known to the authorities. Groups of runaway children had reached unreasonable levels which the administrators had to finally acknowledge. So many children were running away that it could not be ignored. There had to be a reason why it was so predominate. The City Authorities tried hard to cope and their intentions were good. However, trying to balance a financial budget and overwhelmed by sheer numbers of children in care served only to create idiosyncrasies of their system creating an atmosphere of importance to statistics instead of personal contact and love with the child.

The choice of the Matron and some members of staff would by the standard of today leave much to be desired. In one particular case in the 1930's a male member of ground maintenance staff, who had abused young girls in the grounds of Stoke House, was tried and sent to prison. The trial was held "in camera" and not publicised. One witness was a lady whose home had overlooked the grounds of Stoke House. It was she who informed the police of the sexual abuse of the children and the police set up a camera in one of her bedrooms to monitor and photograph the offences. It did succeed in catching the perpetrator and putting the dreadful man in prison for a long time. No doubt that this is one of many hush-hush incidents which, perhaps, helped to secure a seventy five-year closure period on personal records.

Life was very harsh and often a child would be sent to bed without supper for the slightest infringement of rules, and without doubt were not treated as sentient beings. No matter how hard they tried children were always in the wrong! Sweet rations were confiscated and a cold bath would be given if the child showed any sign of temper. Other forms of punishments were applied so that no physical sign would show but the mental scars remain. On occasion a child who did not like the food it was eating was force fed, and made to eat every scrap before leaving the table. This distressed not only the

THE CHILD AND THE LASH

The flagellants of the House of Lords received a severe rebuke from the House of Commons on Thursday.

Their lordships' amendment of the Children Bill which restored the lash to the list of punishments suitable for naughty children was rejected decisively. In the debate, the women members displayed a far wiser psychology as well as a finer humanity than any of the upholders of the " strong arm of the law "— as represented by a burly policeman with a birch in his hand.

They pointed out that if a licking from a schoolmaster or a parent had any virtue at all, it was because the child knew his corrector and understood his motive, and would be in close contact with him thereafter—an entirely different matter from a flogging adjudged to him by a magistrate and administered to him by a constable.

" Judicial " flogging is a futile brutality, a relic from a sorry past, out of harmony with modern ideas of punishment and reformation. Whatever may be said (and it is not much) for flogging adults who commit certain crimes, answering violence with violence, nothing can be said for flogging children. Reclamation, understanding, guidance—these and not the lash are the instruments which will convert the incipient criminal into a decent citizen.

In the 1930's there was still controversy at using physical force against a child as this debate from the Western Independent July 1932 shows. With permission courtesy Plymouth Reference Library.

52

child being forced fed, but also the other children who were made to watch the treatment. Many children wet the bed. The offending child was cruelly punished by being made to stand, wrapped in the wet sheet, in view of all the other children. There was no one to speak for these tormented children and the perpetrators of this punishment should have been ashamed. Children who had normal lives with parents, who lived in the vicinity, were threatened with being sent to Stoke House as punishment if they did not behave. What an indictment on how the public reacted to that large house behind closed walls!

After the change of staff, welfare policies were reconsidered and a tighter control was kept, staff and children were monitored regularly and the abuse stopped. However, occasional beatings still took place, as one or two members of staff were martinets and imposed their physical presence on some of the children that they did not favour. They were careful not to select children who may have had a relative visiting, as they knew that child would tell! Visitors were allowed once a month usually on a Saturday afternoon. There had been fierce debate in July 1932 in the House of Lords, which led to a severe rebuke from the House of Commons on the subject of using physical abuse on children, particularly the use of the lash.

On visiting days all the toys stored were put out on display for the children to play with but as soon as the visitors left they were all taken away and stored out of sight until the following visit. Children in institutions soon learned to be resilient! If children demonstrated initiative they were quickly suppressed and considered too forward or inquisitive. Most children in the institution were considered to be inferior. To get a balanced view, it must be pointed out that some children were difficult and naughty and needed to be corrected, there were also children with mental and emotional difficulties; however, there are ways of correcting children without resorting to physical violence. There were some members of staff who liked the children and would protect their little indiscretions, but who were themselves afraid of the hierarchy in control, and in order to retain their posts kept quiet, rather than risk the wrath of their employers and lose their job. Medical care for children was given more priority; tuberculosis, polio and rickets were widespread amongst the children of the poor in the 1930's, so the welfare authorities appointed Doctor Sandford as Medical Officer in December

1930 at the childrens' home at Stoke House.

There were indeed some happy times too, and when rumours circulated about the problems at Stoke House, some members of the public were angry and others would pass it off with a comment as "Poor little mites" but did nothing! There are limits to the creative vision of quasi-autonomous governmental bodies, and these limitations kept the public from knowing the real situation at Stoke House.

Christmas 1931 the 13th Devonport Brownie Pack under the leadership of Miss Plant whose group attended Saint James the Great church decided to forfeit their Christmas Party to buy presents instead for the Stoke House children. The pack visited Stoke House and quietly placed the presents on the doorstep, then the brownies crouched down behind the wall as the Brown Owl Miss Plant rang the door bell and she dashed behind the wall to join the pack eager to watch what would happen. Someone came to the door and saw the presents on the doorstep, and as they gathered the presents in, they looked around to see whom the mystery caller could be but no one was in sight. Well done that Brownie Pack! Charities on hearing of the unrest began to respond and companies offered some treats. The children and teachers of Ker Street Junior Technical School and the Ker Street Infants School also sent presents. Ker Street Infants school was an Edwardian School constructed in 1903, it closed in 1981 and Devon County Council sold the property.

The Devonport Member of Parliament Major Leslie Hore-Belisha (1923-1945), hearing of the plight of the children also responded. He sent some gifts to Stoke House to be shared amongst the children; he was a genuine man and highly respected by one and all. Although a well liked Minister he was never to fulfil his true political potential, however, he did achieve some measure of fame, as when war started he was Minister of Transport. It was he who introduced the Belisha Beacons at pedestrian crossings. There were many genuine charities and citizens who did much to give the children treats and continued to supply gifts. One very special lady was Lady Astor. The children of Stoke House and Clovelly owe much to this irrepressible citizen; she was to have a profound affect on the quality of their young lives.

Children who came under the care of the Public Assistance Board and the Welfare State were admitted to Stoke House, Ford House or Nazareth House, assessed and relocated to the Scattered Homes in accordance with their grading. New measures were initiated which would improve the education of the children, in July 1931 the decision was made to employ a Teacher with experience of nursery school work to teach the five year olds and under five age group at Stoke House, older children were sent to Somerset Place School, Stoke, Devonport. Selection of children at Stoke House was based on their age on entering the institution those seven years of age and under stayed at Stoke House. Those over seven years old were transferred to either 13 or 36 Hill Park Crescent, Greenbank, Plymouth, for two weeks of observation. Children with problems would be sent to Ford House for further assessment, occasionally young children would be sent to Lady Astor's Childrens' Home and if they did they were very lucky, as those infants were well cared for and her home employed very kind staff.

The decision as to where the child moved next depended on how the Superintendent assessed the child, woe betide the child who spoke out of turn, or did not respond to whatever overtures were put forward, whatever the child did or said then labelled it for life! Many children were labelled maladjusted or misfits because they could not respond to strangers. Often derogatory remarks would be recorded on the child's assessment paper which earmarked that child to the welfare authorities as being difficult, or those dreaded words, sub-normal, retarded or mentally deficient, were written indiscriminately without giving the child a fair assessment, other remarks would be 'dim' or 'stupid'. Already distressed at being left alone in the world some children withdrew into a shell, others responded angrily and became labelled as trouble makers. Some would become emotionally disturbed when all they really wanted was a little love; this was not in the curriculum of Stoke House and the Scattered Homes.

There is a moral here for every generation to learn. Do not demean children or label them or call them names to make them feel inferior, every one is beautiful on the inside and that should be nurtured and not destroyed. It is noted that the matrons and superintendents were all single ladies with no children of their own, they had insular attitudes and a blinkered viewpoint that the appearance of a child contributed directly to whether they would succeed in society. They were dark days, of erratically judging children on how they looked, or even as to what style of clothing they wore when they came into the home, which many times led to a dreadful misjudgement of the child's character. On receiving her record from the Social Services in 1998 one of the senior citizens who had spent her whole life in the Stoke House Orphanage had noted on her records this remark: "This child is socially unsuitable to remain at this school." At the time that the Welfare Worker transcribed this note on the record sheet, the supposed "socially unsuitable" child was three years old! How can a three-year-old child be socially unsuitable?

A CHILDREN'S LOT IN STOKE HOUSE!
Too Fat - Too Thin, Too Stupid - Too Dim, This child is from Sin!
Too Short - Too Tall, Knows nothing at all!
Too slow - Too Dull, Too simple – Too Dumb
No Father – No Mum, A child of the poor- My Label is done!

In fairness it has to be accepted that there were some children who were very difficult to control and some even succumbed to mental illness. Every child craves for some attention and would respond normally to a cuddle or a hug, to be embraced and kissed makes a child feel special. The priorities for spiritual and moral development are a must for children without the love of a normal family home. Emotional guidance and feelings are of paramount importance, however, these were not available to the Scattered Homes children and they soon learnt that they were a name and number and were not granted the emotional comfort they so desired. They were constantly reminded that they were there under sufferance. This was emphasised clearly by the Matron who on speaking to the children would say, "Come here you little sinners!" how can babies and very young children be sinners at that age? Down through the ages many people had quoted from the bible a sentence from the greatest living man of all time. His message was clear and it was he who said, "Suffer little children to come unto me!" Miss M Holden who was the superintendent of Stoke House had spent six months in a special isolation hospital ward, and the motive has to be questionable as to why after six months in hospital for a nervous breakdown she was returned to the post of Matron at Stoke House in charge of vulnerable children.

Life turned for the better in the very late nineteen thirties as lifestyles changed dramatically with the onset of the war and the children of Stoke House were to benefit from the rapid change. More visitors came as children had to be taught where their avenues of escape were in case of fire at the home, instructors taught the children how to wear their gas masks and each child had to have an Identity Card with an allocated number. A greater awareness of the home reached the public and when the children sat down to their meals there was a better quality of food when their meals were put in front of them. Outings were arranged and members of the public would take a child out for the day, perhaps they would take them shopping, or alternatively take them somewhere to be treated to a special tea.

Sports days were organised and usually someone of importance would visit the Childrens' Home to present the prizes, which were usually small sums of money. Summer holidays were spent at Maker Camp just across the water from Plymouth, at the beginning of Cornwall. The children found the event very exciting especially getting everything packed for the trip, clothes were packed in large laundry baskets and sent on ahead. Whilst at Maker Camp they were taken to the beach each day and often a picnic lunch would be taken, usually corned beef sandwiches which tasted lovely, the children would visit Kingsands, Cawsands and Sandy Bay and they would walk on occasion to Ramehead and Whitsand Bay. The children began to mix with other children outside of the institution when at Maker Camp as the Girl Guides and the Boy Scouts used to go there, and they would invite the Stoke House children to join their bonfire and join in the camp fire songs. From their beautiful surroundings they could see the Liner Queen Mary come into Plymouth Sound during the month of August and they would sit on the grass mounds at the bottom of a field and see the Liner all lit up and if the wind was in the right direction the dance music could be heard coming from the ship.

Then came the war and the bombing, and Stoke House was destroyed on St George's Day 23rd April 1941. The children spent the rest of the night in other accommodation. The following day they were transferred to Montpelier Junior & Infant School for girls, Peverell, Plymouth. On the 28th of April 1941 the school received four direct hits from parachute landmines. The terrified children were re-assembled on the 29th April 1941, fed and given clothing and prepared for evacuation. On the 30th April 1941 they were evacuated to Clovelly, North Devon. The children were taken by bus, the girls in one bus, boys in the second bus, and a whole new chapter in their style of living was to change their lives forever.

The Original Stoke House Girls. A Mrs Hitchcock took this photo in 1938 when the girls won the Independent Order of Good Templars Shield. All Rows read from the left. Front Row 1. Pat Richards, 2. Pat Roberts (RIP). 3. Doris Hicks. 4. Betty Newham. Middle Row. 1. Ethel Gerry. 2. Lily Evans. 3. Margaret Bailey (head turned) 4. Ellen Saul. 5. Pearl Rickard. 6. Lucy Evens. Back Row 1. Rosemary Buckingham (top of head only) 2. Sybil Bond. 3. Dorothy Saul. (RIP) 4. Margaret Pester. (RIP) 5. Gwendoline Tyrell.

Photo courtesy of Mrs Gwendoline Collihole (nee Tyrell)

CHAPTER EIGHT

LIFE IN THE NINETEEN THIRTIES

J.R. Herklots former Vicar of St Bartholomew's Church Plymouth wisely said in 1965 "If we are to understand the present, we must know and respect the past."

Any child born in Plymouth during the 1930's was to experience the years of the depression when families were poor and the welfare state as we know it today was not so affluent. Large families existed and birth control clinics were not available for all women in those days, it was a newly formed department and not yet established throughout the country. Children born out of wedlock were stigmatised and unmarried mothers were forced to give up their babies because there was no social system to support them and if the young mother's own parents disowned her, that exacerbated the situation even more. An unwanted child born in the 1930's found themselves in an environment that was far from stable on just about every emotional and financial level. Top class medical care was not available for the very poor and the health of the local population was cause for concern. For those who could pay their chances were better.

Plymouth did lead the way in one unique situation and that was in 1935 when the most modern Ambulance Station in the country was located in the district of Greenbank. It had installed the new revolutionary Novox Resuscitation Apparatus and was manned by St John's Ambulance volunteers. Unemployment was high with two million of the population out of work, in Plymouth twenty per cent of the population was unemployed. Plymouth in the 1930's was a non-industrial, provincial city, its population comprised of a large number of military personnel. However, looking back at the life style of the thirties does reveal a nostalgic era, which we will not see again, when the prices of goods and food were deemed reasonable if you had the money! New ideas were available for the everyday housewife, sliced bread was introduced in 1930 and Lyons Kut-Bread proved a real novelty and the introduction of the new Pyrex dishes were all the rage in the kitchen. Nylon was invented and by taking the initials from London and New York (as both countries had created the invention in the same year) meant that honour was shared, Dupont later patented their new miracle fibre nylon in 1937.

The new Central Park in Plymouth was opened in 1931 for the citizens and children to enjoy. Two hundred acres of land had been bought from Baron St. Levan, and many a happy hour was to be spent playing in the paddling and boating pools and infants cherished the use of the swings. Another favourite spot was the open air bathing pools at Mount Wise, and the recently opened Lido pool on Plymouth Hoe. For those who did not like swimming, walks were very popular. As film shows were to become one of the most popular means of entertainment during the 1930's in Plymouth the population were pleased to note the opening of the new Gaumont Cinema in 1931.

Children have always loved having stories read to them. The evening edition of a local Plymouth paper had a special feature called 'The Wendy Hut Children's Corner.' Some children enjoyed reading it for themselves but there were many more who persisted until an adult was persuaded to read the contents to them. The stories were always called 'Told by the Brownie.' Simple things pleased children in those days. I remember the 'The Tinker Bell Badge Club.' It was so popular that the paper was overwhelmed by the number of applicants. In order to sort the membership out they issued a surname letter each week and children had to wait until their initial appeared before they were able to have the coveted badge and promise to do a kind deed each day, which was the membership requirement. Comics were popular; the weekly 'Dandy' was published for the first time in 1937 and 'Beano' in 1938. A special treat at Christmas was the 'Beano' annual. For girls the 'Girls Crystal' was coveted and boys saved sixpence to have the monthly 'Boys Own.' If they ordered the magazine for one year then they were awarded a membership card and a special badge.

There were many more comics and magazines in the 1930's. For those who could afford it the girl's monthly 'The Merry-Go-Round' crammed full of children's stories cost one shilling. Hotspur, Triumph, Champion and the Rover, were all names to be conjured with. Costing one penny, the boy's comic 'Tip Top' appeared every Wednesday. Other favourites were Chick's Own, Playbox, Tiny Tots, Knockout, and Comics Cuts. Another penny favourite was the illustrated 'Chips', which featured 'Weary Willie and Tired Tim' the world famous tramps. For twopence you could buy 'Puck', which came out every Tuesday. 'Jingles Jolly Circus' was full of fun and frolic with the merry makers and the most expensive of all, 'Rainbow' costing three shillings and sixpence was in the newsagents every Monday featuring Tiger Tim. Annuals were cherished Christmas presents, especially 'Pip, Squeak and Wilfred.' It was in this era that the 'Rupert Bear' books and the still popular weekly 'Sunny Stories' by Enid Blyton became firm favourites with children. A totally different magazine, 'The Aircraft Recognition Book' taught boys about the types of aircraft and with war in the offing it proved a strong competitor in the children's publication market place.

Children did not have the monopoly on magazines. They were avidly read by women particularly Woman or Women's Own for two pence each. Film Magazines telling the stories of forthcoming films and the gossip that exuded from the glamorous world of Hollywood were incredibly popular. Film Weekly, the fortnightly Picturegoer, Film Pictorial every Thursday together with the more serious Picture Post at tuppence, headed the list. Annually one could buy for three shillings the film Pictorial. Every month for one shilling the magazine 'Everywoman's' was published. Full of fashion features, romantic stories, up to date household items and colourful advertisements, it was one of the most popular. Later in the nineteen forties the war brought paper shortages and strict control by the Government Departments. This caused the demise of some magazines and others merged like Film Weekly and Picturegoer. To get your regular copy you had to be registered with the General Post Office. Film stars have dictated fashion to a certain extent and during the war, the actress Priscilla Lane's hair style and clothes were widely copied. Many girls were christened Priscilla.

Some food brands names are still with us today and some have disappeared. You never hear of infants being fed with Doctor Eales-Goodbodys biscuits at one shilling per packet but Farley's Rusks are still with us. Wanting to lose weight has gone on for centuries. In the 30s and 40s diets were assisted by Energen Rolls, McVita, Darvita, Vitawheat and Ryvita Biscuits. Weetabix launched their cereal in 1930 followed later by Quaker Puffed Wheat. Shirley Temple promoted their cereal with her photograph on the front of the packet. Crawford the biscuit manufacturer launched what were to become the well-known tins of Rover Biscuits. Hartley's table jellies were four pence each, a children's delight. Ah! Those were the days! Housewives had a yearning for Typhoo Tea as it was said to relieve indigestion and it was available sold loose or in quarter pound packets. Men who smoked cigarettes favoured Wills Wild Woodbines by WD & HO Wills, which could be bought from a vending machine for the price of five for tuppence. Player's Navy Cut or Players Weights by John Players and Sons, were sold as ten for sixpence; another popular brand for the working class were Park Drive cigarettes by Gallahers. For those who liked to roll their own, Old Holborn or A1 shag tobacco with red Ritz papers would satisfy their craving for a smoke. Ladies who smoked favoured "Craven A" Virginia Cigarettes by Carreras Limited, "Tenner" by Churchman's, or Honey Dew "Gold Flake" by WD. & HO. Wills. The De-Reske cigarettes had a catch phrase popular with smokers known as 'A ten minute smoke for intelligent folk, mine's a minor'. Not many housewives of the 1930's could afford to smoke and it was not deemed morally right to smoke in front of the children.

A 1930's advert depicting the value of children drinking Horlicks as a bedtime drink.

Camp and Chicory coffee was being accepted as an alternative drink to tea by the average household. The Scottish Regiment "The Gordon Highlanders" formerly used Camp coffee when they were in India in 1885. Coffee was considered a real luxury, during the late 1930's Nescafe Instant Coffee made its debut, any child who managed to obtain a cup of coffee was deemed upper class. Small tins of Bantam Coffee could be bought which contained pure grounds. Other children were content with their cup of Bournvita, which came on the market in 1933, some parents preferred to give their children Horlicks as it was recommended for highly strung children, others preferred Fry's Cocoa.

A favourite night time drink for children was a cup of Ovaltine, and of course they would gleefully sing "We are the OvalTineys, little girls and boys" as that was the song at the time. Radio Luxembourg had promoted

Ovaltine, which had been on the market since 1909 and was to be the children's favourite drink in the 1930's. Five million children were to become exclusive members in 1935 of the "League of Oval Tineys" which enhanced its popularity. Children were seen proudly wearing their Ovaltine Badge, every member was expected to follow a code of conduct and observe high moral principles. The adult population tuned in regularly to the show, which had its first transmission in 1935; it proved immensely popular with millions of families of depressed pre-war Britain. Many without jobs, tuned into the wireless Radio Luxembourg every Sunday, the wireless programmes were recorded on large wax discs but the show was always faultless. Children would sing along with the two most popular songs "Happy Days are here again" and "Painting the Clouds with Sunshine". The programme featured riddles, a serial, coded messages and advertising; the children would be glued to the programme with their code sheets and writing paper to record the answers. Broadcasting personality Clarence Wright was compere and well-known talented people were to make their mark in time by broadcasting on the show. Many will remember Jack Carlton who was the chief Ovaltiney, Leslie Crowther, Jean Stone, Jack Warner (who later became Britains famous policeman, Dixon of Dock Green), Dick Bentley, and Bernice Davis, the performing child dancer (later to become the wife of the entertainer Norman Vaughan) and Jimmy Edwards. Another drink was the very popular Cadbury's Bournville Cocoa; each tin had a lead free metal animal toy inside which children loved to collect. It had its own exact measure spoon which was bought with the tin, a dessert spoon with a short stubby handle with Cadbury's Bournville stamped on it, I still have my mum's to this day. In competition to the Ovaltine Company Cadbury's launched their club for children called "The Cococubs Club" it too issued a badge and a monthly magazine. Passwords, secret signs and coded messages were also featured on Radio Luxembourg in 1935. Sadly the outbreak of the Second World War brought an end to the shows. Historical, local, and national events in the nineteen thirties were to have quite a bearing on the future of many children.

On the local front, a Plymouth newspaper article revealed that Albert Casanova Ballard, President of the Plymouth Argyle Football Club, and owner of a well known boy's club, reacted strongly to Lady Nancy Astor's quote from her speech at a garden fete which had castigated his views on

LADY ASTOR ON THE SEX FILM

———◆———

Commercialisation and Its Evils

———

NEW CONTROL NEEDED

———

ECONOMY AND SOCIAL SERVICES

LADY ASTOR hit out last night at the commercialisation of "sex-appeal" in the cinemas.

She called it "degrading and disgusting." "I love a good cinema, but there are certain forms of cinema which are not good for young people," she said in a speech at the annual meeting of the Beaconsfield Habitation of the Primrose League, when Lord Astor presided. "We in the House of Commons are not at all satisfied about some of the films which are being shown in this country. I have always said that for the film trade to appoint a Censor themselves is perfectly ridiculous. The Government ought to have some control over it as they have over the B.B.C. I am not a prude or anything like that, but I am appalled at some of the things young people see.

THE INTERESTS OF CHILDREN

"I know that there are American films shown in this country that cannot be shown in America. Just look at some of the posters and think whether they are very inspiring or good for the children. Why, they do not have that in Russia! They may have too much propaganda, but at least the cinemas do not degrade the people.

Lady Astor confessed that she personally hated watching "those vamps," but had a weakness for cowboys. "It's all that unattractive sex appeal I am complaining about," she said. "I am not attacking cinemas as a whole. I think they are going to be wonderfully useful. Grown-ups can see what they like. What I am concerned with is the children."

Lady Astor's views on the sex appeal films being shown in the Cinemas. She was speaking at the Primrose League meeting in Plymouth July 1932. Courtesy Western Independent & the Plymouth Reference Library. File 0007 CD.

children's attitudes. Lady Astor was a tireless champion for the children, admitted she courted criticism, but her loyalty to Plymouth was never challenged. In another speech at the Primrose League Convention in Plymouth, she also admonished the cinemas, as she objected strongly to the "sex-appeal" in the films of the day. She called the sex-suggested scenes presented in some of the films, as degrading and disgusting, and added that it was not good for young childrens' moral upbringing. With the diminishing standards of morality in this day and age, and with the United Kingdom having the highest incidence of teenage pregnancies in the world, and children having children, what would be her views today if she saw the shocking and degenerate scenes that we see in today's films and television? Some would say we have become more extrovert in our views on sex. Have we really? Or is it an excuse to appease those who participate in unhealthy relationships debasing the moral judgement of our society? These two great philanthropists were always bickering on various subjects, each in their own way were sincere citizens, they had very strong views and both protagonists had dominating personalities. Lady Astor opened a "Country Fair" at Virginia House that was a local community centre for the poor in Plymouth. She fought hard and long for poor families living in such bad conditions and won the fight by forcing the Council to build more houses with better living standards. She set a good example by having built in Mount Gould 80 three and four-bedroom houses for poorer families with children from the Barbican area. This lady was a great champion for children. Lady Astor became the first female Freeman of Plymouth in July 1959. She had served as Member of Parliament for twenty-five years. Her death in 1964 was a great loss not only to her family but also to Plymothians.

Lady Astor at Virginia House Plymouth July 1932. A great champion for the children of the poor. The working classes had great respect for this formidable lady. Courtesy Western Independent & the Plymouth Reference Library.

Fascinating too was the talk and consideration of the Plymouth City Council of moving Derry's Clock, which is a very important landmark in Plymouth. The clock ensconced in its privileged position since 1862 was a secret meeting point for many lovers' trysts. It is a much-loved symbol and holds a special place in the hearts of all Plymouth citizens, and many a romance started from there. The clock was affectionately known as the "Four faced Deceiver" as each clock face contradicted the time. It was an historic monument built as a gift by William Derry the Mayor of Plymouth. Constantly a scource of controversy, even today the talk is still about moving this precious landmark, which had survived the Second World War relatively unscathed, some minor damage had been done to the clock faces. The citizens of Plymouth have fought a one hundred and thirty-nine-year battle to protect the clock. The Plymouth City Council Minutes in 1926 show that a working committee had advocated moving the clock, and discussed the possibility for its removal to another area. However, the plan was turned down.

In January 1932 the uprising and Dartmoor Princetown Prison Mutiny took place and for a while the local population were on edge. Finally police from Exeter and Plymouth were brought in to restore order. Plymouth Firemen had to extinguish many fires as the prisoners had set fire to the main buildings. Plymouth experienced the first visit of the popular Duke and Duchess of York; they had come to open the Orthopaedic (Mount Gould) Hospital. Great Western Railway announced the inauguration of a new Air Service between Plymouth and Cardiff. Nationally in 1932 Sir Oswold Mosley, the former Labour Minister, formed the British Union of Fascists (Blackshirts) and the people voiced their anger and dissent, his party was monitored quite carefully after its formation as it was considered a National

An 1899 scene depicting the Railway Offices. The building on the opposite corner was a bank and standing in the centre is Derry's Clock.

security risk. Their marches through the cities registered a deep disquiet among ordinary citizens until the Home Secretary issued a Public Order Act in 1936, which proved successful in providing new powers for banning provocative uniforms and controlling marches.

The same year saw the tragic loss of a Royal Naval Submarine M2 with the loss of all its crew. One interesting article in the 1932 local paper reminding citizens of a mystery which has never been solved, it was about the disappearance of the frigate "Atalanta" which vanished in 1880. This loss still remains one of the unsolved mysteries of the British Navy. The ship had been previously commissioned by the Crown Emigration Commissioners to convey passengers during 1860 from Plymouth to Australia. However, whilst being used as a British training ship in 1880 she was presumed lost at sea as she had departed from Bermuda for England with 290 young naval cadets and was never seen again. It was declared a national catastrophe with many families losing a loved one. Also in July 1932, the Royal Navy had their moment of entertainment when King George V the Sailor King inspected the Fleet before taking command of his ships in the channel for naval manoeuvres. The King was piped aboard HMS Nelson, flagship of the Home Fleet where he was greeted with due ceremony. Bill the Bulldog, the ship's mascot, had a less formal way of greeting his Monarch. He jumped on to the dais and frisked around the King's legs, the King bent down and patted him thus Knighting the dog. He was known from then on as "Sir William" and the whole fleet laughed for a long time over the incident.

History was made in 1932 when King George V issued his first Christmas Broadcast on Radio to the nation. Significant too in 1932 was the courageous flying success undertaken by England's own lady flyer Amy Johnson who completed a ten thousand-mile trip to Australia alone in a single engine Gypsy Moth plane, named Jason, her commercial flying days

England's own lady flyer of aviation Amy Johnson. She flew to Australia in a single engine Gypsy Moth plane in 1932.

ended with the outbreak of war in 1939. During the Second World War Amy Johnson CBE joined the Air Transport Auxiliary (ATA) a pool of experienced pilots who were ineligible for RAF service. Her duties comprised ferrying aircraft from factory airstrips to RAF bases and it was on one of these flights whilst performing her duty that she was lost on January 5, 1941. The aircraft she was flying had run out of fuel and with no radio communication she was unable to report her predicament. The plane crashed into the Thames Estuary and she was believed drowned at sea, a tragic end to the life of England's most famous woman pilot.

Sport in Plymouth was in its heyday. The local Plymouth Argyle Soccer Team was in Division Two finishing fourth in their league. Their Manager, Robert Jack served for twenty-eight years in that post. One of the cup matches the team played in the 1931/1932 season was against Manchester United, which Argyle won by four goals to one. As a yearly season ticket holder of "The Pilgrims" football club today, I wish those days were here again. It was not unusual to have crowds of over forty thousand. If the present day Argyle board had just one match with that number of fans they would be extremely pleased. Plymouth had good rugby union teams in Plymouth Albion and Devonport Services, whose team was drawn from Naval and Marine personnel. Both teams would play strong teams from other parts of the country, teams with a long history with powerful players. Regular visiting competitors came from Cardiff, Swansea, Newport, Pontypool, Leicester, Bristol and Blackheath and at one time Plymouth Albion celebrated having five men in the England team. As I young child my folks would take me to watch the rugby team play at Beacon Park, and I can remember a member of the Plymouth Albion Committee standing on the touchline shouting to the team "Wakey-Wakey Albion!" The very popular local boxer Len Harvey undertook another sporting event; (Although born in Golberdon near Callington in Cornwall he had lived most of his life in Plymouth). He was England's former Middleweight Boxing Champion, who had failed in his bid to win back the title after losing on points to Marcel Thil of France.

Local politics saw Isaac Foot; father of Michael Foot, who was Secretary for Mines, discussing the alternative use of coal. The research laboraties had started to use pulverised coal and oil. It was suggested that compressed coal gas for use in motor cars could be considered. Science indeed was marching on! On the world front in July the International World Trade meeting in Switzerland, received a boost with the signing and acceptance of the "Lausanne Agreement" for the recovery of world trade. It had been brilliantly negotiated by the then Prime Minister Mr Ramsay MacDonald who quoted "Europe cannot exist alone." The German Trade Industry were very happy at its acceptance, but when Herr Hitler heard of the agreement, it was said he went into a rage and deeply resented its success. The Nazis were furious at the signing of the treaty.

July 1932 saw the summing up of the infamous Lindbergh child murder case and the trial was finally concluded. In Plymouth a well known dealer,

Austin Seven 1935 Model with its original registration number. Photo courtesy of Mr Jeremy Palmer Plymouth.

Barton's Motor Company at Hyde Park Corner had on offer a new Morris Car guaranteed for two years at a price of one hundred pounds. Nationally, a special all weather automatic design Rolls Royce sold for £1,595 and a Bentley new 8-litre sports four door saloon could be obtained for £1,795. In 1935 came the very popular family car the Austin Seven, which could be bought for £135. In those days the road tax for this little car was £8. Another impressive motor car was the Austin Cambridge 10, which was available for those who could afford it in 1936. For the average working family; buses were their mode of transport. On the communication front the press would have their news and events printed in a local newspaper that could be bought for one penny.

For entertainment the most enjoyable pastime for the Plymothians were the popular promenade dances held regularly at the Plymouth Guildhall. Dances were also held at the old Plymouth Corn Exchange and all the local bands would play there. Dance Bands were very popular around the country and became well known on the wireless. The BBC featured professionals like Henry Hall and Ambrose, and not forgetting the popular master of ballroom dancing, Victor Sylvester who had formed his own orchestra in 1935. Henry Hall's dance band left the BBC in 1938 to tour the country and perform in local theatres. Families, who could afford a wireless, would listen avidly to selected programmes and one favourite programme was the Sunday afternoon transmission called "The week in the garden" which featured from 1931 until 1934. In the thirties everyone dreamt of one day owning their own home with a little garden included. Later in 1935 the programme was changed and named "In your Garden." The broadcaster Cecil H.Middleton, known for his soothing, drawling regional accent, captured the hearts of ordinary every day folk in homes across the nation. As soon as his programme was due on the air a hush descended in the home and we children were forbidden to talk while he spoke of the love of his flowers and vegetables. From the war years his programme had backed the "Dig for Victory" campaign and this BBC programme was to remain on the wireless until his death in 1945.

Jackie Searle, Mitzi Green, Jackie Coogan, and Junior Durkin in " Huckleberry Finn," at the Tivoli this week

Film entertainment for children at the Tivoli Cinema 1932. File 0005 from CD. Article from the Western Independent July 1932. Courtesy of Sunday Independent & the Plymouth Reference Library.

Special programmes for children followed in episodes from the BBC of "The Light Keeper" which was in Children's Hour broadcasted at 5.15pm each evening. Children would love to listen. A wireless was considered a luxury in the home and listeners would be glued to the programme. As money was short the working class favoured the arched shaped attractive Philips wireless with the lattice-front speaker or the Ekco Bakelite round shape wireless. Some families who could not afford to buy a wireless would rent one for one shilling and eleven pence per week, and most families would listen to the BBC Home Service (formerly Regional Programme) and the Light Programme (formerly National Programme). Adults loved "In Town Tonight" on Saturday night, which in 1933 had taken the listening patrons to its heart with the distinctive Eric Coates musical signature tune. Another local entertainment event was a "Cavalcade and Parliament" programme for Plymouth week. At the Tivoli Cinema the well known child actors, Jackie Searle, Jackie Cooper, Junior

Durkin and Mitzi Green were appearing in the film "Huckleberry Finn." On the theatre front in England in 1932 the formation of the Crazy Gang took place and they were to spread mirth and happiness to thousands of theatregoers for many years.

In August of 1932 the famous canine star Rin-Tin-Tin died aged fourteen. Many a silent tear was shed for him. The sweethearts of the silver screen

Barbara Stanwyck a classic dramatic actress. An orphan at two, throughout her childhood she longed to be a dancer and her heroine was Isadora Duncan. The gritty actress was formerly a telephone operator before becoming a Ziegfeld girl and finally a superb dramatic actress.

were Jeanette MacDonald and Nelson Eddy. As a singing couple they were to give patrons happiness for many years. Their films and music brought moments of escape into a fantasy world. 1932 saw the birth of England's Petula Clark who was to become a famous singer and actress. American actors such as John Wayne, recognised as the quintessential cowboy, the romantic Clark Gable, and the up and coming actors Henry Fonda, Tyrone Power, Gary Cooper, James Stewart, Errol Flynn and Dana Andrews were idols of the screen. Dramatic actor Spencer Tracy was well liked and the film in which he starred "Boys Town" in 1938 proved most popular. Barbara Stanwyck the smouldering magnetic star was already a fine actress. Powerful drama came from classic actresses Katherine Hepburn, Joan Crawford, and the inimitable Bette Davis. America's musical stars were Mickey Rooney, Judy Garland and James Cagney who later became a serious actor. All of them were destined to become screen legends. Children adored the curly haired child star Shirley Temple who at the age of six sang her song "On the good ship Lollipop" in the 1934 film "Bright Eyes."

The fabulous dancing partnership of Fred Astaire and Ginger Rogers in the nineteen thirties were legends in their own right, as were the Busby Berkelelys 'Broadway Melodies' films. England's own film stars were Anna Neagle, Vivian Leigh, Laurence Olivier, David Niven and James Mason. Who can forget the very talented and flamboyant playwright, songwriter, raconteur and actor Noel Coward? These performers entertained cinema patrons giving them a mood of escapism as in the nineteen thirties Cinema was part of everyone's life. Many craved for the velvet crooning voice of Bing Crosby, who sang his way to stardom, and swooned at the ballads, sung by the new singer Frank Sinatra. Both became famous and the rest is history. Young teenagers of the 1930's were to become pin-ups in the 1940's like the sultry Veronica Lake with her distinctive hairstyle, Betty Grable whose legs were insured for a million dollars and Ava Gardener considered the most beautiful of them all.

On the national political front, Lord Salisbury's views on the Reform of the House of Lords were considered, and the Government announced an offer to convert the War Loan from three and a half to five per cent. The then Chancellor of the Exchequer Mr Neville Chamberlain announced his plans to cut rates and taxes! Germany was already showing the world her sea power as in 1932 the German built ship "Europa" won the Blue Riband by crossing the Atlantic in fifteen hours and fifty-six minutes. A national newspaper report covered an event that should have fore-warned the world of an impending conflict, this was the Nazis march through Munich wearing their uniforms for the first time, which, they had received the right to wear in the first legal uniformed parade in Bavaria. Twelve thousand uniformed Nazis marched whilst a counter demonstration of seven thousand members of the Iron Front took place. Careful handling by the police prevented any possible confrontation at that time. The threat of the Nazis did not go unnoticed by knowledgeable writers in the press, as proven by H.E. Peters article in a local newspaper, he was the British United Press Correspondent in 1932, and he wrote: "Who are the Nazis? What kind of men make up the party which may soon be playing a leading part in the moulding of the new Germany?" Already the seeds of fear were sown and the democratic citizens registered a deep disquiet. Another important political

Who are the Nazis? File 0008 from CD. Article from the Western Independent July 1932. Courtesy of Sunday Independent & the Plymouth Reference Library.

happening was the Annual Meeting of the General Council of the League of Nations Union dealing with the question of disarmament, in 1933 Nazi Germany announced its withdrawal from the League of Nations. Also in 1933 the German Parliament had passed a bill, granting Adolf Hitler dictatorial powers which gave him freedom to apply his political views which one day would disrupt the world. Significantly in 1933 the British Army were issued with new uniforms. More underhanded politics took place in Germany in June 1934 as Adolf Hitler had all the political opponents to his views killed in the infamous "Night of the Long Knives." Meanwhile Germany confirmed in 1935 the creation of her powerful Air Force named "The Luftwaffe" and its formation led to the chilling infamy of war.

Back in England a newly produced Radio Detection and Ranging (Radar) instrument was demonstrated with the citizens unaware of the impact it was to have in 1940 in winning the crucial battle of Britain. In November 1935 the senior Test Pilot Paul Bulman made the first flight in the plane that was to make its mark in history, the Hawker Hurricane! In 1935 women were beginning to lead the way in other skilful pursuits other than being merely housewives and showing their courage as being equal to the male population. Amelia Earhart, the woman pilot from America, achieved the first successful solo flight across the Pacific Ocean. Sadly she was killed in 1937 whilst attempting to fly around the world.

In England 1935 the Silver Jubilee of King George V took place and many celebrations across the country were held and children received a special designed mug as a souvenir. It was in 1935 that Aircraftman Shaw, (T.E. Lawrence) known as Lawrence of Arabia was killed in a motorcycle accident, a sad loss to the nation. The year of 1936 was to be a grim year for the people of Britain as the death of King George V brought changes to the monarchy that were to alter the course of history. The very popular Prince Edward was crowned King Edward the Eighth. The reign was short lived as he chose to abdicate in December 1936 scorning the throne for the love of  the American divorcee, Wallis Simpson. This met with disapproval from many quarters but little did we know that it was probably the best thing that could have happened. His brother, Bertie ascended the throne on Edward's abdication becoming GeorgeV1 with his consort Queen Elizabeth, our beloved Queen Mother.

One very interesting event in England 1936 were the maiden flights of the new all metal fighter plane the "Spitfire" which later proved to be one of the most brilliant defensive weapons of its time. RJ Mitchell designed it. The Spitfire with its Rolls Royce Merlin twelve-cylinder liquid cooling Vee Engine developing a one thousand-horse power was to prove Britain's lifeline.

Citizens found relief in screen entertainment from the film "Rose Marie" featuring Nelson Eddy and Janette McDonald and their songs were sung in many homes. In May 1937 the icon of Nazi Germany the airship "Hindenburg" burst into flames before landing in New Jersey and thirty-seven people lost their lives. Even to this day a disaster that is still surrounded in mystery. The Coronation took place in 1937 of King George .V1 and Queen Elizabeth who were to prove the mainstay of the nation as they faced with their people a very grave future. The classic French passenger Liner Normandie entered the port of Plymouth after her record breaking run from New York. Children welcomed the release of Walt Disney's first full-length animated colour feature film in 1937 "Snow White and the Seven Dwarfs."

In July 1938 British Engineering and the Railway were to have their moment of glory for steam trains, as a Gresley A4 Pacific Class streamlined locomotive Mallard obtained a new world speed record of 126 mph. Another invention by the Great Western Railway (GWR) or God's Wonderful Railway as railway buffs in the Westcountry called it, boasted of their new braking power nick-named "Dead Man's Handle" which automatically applied the brakes if a warning signal was breached. In the sporting field England's Cricketer Len Hutton scored his famous 364 runs against Australia.

Children were issued with gas masks in 1938 and training began in schools on how to wear them. The youngest children had special red and blue "Mickey Mouse" gas masks, which had separate eyepieces, and a little nose to encourage the little ones to wear them; older children were issued with a standard type. The newly formed Air Raid Personnel section with Plymouth's Armed Forces had a combined exercise as a practice run. The idea was to warn the population of an impending attack. To simulate the bombing the RAF allowed their Whitley Bombers to drop white paper bags full of flour as dummy bombs. What a mess the flour bags made as they burst all over the City! Politics were making history when Anthony Eden, the Secretary of State for Dominion Affairs resigned his post in 1938. The Foreign Office had been embroiled in political intrigue and he had been angered at the appeasement policies invoked by the now Prime Minister Neville Chamberlain. He had promised after the infamous Munich Summit meeting in 1938 that we would have "Peace in our time" which by 1939 had proved to be only a pacifist statesman's dream. He must have been a broken hearted man as he was a genuine peacemaker. Meanwhile, the British Government ordered one thousand Spitfire planes for national defence and the chilling reality of a world war was becoming evident.

The General Post Office (GPO) issued weekly an officially registered paper magazine called "The War Illustrated" at four pence (later increased to sixpence) in which advice and instructions were issued in preparation for war, so the authorities were already planning security with the likelihood of war on the horizon. The (LDV) Local Defence Volunteers, nick-named the "Look, Duck and Vanish Brigade" was formed in 1939. They were instructed to learn the Morse code coupled with other duties, as they were expected to respond in any emergency and proved to be a blessing in their tasks which they performed with honour until disbanded in 1944.

In March 1939 the Spanish Civil War finally ended. Little was the world to know that a few months later a world war would envelop many nations. From 1939 the Sunderland Flying Boats Squadron began their convoy escort duties and patrols. The Sunderland Aircraft looked majestic moored in Plymouth Sound and drew many visitors to view the unusual sight of these planes as they skimmed across the Sound before taking off. By April 1939 mechanical diggers started digging pits in the public parks for Air Raid Shelters. Plymouth had succeeded in building 488 public shelters by the outbreak of war and had arranged for 14,000 Anderson shelters to be delivered to the City. Named after the Minister for Civil Defence, Sir John Anderson, they were to be issued to as many households as possible. Made of corrugated iron the instructions were to bury them deep in the gardens and to layer earth on top for maximum safety. Families made them as homely as they could with additions for comfort.

A ray of sunshine appeared on the fashion front in 1939 for women as a new clothing wonder was released on the market; the wonderful Nylon stocking had arrived! The decade of the 1930's was an age of advancements in technology and engineering, it was also the provider of some momentous events which led to the build up to war and which helped to shape our history. With the declaration of war on the 3rd September 1939, the thirties decade was coming to a close and the future looked grim.

In October 1939 the RAF shot down on British soil the first German Plane, a Heinkel Bomber which had been on reconnaissance. It carried a crew of four, two were killed and two taken prisoner. News came of other tragedies of war in October 1939, two British Liners "Yorkshire" and "City of Mandalay" were torpedoed by a German U-boat, aboard were wives and children of soldiers returning to Britain from the East. The King made a secret visit to the port of Plymouth in December to meet officers and men of the Royal Navy. In December 1939 Canadian troops arrived in the Westcountry and found the cold more trying than that of their native land. History and class barriers were taking a pounding as for the first time women came into focus as being capable of taking responsibility and they were to achieve new distinctions in military and civil life. Forward-looking decisions were taken by appointing them in positions of Education, Engineering and Civil Defence. Women became Directors and Controllers of Women's Auxiliary Air Force, (WAAF) Auxiliary Territorial Service, (ATS) Women's Land Army and the Civil Service. Two hundred children took part in a Gala night at the Jubilee Centre in Plymouth, for many of the children life would not be the same as some children who had parents were evacuated under their own private arrangements shortly afterwards.

The release of the classic fantasy film "The Wizard of Oz" which starred Judy Garland brought light relief for the children who were yet to feel the full force of the impending war. Just two months after war was declared the biggest screen version of the American Civil War was released with heartthrob Clark Gable in the lead role, an epic film that described the destruction of its way of life through war. The irony was that this is what happened to the normal childhood of children in the late 1930's and the 1940's as their lives changed forever and the childhood that they had known was "Gone with the Wind." All children throughout the country were to experience a shocking social change in their life styles; it was a shame, for children who had a right to better things had had that right taken from them by the onset of war. For the children of this era it was to prove one of the most devastating reasons for disruption of family life, which ultimately led to many children becoming members of "The Lost Generation."

What entertainment was available at the Picture houses circa July 1932. Courtesy Western Independent & the Plymouth Reference Library.

"We are the OvalTineys" song is remembered by a whole generation of people from 1935 when thousands of children were members of the select club. The opening Song sheet courtesy of Novartis Nutrition UK Consumer Relations Office.

77

The closing song that the Ovaltineys sang when the programme ended. A Wander Ltd published the song in 1935. Courtesy of Novartis Nutrition UK Consumer Relations Office.

CHAPTER NINE

THE FOSTER CHILD

Children in institutions in the 1930's/1940's would often fantasise; creating dreams in their minds with the hope that they would one day be realised. The disadvantages suffered by children and young people in residential care are well known. The arrant destruction of a child's personality in an institution can lead to subtle inner changes in later life; it could also risk mental disorganisation for years to come. The rejected child feels helpless, afraid, angry and confused. In turn this leads to grief, rage and distress, in many instances the trust between adults in authority and children in care were betrayed. Healthy and intelligent children were labelled to appease the need to isolate children from relatives who posed a threat to the authorities, and religion was certainly a governing factor when placing children in homes. There was a continued silence in the corridors of power to avoid awkward questions being submitted by relatives seeking a lost child. Records were withheld and mistakes covered up, everything was earmarked by financial expediency. Names would be changed or the child would be called by another Christian name from their birth details, thus causing confusion in record keeping, and when enquiries about a child was submitted their records could not be located, meanwhile the child would have been transferred to another home.

A child should expect a loving environment with stability and routine, from that trait should emerge confidence, which in turn helps to mould the character of a child. When committed to an institution in the 1930's/1940's the children received no support from a psychotherapy mentor and often the child would become labelled as difficult. Sometimes a girl or boy would wish someone would come along and adopt him or her. On occasion this did happen, but the 1930's and 1940's presented a social restriction, which did not allow a child to be emotionally supported. Full family support was not given and fostered children were kept apart from sibling sisters and brothers. Carers of fostered children were not counselled in child protection.

How could the controlling department at the time defend its failure to keep sisters and brothers together? The social structure even with the 1933

79

childrens' act had many shortcomings; lack of proper training and counselling of social workers rebounded on the children in care. Adopted and fostered children were not always told of their background, which led to many emotional upsets in later years. Fostered children will have the thought of who they really are and where they came from at the back of their minds, and the uncertainty and the wonder never leave them. Adopted children would find themselves as adults desperately seeking their biological parents searching for a sense of their own identity only to find that family shame was the sole reason for their abandonment as a child.

Holders of the records and adoptive parents refused to answer questions on that child's background, leaving the feeling of uncertainty and being the second best. Too often children, who were from institutions suffered in their education, constantly characterised by fragmentation, which led to unacceptable levels of failure. Individual talents were never allowed to develop, and the child would become unstable and lose out later in life, no one would listen to the children. Young adolescents had to fight an uphill struggle to achieve anything in life, and sadly, many fell by the wayside having never realised their full potential, their very upbringing did not afford equal opportunities.

Until these issues are addressed the "Culture of Dependency" created by social welfare will continue for disadvantaged children. It is not always easy to do the right thing and sometimes the system does get it wrong. It is true that social services are often blamed for insensitive handling of children. On the surface their departments would appear to be easy targets, however, it is not without good reason that they are blamed as the lost generation of the nineteen thirties and the nineteen forties will confirm. It was sad that effective counselling was not available in the nineteen thirties, the system in that day and age did not identify the key human needs of the children who suddenly found themselves unwanted or orphaned. They faced alone the trauma of depression, grief, anger, abuse, anxiety and rejection. Some children would think or believe that their real parents may have been wealthy, royalty, or film stars. Many faced the sad truth that they were illegitimate, some children found that they had come from a family who were just ordinary people who could not cope, others were merely victims of circumstances. Many adopted and fostered children could ask for more details when they reached the age of eighteen, but if they made enquiries only met a wall of beaucracy, and secrecy, and some only found out when they married, or sensed that there was something different about their upbringing, and continued to pressurise the authorities to obtain their records.

Boarding out was another method of easing the overcrowded childrens' homes. In 1938-1940 Stoke House was facing a crisis with so many children in their care, there was a forgotten army of orphan children. An appeal was made to parents who were resident in the locality to remove their children from the home to make way for orphaned children who had lost both parents, (one parent families who had to work left their children in the home as no other relative could help with their care). Many times in the 1930's and 1940's a child would be boarded out with a family it had never seen or met. This was often abused and the monetary gain was their main reason in applying for a child to foster. Families who boarded children were given maintenance and clothing allowance. There were those who saw the pound sign first and the child second, others loved the child in their care and just managed with the allocated allowance. Willing foster parents tried to give a child a normal life but found they could not cope with the difficult child. The adopted child fared best as the parents were prepared to meet the full cost and share their love giving the child a sense of really belonging. Fostered children are difficult to monitor and control and need to be handled with immense sensitivity. Some foster parents realised that they could not cope with these traumatised children and returned them to the institution. The girls and boys from orphanages were especially at risk and were exploited without means of defence. The children would be used as cheap labour or as an excuse to obtain a bigger flat or house on the logic of having another child. So deep are first impressions made on a child's mind that many children reached an emotional nadir at a very early age. They became wary of adults especially if that adult had not built up a trust with the child. Many people were horrified by cruelty to children but did nothing, either through fear or simply not knowing what to do. Adult cruelty, and abuse to children whether sexual or physical, is a subject which arouses strong emotions. Some children would end up being boarded out with four or five foster carers and that child would be emotionally disturbed.

When children were fostered or adopted and that family had a child of their own, the foster child was looked upon as an intruder and would often have to bear cruel remarks from the other child with whom they lived. This led to pangs of jealousy among shared families. Attention seeking is a common trait among transplanted children. Sometimes the spoilt child would play off one against the other and it was always the blood kin child who was considered right. It must be difficult for foster parents to show love to a child that is not theirs, but having chosen that child to foster it was imperative to show some measure of love. A child is very sensitive and can quickly pick up any action that indicates rejection; any sign of lost trust is immediately followed by worry and isolation. A child's emotional and spiritual health is an equally important development as is its physical health. However, sometimes a child struck lucky and had lovely foster and adoptive parents who they admired and loved till the end of their days, unfortunately, few and far between.

Frustrating too, was when a child had been placed with foster carers they liked, and the authorities for some inexplicable reason would suddenly take them away, sometimes on such spurious grounds known only to the welfare authorities whose assessment was a short term palliative. Often bad decisions were made by one person's viewpoint and not taking in the consideration of the child's feelings. Campaigns to find foster carers for hundreds of vulnerable children reached nearly every home in Plymouth in the 1930's/1940's, anyone could apply and the vetting was not properly conducted. All one had to do was to give two names of citizens as referees, who would confirm that they considered the applicant capable of being a suitable person to foster a child. The welfare workers would inspect the home to see that the applicants had enough rooms to accommodate the child but never questioned their ability to apply emotional and loving support.

With the authorities overwhelmed by the number of children in welfare care and the high cost to the public purse, it was obvious some other source of home life had to be found. Maintenance to foster parents varied according to age, this was called boarding out allowance. In 1931, children under twelve years were allocated 12/6 per week with 30/- per quarter clothing allowance. Children over twelve years 15/- per week with 40/- clothing per quarter, this would be in addition to the 7/6 per week orphans' pension, pocket money for a child was assessed at one penny per week (under twelve) and threepence per week (over twelve). Clothing allowance was deemed as "For repair and renewals after the first outfit made by the committee as per lists" the payment to be made after the first birthday and issue of first outfit. (Include lists of clothing here). Additional reasonable payments would be made for any child in need of medical treatment or extra nourishment provided a recognised medical practitioner approved it. This was important as poor families had to pay for medical treatment and for a Doctor's visit, so these were constructive improvements by the welfare to increase the quality of life for the children.

Today as we have reached the twenty-first century, foster carers are put through a rigorous assessment to ensure that they are capable and clear about their task and provide a safe and caring environment for the child. Normal age-related fostering allowances for a child now boarded out with a foster family can be between £140-£204 per week and for the fostering of troubled youngsters foster carers will have a weekly wage of between £325-£450 on top of their normal age-related allowances. A ground breaking decision was taken by the social services in the year 2000 when specialist foster care staff took the unusual step of advertising in the jobs advertisement pages of the national and local newspapers in appealing for foster parents to look after troubled youngsters with a committed wage. This was indeed a very courageous and forward-looking project and it is hoped it will bring success.

Consideration is given to the child's self esteem, self respect of the child is very important. The one crucial factor in this modern age, thank goodness, is that sisters and brothers are not deliberately split up, attempts are made to foster or home them as a complete family, a far cry from our tragic days when siblings were separated for life. Some Scattered Homes accommodated ten or fifteen children so there was no excuse for separating brothers or sisters. True, the children were clothed, fed and kept pristine clean, and were instructed in religion, but their character development and emotional guidance were non existent. Children must have guidance and boundaries on behaviour as without these they get confused and behave badly. On the other hand peer pressure can overwhelm the child's reasoning if not handled discreetly and tempered with kindness.

Public Assistance Committees later to be known as Welfare or Social Services replaced the old Board of Guardians in providing poor relief and related services, after the Local Government Act 1929 and The Poor Law Act 1930. They were responsible for Out-Relief, Adoptions, Maintenance, and Administration of the Institutions and Workhouses. Later in 1933 came the Place of Safety of Young Persons Act. In 1942 education experts of nineteen nations met in London and prepared the "Children's Charter." Six rules were listed and accepted and this charter crystallised modern opinion on the care of the children for the future. Each child was to have proper food, clothing and shelter, medical attention and treatment, full time schooling, religious training and that full consideration would be given to recognize the personality of the child as sacred. The rights of adopted children were set out separately three years later, it emphasized the importance that adoption should benefit the child rather than the child should add to the adopter's own prestige or comfort. The Department of Health, for her Majesty's Stationery Office printed an introduction to the Children's Act 1989 highlighting a new framework for the care and upbringing of children. Selected comments show a different approach to the welfare of children that the older generation did not experience. Most interesting was the following: "The child and his/her views in proceedings." The checklist of particular matters to which the court is to have regard in reaching decisions about the child is headed by the child's wishes and feelings and highlights the great importance attached to them! The law seeks to strike a balance between the need to recognize the child as an independent person and to ensure the child's views are fully taken into account. For a child in need who is living away from his family the local authority must take such steps as are reasonably practicable to enable him/her to live with his/her family or to promote contact between the child and the family."

The new policies of Social Welfare and the National Society for the Protection of Cruelty to Children are working together with Local Councils to improve the quality of life for the fostered or adopted child, and this shows a marked improvement on those early years of the 1930's/1940's. Family support is considered essential, and in the year 2000 Plymouth Family Support Services became an independent local charity. Formerly part of the NSPCC the change was due to restructuring of their work, although independent they will still remain endorsed by the NSPCC. It is hoped that this will meet the needs of the local community to provide the much needed support for children and their carers, pleasing too is the policy of a specialised counseling service for adults, and young teenagers who suffered abuse and bullying as a child.

Children and social workers find themselves in situations that are already amongst the most stressful and complex imaginable; care workers could not respond to the unique circumstances of an individual child when trying to balance economy and efficiency with a limited financial budget. Furthermore, children were helpless in the face of irrationality and the omnipotence of bureaucracy, and inevitably it was the child who was the loser. It is pleasing to note that the Waterhouse Report in February 2000 highlighted the plight of children in care in an institution governed by cruel and abusive carers over children of vulnerability, in the 1930's/1940's cruelty and abuse in institutions was covered up and withheld from the public.

Children must be heard and their rights adhered to, welfare care should be provided without stigma and without removing dignity. Fewer children in the United Kingdom are being adopted and fostered and the waiting list of children in England in the year two thousand is known to be in the region of nearly fifty-five thousand. It is distressing for would be parents to be constantly overlooked for some of the most ridiculous and frustrating reasons and the process is far too long. When applicants appear successful with their social assessor they have to wait for the independent panel chosen from agencies to accept them as prospective parents and some face the heartache of being rejected or earmarked as case deferred. Often applicants wishing to adopt a child are rejected because of cultural or multicultural backgrounds and even religion is seen as a barrier. The criterion of political correctness must be observed and this can lead to excessive bureaucracy. Adoption is so complicated and drawn out that everyone forgets the most important factor-the child! For most looked-after children adoption is not a panacea, but there are many children for whom it is the answer. If children can be brought up in a family environment with parental love and care it is so much better for them. Adopted children do better in school and suffer fewer emotional problems if adoptions fill their physical and mental needs.

Thankfully today, a better emphasis is put on the child's rights, as the children's organisation named after Article 12 of the United Nations Convention reveals. It refers to the rights of the child adopted by the British Government in 1991. Childrens' rights are the key issues and the convention gives the children the right to express their views and have them taken into account on all matters, which affect them. Article 23 of a recent European Charter, has advocated a rule that children must be 'Treated as Equals' however, this statement should be viewed with caution, as it could be restrictive in maintaining discipline. It is accepted that adults should be the link in teaching and guiding children through the early years of their lives, and the rapport between child and adult is of paramount importance. Therefore, the application of 'Equality before Maturity' could undermine the accepted levels of social behaviour. Young people want more of a say in family, school, community, media and political matters in this day and age, these young people are the future generation and on their shoulders is placed the responsibility and welfare of our nation. Do we help them to achieve this aim? Or do we let them sink into the abyss of indifference. A new exciting event is now in progress with the birth of the first United Kingdom Youth Parliament set up in July 1999 which means teenagers between the ages of eleven to sixteen can be elected to have a voice in the area in which they live. They will have a larger role in national politics; the four hundred and fifteen-member parliament will create a youth manifesto to be presented to the Government.

With the decline of adoptions in the United Kingdom and so many children in care, perhaps the Government could consider setting up a committee to investigate and control the adoption procedures. Should there be a national voice? In August 2001 a most welcome decision was taken when the welfare authorities agreed to have a new register to speed up the adoption of children needing new families. The national adoption register will carry details of all children seeking adoptions, along with couples approved to adopt, making it easier to match prospective parents.

State care has failed so many young people in the past, as generations of orphaned and fostered children have suffered the agony of rejection through delay and inconsistency. Children need and want a Children's Commissioner, someone who is non-political and totally independent to protect their welfare. Children became 'Pawns on the move' when all they really wanted was a 'Forever' family. We see many charities today assisting children of the world who have suffered from war, cruelty and abuse. Citizens of the Western World adopt many children from foreign lands. One cannot help and think, however, with so many children in need of adoption and care in our own country, would it not be prudent to put our own house in order first?

Regulations and stringent restrictions to information on adopted children deter relatives who are searching for lost children. Under the Adoption Act original families of adopted children have no right to information on them, even when they are grown up. However, there is a clause in the Act that would allow vital documents to be released in exceptional cases subject to a decision by a High Court Judge. There is also a National Organisation for counselling adoptees and parents called Norcap who continues to campaign for changes to the Adoption and Childrens' Bill to enable siblings separated by adoption to initiate renewed contact with kin without the need to take their case to the High Court.

The catalogue of failings by the welfare authorities in years past is well known. In the 1930's/1940's there were stringent rules and no flexible guidelines. The lost generation will continue to seek the truth as they search for their records, which are still held by the authorities under a seventy-five year restriction. Surely the government's own deception will one day be answered as breaching the rights of thousands of former children in care is not acceptable in today's society and it is time to face our past. We are very conservative in our way of living and traditionally slow to adapt to new and progressive ideas, so it was with social welfare, and the children were caught in the dreadful trap of an institution, which set financial considerations before the needs of vulnerable children.

How the fostered child placed with a family with a child of their own often felt!

A CHILD IS WAITING.
(© Copyright Veronica Norman)

1. I AM A CHILD AND I NEED A MUM.
WILL YOU ADOPT ME? OH WHAT FUN!
PLEASE APPLY TO WELFARE CARE
AND TELL THEM THAT YOU WANT TO SHARE
YOUR HOME AND FAMILY JUST WITH ME,
WITH LOVE TO GIVE - PLEASE LET IT BE!

2. WOULD BE PARENTS DO NOT BE LATE
I HAVE THE TIME TO WATCH AND WAIT.
HAVE YOU ASKED? THAT IS FINE-
IT WILL NOT BE LONG BEFORE YOU'RE MINE.
HAVE YOU MET THE RULES JUST RIGHT?
DID YOU BEAT THE SYSTEM'S MIGHT?

3. MANY QUESTIONS THERE WILL BE
BEFORE THE DREAM IS AGREED.
NOT TOO YOUNG OR NOT TOO OLD-
ARE YOU QUIET OR TOO BOLD?
ARE YOU FAT OR ARE YOU THIN?
WHAT IS THE COLOUR OF YOUR SKIN?

4. RELIGION AS A RULE IS MUST,
IF YOU WANT TO WIN THE TRUST-
OF PEERS WHO SET THE RULES OF STATE,
MEANWHILE I WILL WATCH AND WAIT!
TO SEE MY CHILDHOOD SOAR SO HIGH
WITH A FAMILY SHIELD OH SO NIGH!
MAKES MY HEART MISS A BEAT
SOON I WILL HAVE A FAMILY SEAT.

5. WHAT DID YOU SAY-THERE IS A BLOT?
DO YOU SMOKE OR DRINK A LOT?
I SIT AND WAIT ALL IN A FLURRY-
I WISH THE POWERS THAT BE WOULD HURRY.
A YEAR HAS PAST SO VERY QUICK-
BUT STILL NO PARENTS HAVE BEEN PICKED.
WOULD BE PARENTS DO NOT FRET –
AS YOU ARE TOLD "NOT YOUR TURN YET!"

6. WHAT ARE YOUR FAILURES NOW I ASK-
IT'S TIME I TOOK SOMEONE TO TASK!
TOO WELL QUALIFIED DID YOU SAY?
I WILL BE PATIENT AS I WAIT EACH DAY!
THIS COULD CAUSE DELAY AND STRIFE
DO YOU HAVE A NORMAL SEX LIFE?
ARE YOU MULTI CULTURAL OR GAY?
AS THE CHILD CAN I HAVE A SAY?

7. HOW MANY TIMES WERE YOU WED?
CAN YOU KEEP YOUR FAMILY FED?
PANIC THOUGHTS AND ACHING HEART
WHEN IS MY FAMILY GOING TO START?
'THEM AND US' IS WHAT WE FACE
YOU NEED GOOD MARKS TO WIN THE RACE!

8. FAMILY LINKS AND THE CHURCH
WILL BE CONSIDERED IN YOUR SEARCH.
SELECTION PROCESS MAY TAKE A YEAR
BUT THINGS LOOK GOOD, SO DO NOT FEAR.
LOVE IS EVERYTHING – IT'S A FACT
BUT IT TAKES MUCH MORE THAN THAT!

9. HOME STUDIES IS THE FENCE TO JUMP
AND THEN THE INTERVIEWS WILL PUMP
THE INFORMATION NEEDED BY -
THE SOCIAL WORKER WHO IS YOUR GUIDE.
POLICE AND DOCTORS ARE QUESTIONS ASKED
ARE YOU SUITABLE FOR THE TASK?
SOCIAL WORKER NOW AGREES
AND RECCOMMENDS THE POWER THAT BE
THAT YOU HAVE MADE THE FINAL GRADE
AND THAT YOU HAVE A LOVE TO TRADE.

10. REPORTS WILL FILTER FROM SOCIAL CARE
TO PROVE THAT YOU ARE FIT TO SHARE
INTRUSIVE PROCESS WOUNDS THE WILLING HEART-
AND SOWS THE SEED OF DOUBT OF TAKING PART.
DOES ONE EXPECT THE PERFECT MUM?
AND THE PERFECT DAD?
IF ONE DOES-THE CHILD IS LOST-
AND THAT CAN BE SO SAD.
SEEK YE NOT A PERFECT CHILD-
THERE WAS ONLY EVER ONE.
BORN SON OF GOD –THE GREATEST YET-
LET THY KINGDOM COME.

11. SOCIAL PEERS HEED COMMON FOLK
FOR THEY HAVE SPECIAL TRAITS
DO NOT TAKE SO LONG TO JUDGE
A LONELY CHILD JUST WAITS.
OH MY GOODNESS THE YEARS HAVE FLOWN!
MEANWHILE THE WAITING CHILD HAS GROWN.
MANY YEARS HAVE NOW GONE BY
WAS IT REALLY JUST A LIE?
THE ADOPTION NOW IS FAR TOO LATE
ALL THE CHILD DID WAS TO WATCH AND WAIT!

CHAPTER TEN

GAMES WE PLAYED

> No, no, let us play, for it is yet day,
> And we cannot go to sleep:
>
> Besides, in the sky the little birds fly,
> And the hills are all covered with sheep.
>
> William Blake.

Children of the nineteen thirties and forties did not have television or computers and working folk in those days could not afford to buy toys as they struggled to survive and to feed and clothe their children. Most children made their own fun and the games and toys available to our generation were simple, but nevertheless, gave us many hours of pleasure, only the children of well to do parents or relations received expensive toys.

As I write I can visualise so many of the games. Young girls would make a cat's cradle with string, or alternatively with wool or cotton threaded through their hands to make the cradle, they would criss-cross the yarn to make patterned shapes and one of these would look like a cradle. Many whiled away the hours doing French knitting. This involved taking a cotton reel and putting in four nails at the top, and then the wool would be looped over the nails. On each round the stitch would be picked up which gradually formed a woollen tube through the hole of the cotton reel; these would then be stitched together in a circle making a place mat, or alternatively, to make woollen dolls. Given a pair of scissors girls and boys would cut out dolls or aeroplane paper shapes from newspapers, this game was called Origami which was a Japanese decorative art of paper folding.

A much quieter pastime on wet and miserable days would be a jigsaw puzzle. We were not always too patient with all the little bits and pieces but we did like seeing the finished picture. They say that necessity is the mother of invention and we would good at invention. Comb and tissue paper to play music was the only musical instrument the institute children would have, they soon learnt the art of playing well-known tunes. Games which could be played by more than one person were Tiddlywinks, Ludo, Snap, Snakes and Ladders, Shove Ha'penny or Hide and seek, Pass the Parcel or Hunt the Thimble. Another pastime was the simple game Spot the Items. For this game there would be a number of items placed on a tray. You would look at it, then it would be taken away, and you would have to remember as many items that you could. Pin the Tail on a Donkey brought endless peals of laughter as a blindfolded person, having been spun around to disorientate them, would try to pin the tail of the Donkey in the right place. Not easy.

Musical Chairs was another favourite but could be quite rough at times as elbows, feet and any other part of the anatomy would be used to commandeer the chair first. Squeak-Piggy-Squeak led to riotous moments as a child would be blindfolded while the other children sitting in the chairs would all change seats and the blindfolded child had to guess whose lap they had sat on. In summer months nearly every child frolicked in the fields or on overgrown lawns, to pick and collect daisies to make as large a daisy chain as possible.

More vigorous games were Rounders and Hockey. Older girls played the Chain Top game; a circle of children was formed with one girl placed in the centre. She would shout "Go!" and the girls would disperse in all directions. The girl who had been in the middle had to try and catch the runners and as one and then another was caught, they would hold hands and form a chain, until eventually everyone was caught. Whips and Tops was a favourite game with the girls as the whipping tops would be covered with different coloured chalks and when you whipped the wooden top to gain speed, the pretty coloured chalks would evolve into a profusion of colours. Marbles (or "Alleys" as they were called in Plymouth) were very popular with all children and many deals by exchanging duplicate marbles of the same pattern were undertaken, those who had "Shooters" or "Cat's Eyes" marbles were envied. There were pretty coloured marbles of various sizes; the game was played by hitting your opponents marble from a set distance in the kerbside. If you succeeded, you won. Many children treasured their marbles and guarded them jealously. Another version used was to form a drawn circle and the player would have to knock other player's marbles out of the circle.

Nearly every age group of all generations will have played Conkers! The English Chestnut tree must have been the most loved, and it came under heavy bombardment when the conkers were ripe, as any missile would be utilised to dislodge the chestnut casing from the tree to obtain the biggest Conker. Some children would ask their guardians to bake their conkers to make them stronger, others would soak the conker in vinegar to harden the shell and these proved formidable opponents. Battle would then commence, attached to the end of a long piece of string the conker would be hit by the opponent's conker and the one who could succeed in breaking a conker first would be the winner and the proud owner of King Conker!

Cocky Fivers, also known as Fivestones, Jacks or Dibs, depending on what part of the country one came from were played by girls and boys alike. This was a game played on the ground. You needed a bouncy ball and five small stones, or alternatively pebbles. The latter were preferred, as they were rounded and more compact to pick up. The player would throw the stones on the ground and toss the ball into the air and try to pick up the first stone, then catch the ball. Then you had to try with two, three, and four stones. Eventually the player attempts to gather the remaining five stones set in a pattern on the ground with one toss. Easy? Try It!

Home made Kites were the in-thing with the boys, as they would try to outdo their friends with different designs and shapes. On a windy day the kites, on yards of string to obtain maximum height, would soar into the sky, guided by their owners. With a small mirror or tin plate the reflective game of Johnny Noddy could be played provided the sun was shining! The sunray would flash as a round reflection in the bright sunlight, and the Johnny Noddy would bounce off the house walls and windows. Another favourite pastime was the makeshift swing we would create on the street lamplights, which had two metal arms sticking out. This would allow the children to tie their old clothes lines on to them and swing around; of course you had to make sure the lamplighter was not in sight to catch one doing it.

Simple items could give immense pleasure for a while as both girls and boys would scrounge an old lid from a tin of polish from their guardians. Then a hole would be made in the middle with a long string inserted and tied with a knot, and one could run along with it as a wheel making a clanging noise as we ran. Most children were naturally noisy and in addition, the wheel would be dragged along whilst whizzing along on roller skates, for those children lucky enough to have a pair!

Some of the games we played have continued into the twenty-first century as recently I saw some children playing Hopscotch, a game where squares are chalked on the pavement. Each square is numbered. A child must throw a stone into the correct square and then hop from square to square without stepping on the lines. The game of chase was always popular and the loud singing of "pitter-patter on my shoulder" could be heard in many a playground.

Ball Games could be most enjoyable as the lonely child could play quite happily. Chants of One-Two-Three Alera, I saw my sister Sarah, sitting on the bumbalera, outside a penny bazaar! would be sung, meanwhile bouncing the ball on the pavement by using the hand as a bat. Cocking one leg for the ball to pass under without losing its rhythm and Double Balls were played by bouncing the two balls alternatively against a wall.

Cigarette Cards or Flickers was a game employed by using cigarette or bubblegum cards and at times even cardboard milk tops up against the wall. The one claiming the most number of cards or tops on opponent's cards would be the winner. Remember the Players Cigarette cards in the 1930's, which featured aviary and cage birds, Aircraft of the RAF, Motor Cars and Film Stars? What about the Churchman cigarette cards? They featured cricket players and film stars too. Then there were the very popular WD & HO Wills cigarette cards featuring the Air Raid Precautions, Film Stars, Flowers and famous sporting personalities, sadly no further cigarette cards were issued after 1939 because of the world shortage of paper. For children who had parents who could afford to pay there was a game called "Pinocchio" a Walt Disney card game, which became very popular with the girls lucky enough to have the forty-five pack coloured cards at one shilling and sixpence. Each card had a letter printed in the top corner and you had to bring the doll to life by collecting the completed name.

Every child had their own Walt Disney animal character that they loved and the Disney phenomenon was to bring joy to thousands. Today the emphasis is on Pokemon Cards and in years to come there will be collectors who will look back on them with nostalgia. Skipping Games were for the girls who would use a long rope with someone on each end turning it. One game was called Higher and Lower, consisted of starting with the skipping rope at the lowest level and gradually raising the level until the last girl was out. One favourite skipping game was accompanied by singing "All the girls of England ". Skipping ropes came in all types and sizes, from smaller ones with wooden handles to larger discarded clotheslines, or odd bits of rope tied together. A fast skipping rope game was called "Bumps" where a single rope was passed rapidly twice under the feet on each jump whilst the girls were singing various chants. One chant vividly remembered was:

ONE TWO - BUCKLE MY SHOE,
THREE FOUR – KNOCK ON THE DOOR,
FIVE SIX – PICK UP THE STICK,
SEVEN EIGHT – SHUT THE GATE,
NINE TEN – BIG FAT HEN!

Another game favoured by the girls was called "Whizz!" This required taking a stick about eighteen inches long and tying coloured strips of paper to one end of the stick with a small stone attached on the end of the paper. Then the girls would whirl and spin it around at speed to make pretty patterns. The faster you spun the prettier the pattern.

Boys would have go-carts, made from planks of wood and old wooden boxes fitted with discarded pram wheels, or old bike wheels. Hoops were rescued from any back yard and then by using a piece of stick to guide and pick up speed, they would race each other down the hills. Catapults the boy's favourite weapon (Especially to torment the girls!) were made from V shaped twigs, an old piece of leather shoe tongue or strong rubber bands, they were used to fire stones at old tin cans set up at gate posts or walls, ideal too for targeting an enemy or a person they disliked. Yes! Simple Games! But games that brought endless hours of fun as children in the 1930''s/1940''s had to make the best of what little treasures they had. One rarely heard children of our generation say, "We are bored!" If a child did show any sign of boredom an adult would quickly solve the situation by detailing little household chores and I know which choice most children of our generation preferred!

CHAPTER ELEVEN

BLITZ MEMORIES

No peace lies in the future, which is not hidden in this present instant.Take Peace. (Fra Giovanni AD 1513)

The outbreak of war in September 1939 was to touch every family as social history suffered a dramatic change. It proved to be the greatest social revolution of all times, yet in its way, made life better for the poor families. The upper classes found themselves having to contribute to the war effort which brought them into contact with all types of people with whom they would not normally associate, and Plymouth citizens were to experience these dramatic changes. World War Two was a frightening time to be a child, children found themselves evacuated and separated from parents; brothers, sisters, and school friends, sent to live with perfect strangers with whom, in many cases, they were not compatible. The Second World War was different from every war the British people had ever been in before. It was not just servicemen who faced injury and death every day as ordinary citizens were also affected and it embraced the whole population irrespective of age or class. The people who stayed at home had their courage tested to the full, as was their patience, honesty, determination and their sense of humour; the children too encapsulated that spirit.

Strange things were happening like the removal of road signs and the church bells stopped ringing, citizens were told if the church bells rang it was a warning that the Germans had landed on British soil. In 1940 we stood alone our backs to the wall, but we would not be beaten! Some used the war to make money and became black market profiteers, and the fifth columnists tried to undermine the social structure of our society, but they had underestimated the steadfastness of the British people. The sleeping Lion had been awakened and the enemies of England were to hear its roar, with the rescue of our troops at Dunkirk and the appointment of our new leader Prime Minister Winston Churchill in May 1940. The whole nation was united in the common cause. In June 1940, following the tragic sinking of the troopship HMT Lancastria, survivors were landed in Plymouth. Five thousand men died in this our biggest maritime disaster. The tragedy was so shocking that Winston Churchill ordered the event to be kept secret. To this day many families do not know how their loved ones were lost.

In Plymouth, bombing took toll of more lives. The Public Assistance Institution Ford House received direct hits from bombs in a raid during July 1940 and thirteen women residents were killed, but the children's wing remained safe. Another bombing raid sent the citizens scurrying to their shelters only to find it was a leaflet drop by the Germans as a propaganda exercise. The leaflet was entitled "Last Appeal to Reason" Plymouth citizens gathered in the leaflets, cut them into squares and used the paper for toilet use but one ambitious lady sold the leaflets to interested parties. At home the Royal Air Force fought a magnificent battle in the air to protect our country against the full might of the German Luftwaffe and the Battle of Britain was to immortalise the RAF for all time. Although the Spitfires made a significant contribution, and theirs was the glory, it was the slower workhorse plane the Hawker Hurricane, which accounted for almost three-quarters of the German aircraft destroyed in the battle that clinched the formidable air victory. In an inspirational speech Winston Churchill made it clear that we would fight on, but reality soon struck home as news was received in September 1940 that the liner "City of Benares" carrying ninety evacuee children to Canada was torpedoed. Eighty-three children were lost in this tragic event.

The children of Stoke House and Scattered Homes in Plymouth were inextricably linked with the misfortune of being in an orphanage. Coupled with the horrors of the Second World War this further exacerbated the quality of their young lives. Many children had suffered the loss of their homes, relatives, belongings and pets, and were faced with being evacuated to strange country areas, lodged or fostered with distant relatives, or placed in orphanages. The blitz was unforgettable, a time of terror. Children who lived through those times caught up in the bombing still shake with the memory. Even to this day if one were to observe the generation of that time, they will look and watch when a plane passes over. They will listen for the doleful wailing sound of the siren ready to dash for cover or run if threatened.

Only the citizens who experienced those raids could understand what terror they endured, and how we would shudder at the dreadful droning noise of the Nazi Bombers. For those who did not have Anderson or Public shelters, coal bunkers and wash houses would be converted into a temporary refuge. Sometimes people would make a comfortable space under the stairs; there was also the very strong steel and wire indoor table shelter, which could be assembled in any room, the Morrison Shelter, named after the Minister of Supply Herbert Morrison. Not all shelters were constructed deep underground; many surface concrete shelters were built in the middle of the street. Whatever shelter the population used during the bombing it did not guarantee them complete safety. There was always the hope that the sausage shaped silver coloured barrage balloons floating in the sky over Plymouth Sound and those attached to boats in the River Tamar, would be our defence, and perhaps the bombers would not get through. Such wishful thinking! Frightening too, was the black-out, living in total darkness relying on candles or torches to see the way, afraid to move in case of being caught out in a strange area if the siren sounded. Many civilians sustained injuries during the war from the Blackout. Pedestrians stepped off curbs into the paths of oncoming vehicles; some fell into unfilled pits and craters, or walked into lampposts. Trying to live a normal every day life was extremely dangerous.

Damaged Anderson Shelter in Plymouth after the March/April 1941 Raids. Photo courtesy of Westcountry Publications. ·

When the Siren did sound in Plymouth, it would be quite loud as it operated under a single remote control by an electrical switch, which issued synchronised two-minute air raid warnings from the Greenbank Police Headquarters. All the sirens at key points would go off together warning the population of an impending raid. If sometimes bombers came over without the siren going off, the ARP Wardens had mobile air raid sirens that they could operate manually. Often a German Reconnaissance Dornier plane (Flying Pencil) was the first indication of an impending raid. When the Heinkel 111, Junkers 88, and the Dornier bombers came, during the day or

Mobile Air Raid Warning System. Item courtesy of Mr Dick Eva Plymouth. Photo courtesy Mr Raymond Vittle Plymouth.

through the night, we would be huddled in the shelters and if the bombs dropped too close we would put our fingers in our mouth to protect our ears if a blast did occur. Every family had to have an emergency box comprising of candles, matches, toilet paper, first aid kit, water and a few rations which were to be taken to the shelter when a raid was imminent. ARP wardens could hear us breaking into a musical soiree. We would sing the songs of that era in our cold damp shelter, accompanied by music from the children playing their combs with a piece of tissue paper. Adults brought other musical instruments, sometimes the accordion, sometimes the concertina and mouth organ to try and drown the sound of falling bombs, and the more welcomed sound of our own ships and land batteries firing their Ack-Ack guns. A simple stick with a rubber band joined end to end, tautly extended which became an home made instrument would allow the owner to pluck away at the rubber band creating a musical note.

To keep our spirits up we belted out, "You Are My Sunshine" "In The Quarter Master's Store" "Daisy-Daisy" "Bye-Bye Blackbird" "Run-Rabbit-Run" "I've got Sixpence" "Roll out the Barrel" and Gracie Field's 1939 song "Wish Me Luck as You Wave Me Goodbye." Then there was the 1941 version of "Bless 'Em All" by George Formby and we would try to emulate Flanagan and Allen's 1939 melody "We're Going to Hang Out the washing on the Siegfried Line" and Vera Lynn's classic songs "There Always be an England!" "When They Sound The Last All Clear" "When the Lights Go On Again" and "We'll Meet Again" a song which became one of the songs of the 20th century. Famous too was "Lili Marlene" sung by Anne Shelton.

Vera Lynn. England's own secret weapon during the war years.

This song had been written in Germany yet both nations adopted the song and it was sung by the troops of both countries. Vera Lynn would sing to the children a song from 1940 called "Goodnight Children Everywhere" and throughout the war years her songs were to be significant in keeping the spirits in good stead among civilians and troops alike. Deanna Durbin's dulcet tones sang "Can't help Singing." Adults formed little groups of singers to emulate "The Ink Spots" and they favoured wartime bands like Tommy Dorsey, Geraldo, Ambrose, Joe Loss, Billy Cotton and Glenn Miller with his Army Air Force Band. Most would listen to the ENSA Concerts, Hi-Gang, ITMA, (It's that man again) or listen to Bing Crosby and the Andrew Sisters or England's own singer Al Bowly.

BBC Home Service on the wireless was a lifeline of communication in the war years; it kept everyone updated with the news. Reddifusion broadcasts were linked to the Ministry of Information and it was their task to convey messages of civil importance to the population. The popular Radio Home Service featured Jack Payne's Orchestra, Radio Rhythm Club and Oscar Rabin's Band, and on Saturday night there was the very popular show called Music Hall. Forces Network introduced Henry Hall's Guest Night and the Kentucky Minstrels. Factory workers had a daily programme "Music While You Work" while for the children there was always children's hour at five-fifteen in the evening, providing the bombers gave us a respite to listen. Various forms of entertainment were popular for the adults such as dancing on the Hoe or at the Pier Pavilion for one shilling every Saturday (until its destruction in 1941), and every evening there would be dancing at the Paramount (opposite the Gaumont Cinema in Union Street).

An advert from the Western Evening Herald 9th July 1940 advertising a cup of Oxo in the Shelter. Many citizens did indeed like their cup of hot oxo, it was considered a meal by some. Courtesy Westcountry Publications.

There were times when we would spend hours huddled in the shelter, cold and damp. Relatives or guardians would come prepared with flasks and billycans containing home made soup or hot tea and biscuits, others would prefer their cup of Oxo, or Bovril. We would read comics, play shadow pictures on the wall with our fingers which reflected from the candlelight, or from the sixpenny Beacon Night-Light which with one pennyworth of oil, would burn for many hours, some children would be encouraged to knit. Adults and children alike became quite adept at playing "I spy" during the long hours. On occasion someone would have a Crystal Set Radio Receiver in the shelter which was the 'in thing' for radio enthusiasts and they would keep us updated with the news. At home radios could be bought or rented and there were several well-known types, notably Philips, Philco,

Murphy, Emston, Ekco and Reddifusion.

Sometimes during the early morning or evening when it was still light we could see the dogfights between the German raiders and our Royal Air Force fighters. The classic Spitfires and the workhorses of the RAF the Hawker Hurricanes Mk1&2 would be engaged in single combat weaving intricate trails of smoke into the sky as they pursued the enemy Messerschmitt B/109's fighters (code-named Snappers by the RAF) and the twin engine Heinkels. The rat-tat-tat of the Browning 303 canon fire belching from the Hurricane could not penetrate the armour of the Messerschmitt; nonetheless, our fighters brought down many of the enemy raiders. The Messerschmitt pilots would often strafe the barrage balloons over the city and attack the civilian population in the streets. This angered the RAF pilots so they would make great efforts to destroy the enemy when they could. The Royal Air Force 247 squadron based at Roborough and at St Eval, Newquay, would launch their obsolete Gloster Gladiator planes, which were later replaced by the Hawker Hurricane. We called our RAF men "The Brylcreem Boys" because they would use Brylcreem on their hair to give it a sleek shining appearance, which made them look more handsome in their uniforms.

Gloster Gladiator K6131 superseded by the Hurricane 1 during the early years of the war. Photo by kind permission The Fleet Air Arm Museum Yeovilton.

A wartime blitz spirit developed, the nation pulled together for the war effort, as our Island fought for its very existence, and Winston Churchill introduced the "V for Victory" campaign. Tremendous losses to merchant and Royal Navy ships had been suffered with the German Wolf Packs of U-boats sinking all ships within their torpedo range. However, the Battle of the Atlantic had turned in 1941 with the allies winning the sea battle and more ships with food were able to reach port as the British Armed Services had won the fierce engagement and had succeeded in sinking many German U-boats. The Americans did not come into the war until December 1941, until then we had fought on alone. However, children are very resilient, and even in those terrible times we improvised and created our own fun and values. Children became involved with the war in 1940-1941 when School Squads were formed known as the Junior Service Squads for children between the ages of eleven and fourteen. They were detailed to look after gardens and do farm work, entertain younger children and raise money for war charities. They also delivered messages as the telephone lines were constantly out of order with the bombing. Younger children helped with filling the sandbags, which were used to place around buildings of importance to minimise bomb damage. From the age of eight upward boys and girls were taught how to extinguish an Incendiary Bomb. Senior girls helped to knit socks, balaclavas and cap comforters for the servicemen. Life was hard in the war but adversity in some respects is character forming and that never harmed anyone. Today everything comes too easy to children and their sense of value is so different from ours in the war years.

Plymouth Children practising putting on their Gas Masks 1941. Photo courtesy Mr Eric Wyatt Plymouth.

Not many children of the war years will have forgotten the rubbery sickly smell and the claustrophobic sensation of our gas respirators. When we were told to put them on it was fascinating to see what came out of the little brown cardboard boxes in which we carried our masks, our faces would have a sheepish expression on them, knowing we had been caught as we turned out our treasures. Combs, marbles, sticky sweets, chewing gum, conkers, rubber bands (used to make a catapult or a sling) safety pins, (girls always carried a safety pin in case their knicker elastic broke) and ball bearings to exchange for shrapnel, (jagged pieces of bomb and shell) which gave us an avenue to an alternative currency. Many a penny for pocket money was obtained by this transaction. Some children would have a little tin of Bleach Ointment in their gas mask case, which was supposed to neutralise mustard gas.

The blackouts were scary. No lights could be shown and white lines were painted on the kerbs to avoid stepping into the road. Trees lining the roadside near the kerb had three large white stripes painted on the trunk, and walls had every alternate stone painted white so that important transport could see the way in the blackout. Motorists who could still get petrol painted the mudguards of their cars white so that pedestrians could see them in the black out. Headlights were covered with only a very small aperture cut out to see. Public areas, which had to be lit to some degree, inserted black painted bulbs into lamps and electric lights. During the war, when wave after wave of enemy bombers dropped their parachute flares, incendiaries and high explosive bombs on Plymouth, the evening skies would light up with colourful hues. Vivid in our memories is the colour of the sky, it was blood red and we feared we would never see a blue sky again. Another memory was the stench of burning buildings and the way everything seemed to catch fire so easily. The overpowering smell of sulphur that came from the incendiaries was an experience never to be forgotten. For days after the raids billowing smoke could still be seen. A thick cloak of ash would cover everything and the choking dust made our lives difficult. Talk of the town was when a jewellery shop somewhere in the City in March 1941 had caught fire and the heat had been so intense that the gold melted and flowed away into the gutter. Seventeen days after the heavy raid, and when the rubble had been cleared away, thousands of pounds worth of jewellery was recovered from the strong room under the burnt out shop.

The Nazi bombers had other little tricks that they would unleash from the bellies of their planes, known as booby traps. They were Anti-Personnel Bombs and included items like cheap imitation jewellery bearing inscriptions in German or Italian, or they would appear disguised as a box of matches, or a cigarette packet. Also there were paper covers wrapped around small parcels to make them look like sweets or chocolate bars, there were metal boxes that looked liked cigarette lighters. Cruellest of all were the brightly coloured butterfly splinter bombs the size of a cocoa tin. The slightest vibration would set the fuse off and then they exploded. Invariably it was the children who lost a hand or a foot, or were blinded or killed by these cruel packages. Children were instructed not to pick anything up without asking an adult. Sometimes enemy bombers appeared dropping their bombs when no air raid warning had been sounded. Children and adults were killed in these hit and run raids. It is thought the bombers came in under the radar screen and were over the city before any defensive action could be taken. The delayed action bomb, (Lange Zeil Zunderlong) was a cruel invention, as no warning would be given. These raids tested the human spirit and the level of endurance borne by the citizens gave courage to many who feared the worst. No one could have anticipated the devastation that our city would endure; children played amidst the ruins of bombed out houses treating them as adventure playgrounds, so this then, was our heritage!

Often heavy gunfire, without the siren warning would indicate the first of the pathfinders unloading their high incendiaries bombs to set fire to the city allowing enemy bombers to have a clear view to unload their means of destruction and death. Every part of the city was systematically targeted and Plymouth was to experience three hundred raids from July 1940 until 1944 when the last raid took place. They took a dreadful toll of life and property. The nightmare of bombing produced noises, which almost deafened the eardrums. Many civilians wore earplugs. Who will ever forget the awful whistling sound that the bombs made when they were released by the German planes. It was a test of stamina almost beyond endurance, yet the Plymouth population refused to submit and tried to carry on living as normal as the conditions would allow.

Plymouth did have some Anti-Aircraft gun emplacements; one was at the Royal Engineers College at Manadon, which was manned by the Officers. Other emplacements were at Penlee, at Central Park, and Treville Street operated by Ack-Ack crews. Locals in the Ham Woods area lived with the

constant boom-boom of Big Bertha. Another battery was situated at Colesdown Hill. We could hear the 3.7-inch Ack-Ack guns firing which gave us some measure of satisfaction. However, the gun barrels were worn out with so many heavy raids, that the crew fired practice blanks on occasion, to let the population think they were fighting back! There were other mobile guns operated at various vantage points around the city but it was only a token gesture, as they did not succeed in shooting down many enemy bombers, often we would see the beams of the searchlights probing the sky, trying to mark the German planes to shoot them down. Meanwhile, the Minister of Supply appealed to Plymouth Barbican fishermen and to villages in Devon asking for hundreds of fishing nets to use in camouflaging the guns, the nation was so short of resources. The German Luftwaffe carried out the worst

Damaged House in a Westcountry City after the March/April 1941 Raids. Note the unbroken mirrors & pictures on the wall & the free-standing clock on the mantelpiece over the fireplace, which is untouched by the bombing. Photo courtesy of Westcountry Publications.

of their raids on Plymouth in March 1941 after the King and Queen had left for London after paying a visit to Plymouth. Very heavy bombing with waves of German bombers in the attack unloaded their bombs from heights of 10,000 & 15,000 feet. The German raiders attacked in force over two or three nights then a few days respite until the bombing pattern began again. Hundreds of electron incendiary bombs were dropped which set fire to the city followed by massive high explosive bombs, which left piles of smouldering ruins and razed buildings. Men, women and children were killed or trapped beneath debris, these raids continued into April 1941 and the city was devastated and the death toll reached a staggering 1,178, many families losing everything.

The population were angry with the Ministry of Information who casually issued a bulletin in the press stating that "A short sharp raid had occurred over a South West City." Lady Astor was incensed and criticised the bureaucrats as "The Ministry of Inflammation!" Children and adults were amazed at some bombed out homes as on several occasions the bombs would split the house in two, often with serious casualties. Above the fireplaces would be seen a mantel shelf, the items would still be standing untouched, cups of cocoa and not a drop spilt, china ornaments with no damage, standing steady on the mantel piece. Photographs encased in glass and mirrors would be exactly as they were before the devastation, not even a crack. Every bombed City had its looters and Plymouth was no exception, the authorities tried hard to keep it under control. Gas and electricity supplies were cut off and this meant emergency feeding arrangements had to be organised. With the destruction of many municipal rest homes and the loss of emergency food rations, it left hundreds of homeless people without food or provisions and became an acute problem.

Queen's Messengers set up an emergency field kitchen at Home Park Car Park 1941. Photo courtesy of Westcountry Publications.

Loud speakers toured the city asking that people with empty rooms come forward so that homeless people could have shelter as the billeting department had lost all their records in the March bombing. Hundreds of pets were being destroyed as their owners had been left homeless and the Animal Welfare (RSPCA) was overwhelmed with lost and abandoned pets. There was no pet food, as we know today, feeding comprised of dog or cat biscuits soaked in gravy, boiled rice, on occasion horsemeat, bones, scraps and vegetables. At one time the Ministry of Food considered allowing a small bottle of milk ration to be issued for pets but it never materialised. Homes usually displayed a poster on the house wall indicating the number of people or pets living in the house in the event of it being bombed, to inform would be rescuers who and what to rescue. For housewives who still had a home, normal home life was totally disrupted as no drinking water from the tap was available, mobile water tankers supplied the population where they could. Gas rings could not be lit, and electric lights could not be switched on, trying to produce a meal was proving very difficult. With the April bombing food was in short supply and long queues of people could be seen outside shops that were still open and able to supply food. Sometimes food supplies would be zoned so that the goods were sold only in the areas where ships were able to dock or trains were able to deliver to various towns. Naval authorities came to the rescue when food shops were bombed until Plymouth citizens saw the arrival of Ministry of Food Officials. Meanwhile, private bakeries were organised to cook dinners during the weekend in their coal-heated ovens. The Army and Navy issued boilers, and emergency field soup kitchens were brought in to use to provide hot meals; housewives used Primus stoves or oil cookers and they improvised cooking facilities by converting a biscuit tin. They would stand the tin on its side with the back close to a coal fire, put the lid partly on, so that it was not quite shut, then a shelf would be used from the stove and then they cooked meat, vegetables and even cake! The 'Queen's Messengers' and their flying food squads also supplied meals as they brought in convoys of food to be distributed to the beleaguered City residents from the mobile kitchens that had been set up in car parks.

A new cooking depot was established in Plymouth in school premises for communal meals, citizens could buy a three course meal for nine pence. One particular place was the School of Housecraft at Portland Square and another centre was opened at Plymouth High School for Girls at North Hill. The Women's Voluntary Service (WVS), the British War Relief Society of America, the British Red Cross and the Salvation Army, affectionately called the Sally Ann, helped in supplying food, clothing, comfort and support as they manned the rest centres. What a wonderful body of people

they were as many families were helped by their efforts. On Flag Day in the spring the Salvation Army soldiers sold bunches of primroses on the streets in a desperate attempt to raise funds for their work. Mobile shower and bath vans were placed in strategic areas to allow personnel to shower or bath as a decontamination process. The March/April 1941 terror bombing was when our lovely city of Plymouth was almost totally destroyed. Beautiful architectural buildings were razed to the ground, and so much was irretrievably lost in the devastation. Those well-loved Department Stores Spooners of Plymouth and J.C. Tozer of Devonport were completely destroyed.

The Graphic depicting the Tozer shop in Devonport circa 1930's. Taken from a former invoice courtesy Miss Jean Tozer Justice of the Peace. (Daughter of Sir Clifford & Lady Tozer)

A scene depicting firemen trying to extinguish a road on fire in a Westcountry City after the bombing 1941. Photo courtesy of Westcountry Publications.

No other provincial city suffered more bombing and destruction than Plymouth, yet when the blitzed cities are mentioned in history it is always Coventry, Sheffield, Manchester, Glasgow and London who are noted as being the most heavily bombed, with Plymouth being the forgotten city. The AA Gun crews shot down three enemy bombers in April and the fighting spirit of the civilian population was summed up by a book shop owner called Becker who had been bombed out in March 1941 by this quote. "Old Hitler has bombed our home, but he is a long way from bombing our hearts!" Scenes of destruction and the breakdown of services in Plymouth made living conditions intolerable. Winston Churchill visited Plymouth on the 2nd May 1941, which finally brought about the order from the Government to declare Plymouth an official evacuation area and nine thousand children were evacuated in May. Previously the City had been designated a neutral or safe zone despite being a naval port, many children died in Plymouth from that ill-fated decision.

The heat caused by the burning was terrible, when children came out of their homes to go to school or play, (if the school was still standing) we would find the roads still on fire and we would be walking on burning tar that had still not been extinguished. Noticeable was the choking dust and smoke, the air was so thick one could hardly breathe. Feathers from burnt out mattresses flung in the street were blown about in clouds, almost like a snowstorm. Now and again as we walked to school or to a shop a sudden "Whoosh!" would emanate from the ground followed by a fire shooting up into the air out of control, another gas main had fractured! After a heavy raid on the following day teams of workmen and servicemen would have to clear the rubble to the sides of the road so that people could walk safely, and to allow buses and working transport access to other parts of the city. All citizens and children were told to walk in the middle of the road to avoid being hit by falling masonry. War damaged dangerous buildings were pulled down and the residue removed to allow the citizens to go about their everyday business.

Exhausted Firemen, ARP Wardens and workmen fell asleep on the streets after spending hours, sometimes days, in fighting the fires and clearing the rubble. Children fell asleep during lessons at school tired from so many sleepless nights and workers on their way to their jobs could be seen in buses fast asleep trying desperately to catch up on much needed rest. There was no nine to five working hours during the war; nearly every adult had two jobs, one by day and one by night. In the evening when the dusk drew in, the buses would put up their blackout curtains and blast screens. A team of older men would be seen placing oil lamps at the end of important streets

The Leyland Bus seen in Plymouth during the 1930's/1940's. Civilians could be seen nodding off after nights of heavy bombing. The Drivers often knew their passengers and would awake them when they reached their destination. Photo from a private collection. Photograph courtesy Mr R. F Mack Whitchurch Bristol.

so that vehicles of importance could see where they were going, these lamps could not be seen from the air as they had a special shutter to avoid exposure of unnecessary light. Everyone would help to put on criss-cross sticky tape to protect windows, and children would often help the adults in filling the fire buckets with sand or water, which was pleasing, because most children love to play with sand and water. At night when the fire buckets were empty, we would fill them by candlelight; sometimes the light from the burning buildings would guide us.

Sometimes during a raid we could hear the Air Raid Wardens sounding a series of short blasts on their whistles, this meant many incendiaries had fallen and adults had to come out of the shelters to help put out the fires.

Children rushed to nearby fire bombed homes to claim shrapnel, the green silk parachute cord from land mines, and the fins from incendiary bombs as they were worth a fortune in exchange for currency or black market sweets. Nearly every home kept a tin bath full of water, with a bucket and stirrup pump close by, to be used when incendiary bombs hit the buildings, and no emergency gear would be without an hurricane lamp with its distinctive paraffin smell. Ordinary people would use the 'Minimax' Soda Acid Fire Extinguisher which could be used by one person and was operated by one hand to tackle the Incendiary Bombs. It was so distressing when the fire fighters found that their hoses would not fit the fire hydrants. Fire fighting brigades came from all parts of the Westcountry to help as fires raged in many parts of the city, consequently, they had to stand by helplessly as the buildings burnt and collapsed around them. So brave were the fire fighters, and none braver than the ARP Wardens, the regular National Fire Service and the Auxiliary Fire Service who took tremendous risks to save life and property. Courage of the highest order was displayed by the men of the bomb disposal sections of the Royal Engineers who job it was to dig up and destroy the time-bombs distributed by the Nazi raiders. The number of servicemen killed in the City of Plymouth has never been truly revealed. One incident of a squad of five soldiers killed near the Hoe whilst defusing a time bomb shocked the citizens as was the death of eighty Petty Officers at the Naval Barracks during a heavy raid. The Local Defence Volunteers (LDV) also called "Parashots" were renamed the Home Guard by Winston Churchill in July 1940 as enemy parachute drops were expected that summer. The term Parashot was given to them because they were continually on the lookout for parachute invaders. They were armed with their truncheons and shotguns (those who had one as rifles and guns were in short supply) ready to challenge any landing attempt on British soil. Some

NFS Fireman in wartime uniform. Courtesy of Mr Dick Eva Plymouth.

carried pikes and pitchforks, they were affectionately nicknamed by the ordinary citizens as the "Broom Stick Army" or the "Look, Duck and Vanish Brigade." Plymouth Home Guard known as the City Battalion under the command of Colonel Northcott was attached to 16th Battalion of the Devonshire Regiment. With the fear of invasion instructions had been issued to the Home Guard to leave open all manhole covers, place containers on the road propped up with a stick which was then attached to a piece of string trailed off to an unseen position. This idea was to force the enemy raiders to inspect every area to make them think it was booby-trapped with a live bomb. Residents were informed to prop open windows and place a straight tube out the window to give the appearance that a sniper was in position. Because the Home Guard was made up of ordinary citizens not of fighting age in the services, there were unfortunately mistakes and tragic accidents which cost the lives of many civilians, either shot by mistake or through misunderstandings. Whatever their name they did a wonderful job safeguarding the public and property and no doubt about it, they would have fought with whatever weapons they could find to protect our country and we owe them all a debt of gratitude. Plymouth citizens received the dreadful news that the Devonport based HMS Hood had been sunk on the 24th May in the Denmark Straits and that of her 1,421 gallant crew there were only three survivors. The people of the city and the whole nation were shocked at the terrible naval tragedy.

The forgotten architectural crime of the war in Plymouth was not committed by the enemy bombers but by our own government. The city's ornamental iron works had been a part of our heritage from the early eighteenth century and gave the city character. The requisitioning for the war effort presented the question which had to be asked, "Was it really necessary for our survival?" in view of the public records which show that great mountains of railings and gates were stock piled in various parts of the country and never used, or stored in builders yards and warehouses, then simply left to rust away. This indicates the injustice of the decision and the waste of iron, which only amounted to two per cent of the nation's assets. Stripping the buildings and streets robbed them of their character and sadly streets still show the scars today where they were hacked away. "Turn the iron railings into tanks and guns" was the war cry! Not all railings were removed as those that were considered to be of an artistic or historical merit were spared, but all others made after 1850, however ornate or well crafted had to go.

The war had put pressure on every resource the country had. The press in a wave of patriotism lodged re-cycling drives for papers, bottles, aluminium, and pots and pans for the Spitfire Fund. The idea of requisitioning iron works for the production of munitions was stolen from the enemy. The Minister of Supply Lord Beaverbrook, who was also a newspaper magnate and a close friend of Winston Churchill, was inspired by the re-cycling drive instigated by Hitler and Mussolini, so in the autumn of 1941 the British government made railings and gates requisitioning compulsory. A vast propaganda programme followed as homes, businesses, garden squares and public parks sacrificed their railings and gates for the national good. The Duke of Bedford had refused to have his ornate ironwork removed, as he believed the whole thing was a propaganda scam, so Lord Beaverbrook's newspapers engaged in a press war with the Duke of Bedford, and bitter episodes ensued. After several confrontations the Duke of Bedford submitted and he lost all his railings with the exception of Bedford Square which still stands today, historians will note that his views were so near the truth. Other railings, which escaped the removal rule, were the ornate railings around Dover Castle. They were considered important to the defence of Dover because the underground sections were used by the High Command of the Royal Navy and by the Prime Minister Winston Churchill. The castle overlooked the English Channel and on a clear day France could be seen and any launch of an impending invasion would have to be repelled from this point. The thought of invasion placed a feeling of fear into the hearts of all the citizens, some were seized by panic and despair and decided they would end their lives if the Hun landed on our shores, others were nonchalant and sombre, and many stated they would fight to the death. The threat of invasion was real in 1940.

The Blitz was to bring even further changes to the lives of children, those with parents wrenched from their homes, including children of foster parents and institutions, suddenly found their whole lifestyles totally disrupted. Children were evacuated to villages of safety and placed with strangers whose lifestyles were complete opposite to what they had known. Schools were being bombed, and despite valiant efforts by teachers to run classes in difficult circumstances, many children were to suffer lost education which put them two years behind the standard expected and as (at that time) children were to leave school at fourteen years of age, that loss was to prove costly, as when orphaned children left school and started work they would only be eligible for the most mundane jobs. Boys would go to farms or perhaps be apprenticed to a labourer, and girls were earmarked for domestic work, often they would have to "sleep in" and their board and keep would come out of their pecuniary low wages. Children from institutions were put in "Blind Alley" jobs, and often their assessment was not commensurate with the young person's character or calibre. In 1943 discussions were underway to raise the school leaving age to sixteen, opinion was that it would improve the children's mental health and increase understanding between the social classes. Insularity and snobbishness would be minimised and unemployment reduced, it would allow for better education opening the way to better jobs when children left school. This brought a 'cri-de-coeur' from many a pupil who did not relish the idea of staying at school for two more years.

It was strange that the Whitehall pundits did not consider Plymouth to be a target in the early years of the war, despite the fact the provincial city was home to an army garrison, an air station, and a naval port. The government ministers disassociated Plymouth with the events happening in other parts of the world. Children had been killed in the early bombing of 1940, nevertheless, the authorities in London refused to consent to Plymouth being an evacuation area. The local Plymouth authorities pressed again and again and pleaded for the children to be evacuated through a properly organised evacuation scheme. No plan was forthcoming, so the children would have to take their chances. This angered the local population and I believe that Plymouth has never quite forgotten or forgiven those quangos in London for ignoring the appeal that would have sent their children to the quiet country villages before the dreadful bombing began. There were some children sent away to areas of safety, but these were mostly private arrangements.

With the destruction and damage to so many schools and more children killed in the March/April 1941 bombing, including sixteen very young children and babies at the City Hospital in Plymouth on the 21 March 1941 Whitehall finally relented, but even then it was quite voluntary. The rescue workers, Police, AFS, Civil Defence Workers, Demolitions Squads, Saint Johns Ambulance and Civilians toiled relentlessly. They had to dig out the bodies of six nurses, coupled with the bodies of the children and babies from the Childrens' sick ward and the Nursery and cried openly as their efforts to dig out any alive proved fruitless. With aching hearts it was upsetting to see tough men cry as they tenderly carried the lifeless bodies of the babies. The nurses had refused to abandon their charges and so that their courage and sacrifice will never be forgotten their names are printed here. Staff Midwife Ruth Cardew Williams, Assistant Nurse Emily Helen Kelly, Nursery Nurses, Monica White and Lydia Rebecca Walters, Student Nurses Winifred May McGuirk and Olivia May Willing. It is pleasing to note that sixty years after their sacrifice the Plymouth nurses have been acknowledged by the naming of streets on a new housing estate where the old hospital once stood. On the death certificates of those dear children killed was written death through War Operations. It was indeed senseless slaughter! One of the children killed was three-year-old John Blatchford who was one of the children in scattered homes care, the City Hospital would care for babies up to and including three years of age. History records show that the first official parties to be evacuated from Plymouth was on the 1st May 1941. However, the children of the Scattered Homes and Stoke House which numbered fifty, were evacuated on 30 April 1941, and many more followed in May, as they were gradually withdrawn from their foster homes. The irony is, that the worst of the bombing raids were over, spasmodic raids did continue over Plymouth until April 1944.

In April 1941 the saturation bombing experienced had also destroyed the heritage of Devonport, Plymouth, as it bore the savagery of the bombing. Tozer's was one of the businesses totally destroyed but with a fighting spirit they re-opened with smaller shops in various locations determined not to be beaten by the destruction of their former premises. A small Nissen Hut in Portland Ope was occupied and other smaller shops scattered throughout the City, notably Mutley Plain, Townsend Hill and St Budeaux. Other shops were opened at Torpoint & Camborne in Cornwall and at Tavistock, Devon.

The destroyed JC Tozer shop in Marlborough Street Devonport Plymouth after the April 1941 bombing, Stoke House Orphanage was also fire bombed which had formerly been owned by the Tozer family. Picture with permission from Plymouth Library Services.

It is indeed sad that the secrecy surrounding the children of Stoke House continued even during the war. The staff and children were burnt out of Stoke House on St George's day the 23 April 1941 and transferred to other accommodation for one night. The next day 24th April the children were accommodated in the Emergency Rest Home at Montpelier Junior & Infants School, Peverell, until 28 April 1941 when four parachute landmines exploded on the school causing damage, which made it uninhabitable. The children were caught in the damage, created by an extensive blast from the mines, which buried some of them alive. Some were in the shelter and a few slept in the school. Frantic efforts by fireman, wardens, police, servicemen and civilians, ensued to dig them out. Thankfully no one was killed but the children were so frightened and one member of the staff Nurse Penna had been slightly hurt. The staff had remained very calm under appalling conditions. It is noted that H.P.Twyford who was a journalist, and was the accredited war correspondent for the Western Morning News newspaper for Plymouth in 1939-1945, made quite detailed diary notes recording dates of specific raids. His book called "It came to our Door" highlighted other orphanages, which were affected by the bombing, but no mention was made of the Stoke House incident. The Devon and Cornwall Female Orphanage, Lockyer Street was mentioned, as was the United Services' Girls Orphanage at Stoke, which had been evacuated to their old-time summer residence at Newquay. The Devonport Dockyard Orphanage at Brightside was also highlighted, yet Stoke House being only a street away from the United Services' Girls Orphanage and just up the hill from the Dockyard Orphanage had no mention.

The blitz and the six years of war were the most traumatic years the citizens of Plymouth were to endure. For the scattered homes and Stoke House children and those wrenched from loving foster homes it was to be an emotional nadir in their young lives. For the majority of those children the evacuation to Clovelly, North Devon, once accepted and integrated with village life, achieved a measure of happiness from a violent conflict. In full view of the villagers and not hidden from the public, mixing freely with other people, playing with children from other areas, and the easing of institutional rules, saw a marked improvement in the quality of their lives. It is indeed sad that it took a war to highlight the plight of orphaned and unwanted children.

When in 1944 from a small beleaguered island sprang the mightiest seaborne invasion the world had ever seen it was clear that the tide had turned and in the end our nation with our Allies achieved the final victory. Now at the beginning of the twenty-first century it is hoped that the violent conflicts are over and that the children of the future do not experience the terror of war. There has been enormous development in humanitarian concern and care, and it is important that we are aware of each other's needs. Older citizens are saddened by the wanton vandalism in which some youth of today participate in; perhaps it is because we saw so much destruction in the war that we did not envisage seeing it again in our lifetime. **War is a savage occurrence in time, and whether it is for national survival or political expediency, in war nobody wins!** It is hoped that mankind gains greater respect for the world in which we live. As we look to the future, we long for a New World of peace and freedom, justice and hope, and a normal childhood for each generation of children to come. We must go forward to seek contentment, for in contentment there is peace.

Looking Up Old Town Street Plymouth after the March/April 1941 bombing before the dangerous damaged buildings were pulled down. Note the Guinness Clock. Photo courtesy of Westcountry Publications.

Looking Up Old Town Street 1941 after teams of workmen had pulled down the bomb damaged shells of buildings and cleared away the rubble. Note the Guinness Clock. Photo courtesy of Westcountry Publications.

City Hospital Ward Damage (interior) after the March Raid 1941. One of the scattered homes children John Blatchford aged three was killed. Photo courtesy of Westcountry Publications Plymouth.

Winston Spencer Churchill with his wife Clementine visits war torn Plymouth 1941. Seen here in the company of Lady Nancy Astor leaving Elliot House on the Hoe. This great man united the population when appointed Prime Minister in 1940. His leadership throughout the war years was of paramount importance to a nation almost on its knees. Yes, he made mistakes! Does anyone know a leader who did not make mistakes when at the helm of the nation? Photo courtesy of Westcountry Publications.

Children's Ward (exterior) Plymouth City Hospital after the March 1941 Raid. Children & Nurses killed. Photo courtesy of Westcountry Publications.

Plymouth's precious Derry's Clock after the March 1941 bombing. Opposite corner was the former Lloyds Bank. Note the damaged clock face. Photo courtesy of Westcountry Publications.

Fore Street Devonport after the saturation bombing. Note both shops now completely destroyed next to the Forum Cinema (formerly a Bookseller & Stationery Store) Businesses which suffered were numbers 109, grocery provisions store David Greig. 110, branch of the Singer Sewing Machine Company. 111-112, The Forum. 113, Miss E Blatchford's Devon Tuckshop Confectionery Shop. 116, (which also incorporated numbers 114 & 115) Military Arms Public House. Seen also is the Electric Theatre (formerly the Devonport Public Hall). Note the Servicemen and the WVS Tea Van in attendance. Photo courtesy of Westcountry Publications.

Fore Street Devonport after a night raid April 1941. The terror bombing lasted three nights. Traders, among them David Creig and the Forum Cinema, were badly damaged. People still going about their daily business showing the fortitude that kept them united. Devonport was never the same after the bombing; it lost forever its very special heritage. Photo courtesy of Westcountry Publications.

CHAPTER TWELVE

THE RATIONING

From the outbreak of War 1939 until D-Day 1944 Germany was determined to starve Britain into submission which led to the Government decision to ration all food and goods to ensure that every citizen had a fair share of food and clothes to survive. Nothing could be bought without coupons; thus the onset of rationing began. Government Ministries controlled factory production and set up rationing schemes to distribute scarce foods fairly, in some instances food was sold in zoned areas only. Rationing in Britain lasted for fourteen years from 1940 to 1954, except for bread, which was rationed in 1946 after the war, because of a world shortage of grain, however, who can forget the grey bread of the war years? Some bakers eked out their flour supply by adding potatoes to bread. In March 1942 Lord Woolton announced that nothing white, whether bread, buns, cakes or biscuits would be made from April 1942. It was to be many years before white bread was seen again and bread was finally derationed in 1948.

The Ministry of Food would issue adverts to Newspapers to encourage the population to follow its advice. National Wheatmeal Bread. Ugh! Article courtesy Western Evening Herald dated 21st April 1941.

During the war years home made cake was not so available as with limited sugar housewives resorted to making a very small cake using a grated carrot to sweeten with their meagre rations. Food, clothing and fuel were all rationed; suddenly it brought new words into our daily vocabulary such as coupons, utility and black market. If you knew the right people "Off the Ration" and "Under the Counter" goods and food could be bought from a thriving black market, particularly scarce goods. Petrol was rationed immediately in September 1939 and was to continue until 1950.

In July 1941, domestic users were restricted to a ton of coal or coke a month; the Minister of fuel; light and power instructed users not to exceed 5 inches

The posh soap of the war years! Article courtesy Unilever Historical Archives Merseyside.

of water in their baths. Many citizens drew a Samuel Plimsoll line around the interior of a bath to maintain the regulated five inches allowed. Soap (3 ounces per person) was rationed in February 1942. One popular soap bar was the well-known puritan Soap, which had a little fairy as its logo, another was lifebuoy toilet soap but a little more expensive. Soap rationing did not end until September 1950. Housewives would use crysella soapflakes made by the Co-operative Society (CWS) and Persil to do the washing, another was the ever present Lifebuoy bar of soap considered the best to kill all germs.

The Minister of Food issued a booklet called "Wartime food for growing children" which cost four pence advising parents on various recipes. One of the recipes was called "Woolton Pie" and consisted of vegetables and potatoes only. There were other recipes offered to the public to encourage housewives to make the most of their rations. All housewives had to be registered with one shop to obtain their meat and bacon rations, sometimes if the shopkeepers had extra supplies regular customers would have first choice. It was in 1941 that children were to experience for the first time the dreadful replacement for ice cream as it changed its taste. Now it was made with wheatened flour mixed with water as a substitute for the real ice cream, but most children would eat most anything, as it was better than nothing.

Sugar was one of the first items to be placed on the ration from January 1940, (to September 1953), by the Ministry of Food. Unfortunately, 1940 was to be one of the coldest winters on record, so sugar, which supplied energy, would be missed, and for housewives and children the bitter news that icing sugar was banned also made the future look glum. Butter rationing followed next, Tips on how to make the butter go further were printed in the newspapers, one article appeared as "Eking out Butter" If you have only a little butter left and want to make it go further, mix milk with it to make the required quantity! Bacon and ham were restricted and tea was rationed from July 1940 (to October 1952) the population mostly favoured Typhoo and Mazawattee tea. Other items rationed were jam, marmalade, treacle, syrup and eggs.

During the war years Cadbury's put out advertising leaflets asking the public to keep the chocolate for the children. Well done Cadburys!

Powdered egg imported from the United States was available as a substitute, a packet of powdered egg could be bought for one shilling and three-pence, and was considered to be the equivalent of twelve real eggs. Every month from 1942 a tin of dried egg was offered in addition to the whole egg ration, one fresh egg would cost a farthing in old money. Cheese was rationed from March 1941; however, enormous quantities of cheese arrived from Canada for the population to buy. Sweets and chocolate were also rationed from March 1941 (sweets and chocolate were de-rationed in April 1949). Meat, first rationed in March 1940, was the very last item to be de-rationed, (in June 1954). Housewives would sometimes mince the meat ration and make rissoles in an effort to make the ration go further to feed hungry children. Alternatively, children would be given slices of bread covered in Marmite as a meat substitute, or alternatively a cup of Bovril.

Basic rations for one person per week were obtained by producing the ration book that had coupons covering the different foods, and these were removed when the food was bought. Rations varied as certain foods became available, sometimes you could not use the coupons if the food supply did not get through the English Channel, as Merchant Navy shipping convoys were being sunk by German U-boats at a rate of half a million tons of shipping every month. In the Battle of the Atlantic, in 1942, it reached its peak, and many a brave merchantman gave his life in a valiant effort to get food through to the population.

To add variety and choice the ration was supplemented with additional points and each person was given a supplement ration book to use on instruction only as certain items became available. This gave every person coupons worth sixteen extra points a month, which could be spent on biscuits, cereal, fish, (remember the snook fish rissoles?) fruit or tinned fruit, if you could get it. Fruit was the first early casualty of the war; lemons, oranges, grapefruit, bananas, grapes, and tinned fruit vanished. When the Americans arrived, which we quickly nick-named "The Yanks," they brought their trade marks with them including various brands of cigarettes such as Lucky Strike, Camel, Phillip Morris and Chesterfields.

So now you
DRINK
the glass and
a half of Milk

It is some time since Cadburys had milk for their chocolate, and their supplies of Milk Chocolate are now exhausted. No Milk Chocolate, for the moment, must say 'Farewell.' The milk goes on your doorstep now — half-a-million pints a day of it to help your children's health!

ISSUED BY
CADBURYS
FROM BOURNVILLE — the Factory in a Garden

With chocolate now so scarce Cadbury's issued adverts encouraging children to drink their milk. With grateful thanks to Cadbury Ltd.

Most important for the children however, were the chewing gum and the small bars of nestles milk chocolate that the servicemen had issued in their rations which they quickly passed on to the children. Also they would give Fry's chocolate spread and in a brown paper bag they would give the children Cadbury's Bournville cocoa with sugar. Serviceman would often be issued with items the populace could not get; however, they were indeed very generous to the British children. British cigarettes were Wild Woodbine packs of five, also the Red Label brand. Then there were the Star cigarettes and the well-known Players. Some citizens preferred Callagers Park Drive or Capstan Navy cut, others bought Gold Leaf or Craven "A". Most children would look for an empty packet of Craven "A" on the streets as their packets featured a black cat which children would step on, circle to the left, saying "Lucky black cat" and who can forget the Swan Vestas and Bryant and Mays matches?

The President of the Board of Trade Oliver Lyttelton, rationed clothes in June 1941 with an allowance of sixty-six coupons, (later to be reduced to twenty-eight coupons). Utility clothes were introduced by his successor Hugh Dalton and this caused a great deal of controversy amongst the fashion wearers who were to see the disappearance of pleats and flounces. Hemlines were raised and double-breasted coats were banned and this did not go down too well with the population. From this decision came the freedom that women were to have in wearing trousers, which had been considered not feminine to wear prior to the war years. Women dressed in what had become a virtual uniform, consisting of slacks, sweaters, and a turban to cover their hair.

With the "Make Do and Mend" ethos it was deemed that less fabric was to be used by the housewife when making or altering clothes, and there was a dramatic shortage of children's footwear. Wartime children's clothes were to be reinforced to obtain maximum value from the item. Furthermore, manufacturers now had to display a utility mark and number to prove to government inspectors that regulations had been adhered to, even buttons were restricted; more than four buttons on a costume or coat would raise an eyebrow or two among the inspectors. However, Hugh Dalton was a man who brooked no nonsense and the populace had to accept the sacrifice.

Wartime Ladies Remember?
Advert taken from a 1940's
Picturegoer magazine.

On the lighter side was the rationing of knicker elastic which affected girls and ladies, elastic was very scarce and drapers who did have stock often kept it under the counter. Usually two yards per person was allowed to their regular customers only, a contrast indeed to the present day where elastic is stitched into the garment so it is impossible to replace, and one has to buy a completely new garment. Silk stockings would disappear; occasionally a black marketeer would have some stock at a price. When the Americans arrived in Britain girls could get nylons from their American boyfriends, for other ladies there was always the Nyrona leg tan which was painted on the legs to look like stockings, it would last quite a few days and stayed on until washed off. Civilian and service women used Tangee natural lipstick bought from Naval, Army, Air Force Families Institution canteens to use as make up as creams and lipsticks were scarce.

WHAT WAS THE RATION?

Sugar.	8 oz (225 grams)	Bacon	4 oz (100 grams)
Ham.	4 oz (100 grams) this could be an alternative to bacon.		
Butter.	4 oz (100 grams)	Lard	2 oz (50 grams)
Margarine	4 oz (115 grams)	Cooking Fats.	8 oz (225 grams)
Milk 3 pints. (1.8 litres).		Jam.	4 oz (100 grams)
Tea	2 oz (50 grams) (plus two pints of milk)	Cheese	2 oz (50 grams)

Sweets 2 oz (50 grams) per week or 12 ozs every four weeks. (Zoned)
Eggs. One shell egg a week if available! Eggs were like Gold Dust!
Dried Eggs. One packet every four weeks.

Meat. A set weight was not given (although twelve ounces of minced beef was allocated) as meat was difficult to obtain, the troops had first choice of meat for their rations, so one person could only buy meat to the value of one-shilling (Five new pence). The only people lucky enough to have plenty of meat, were farmers, butchers and the black market traders. Canned Corned Beef, of which one was allowed three pennyworth, became very popular. Imported Supply Pressed American Ham (Spam) was relished as an alternative to meat which looked and tasted like fresh meat and did prove successful. The Lend-Lease Act in March 1941 between America and Great Britain gave food aid to service personnel and civilians alike. Hormel the American firm producing Spam went into immediate wartime production ensuring that Britain had a regular supply and when the first batch of Spam arrived in Britain in 1941 it was an immediate favourite with the housewives. The nation was fed by stringent government control and on reflection the whole population benefited from it, as everyone had a fair share.

Sausages were not rationed but these could only be had on occasion and no one was sure what was in them. Butchers would use a lot of bread and water to make the meat go further, in this instance you were at the mercy of the farmer or the butcher. Families could supplement their food rations by setting up chicken runs in their back garden for hens and poultry and some even had pigs in their plot or garden. If a pig was slaughtered half of the pig was given to the Government men and the owner could keep the other half. Pig and bone bins were placed in the streets to be collected by the local council and everyone who had a plot, garden or allotment, was detailed to turn their garden into growing vegetables for the population. Citizens were regularly monitored by local enforcers appointed by the Government to ensure that every iota of space was being used to grow vegetables. If when on inspection anyone had a tree or a bush, or even a flower bed, that person would be made to dig it up and replace it with an edible plant. They also risked being heavily fined. Ironically, shortages of goods seemed to get worse after the war because there were so many people all over the world at the point of starvation who needed a share of limited resources. The war rationing was deemed fair and kept the nation fed.

CHAPTER THIRTEEN

C(LOVE)LLY!

Clovelly! Known in the Domesday Book as Cleave Leigh, (The Cliff Place) Oh Clovelly! What an impact Clovelly was to have on all the children and adults who were evacuated there from Plymouth a City sixty miles away during the 1939/1945 war. A period of time that was to be imprinted in their memories for life on all who stayed at the village in those memorable years!

A beautiful place of Saxon origin, an ancient and picturesque little fishing village on the North Devon coast between Hartland Point and Bideford whose history originates from the fourteenth century. Its cobbled streets created from the very pebbles taken from the shore, built by hand and still as sturdy today. Clovelly's livelihood was coupled with the fishing industry, famous for it's small fishing boats and the shoals of herring that was part of their lives. The Lords and Ladies of the Clovelly Court Manor governed for four centuries, linked in the eleventh century with the family Giffards it then passed to the Fane-Cary family who held it in their family tree for seven generations. On their demise it transferred to the Hamlyns and Christine Fane Hamlyn although small in stature was the most loved of all as she did much to improve the living conditions of her villagers.

It was her courageous decision to turn the estate into a company in 1928 that changed the life of the village forever. She was forced to make this judgement because of high taxes and death duties, which made prospects for private landowners very bleak. On her death the estate came into the hands of her niece the Honourable Mrs Betty Asquith and her husband Arthur, later their daughter the Honourable Mrs Keith Rous inherited the estate. Now the Honourable Mr John Rous controls the estate and he has the future of Clovelly in his hands, indeed a very heavy responsibility. Clovelly is steeped in history and is a small and self-contained village with a strong family community. Throughout the years the management of the tiny village has relied on these families and it is through their efforts that the village has retained its uniqueness and long may it reign.

The Clovelly Dykes or Ditchen Hills are believed to be ancient Roman earthworks. The Clovelly people are so different from city folk, as in their genes and bloodlines will be found seeds of Roman, Celtic, Spanish, Norman and Saxon heritage. Their temperaments embraced the folklore, and they paid great heed to myths, superstition and legend. In Upper Clovelly is the lovely Clovelly Court, which is synonymous with nature. As soon as one enters the estate it offers a gentle reminder that one is immediately in a special place. Here where the smell of the blossom on the trees give a scent of appreciation and the wonderment of nature amongst the mature lime trees and the grassy banks covered in wild flowers bordered with hydrangea and fuschia hedges. Nearby are the fields, which during the war years grew crops of vegetables, barley, maize, wheat and corn, not like today where fields consist mainly of crops of fodder peas, oil seed rape and linseed or flax.

The early years of the war saw Clovelly Court as a centre point for the British Red Cross with its convalescent home. It became involved in village activities but sadly in December 1943 part of the house was destroyed by fire and the Red Cross had to move to other premises. Further up the hill toward Slerra lies the lovely Norman All Saints Church with its ancient lych gate, a vignette from the past, surrounded by old yew trees which bordered the church grounds and when you entered the church there was an aura of peace. The cemetery outside the church, on inspection of the gravestones, revealed names from families of distinction indicating a very special history.

ARP and Red Cross Post Clovelly June 1942. Boy in front Bobby Couchman (London) From the Left. Second row. 1.Miss Horncastle (Clovelly) 2. Pamela Williams (Plymouth) 3. Rose Cruse (Clovelly) 4. Miss Scott (Clovelly) 5. Mary Cruse (Clovelly) 6. Mr Albert Lyddon (Clovelly) Standing in doorway Charlie Synes (Clovelly).

Inside the church is a Saxon font, and it was in this church, during the war years that the institution children from the New Inn sang in the choir or worshipped in the pews as they were taught to chant "The Creed." At least the orphan children were allowed to sit in the pews with every one else and not relegated to the paupers' bracket seats!

Further down the cobbled High Street is the New Inn, which nestles in what is known as "Up-along" with a glorious view out to sea overlooking Bideford Bay. In ancient times the present village High Street where the New Inn is situated was a stream, which now finds its way to the sea from behind the houses. The houses in High Street are built each on a different level along 'Up-a-long' or 'Down-a-long' and each house has its own character. The New Inn, which has been a Hostelry for over 100 years, was rebuilt on the site of the 17th Century Inn. The bar was unique with its floor of Cornish Delabole slate and carpentry of elm and oak crafted by local carpenters. The Edinburgh Architect Mister Burnett Orphoot keeping to the style of William Morris with a London firm of builders started to rebuild the Hotel in January 1914 and his stage of the work was completed by May of the same year. The Great War did not interfere with the building of the New Inn Hotel as the local estate workers were employed to build the laundry and garage which was by 1915 finally completed.

The reconstruction of the New Inn was indeed a clever piece of work by the Architect considering the awkwardness of its position on a steep hill. As a new kitchen had been installed on the opposite side of the High Street and the main dining room was sited there the decision was taken to move the sign to its present site. The annexe on the opposite side is where the licensees have their living quarters and there are also self-contained flats. The re-siting of the sign was clearer for all visitors to see when making their way to the High Street. Many visitors throughout the years have wondered about the picture postcards depicting the New Inn sign on one side when other cards show it on the opposite side of the High Street. The New Inn was a popular meeting point for the village folk who enjoyed their pint of beer at the bar, and its picture is found on many a postcard ensuring its place in history.

The Plymouth children billeted at the New Inn during the war years remember the large picture of Christine Hamlyn, which hung on the wall in the dining room, and to this day it is still there. In 1924 Mr and Mrs Paul Ellis opened their little shop opposite the New Inn, later they had two children John and Sheila Ellis. The shop was to prove a very precious link to the orphaned children from Plymouth in the war years.

The New Inn had bread delivered every day to feed the ever-hungry orphaned evacuees, and the butcher Mr James Cruse supplied meat paid for

123

This scene was taken in 1950 and clearly shows the New Inn sign changed to a Cormorant. I wonder how the villagers felt about that! Note the Ellis Shop in all its splendour the sweet haven for the New Inn children during the war years 1941-1945. The Author extends an apology for any copyright breach as this postcard did not indicate the name or address of the copyright holder, only an M&L sign. Postcard from a private collection.

by the Plymouth City Treasury. Plymouth City Council had requisitioned the New Inn from the Clovelly Estate as a temporary home for the orphaned, unwanted and evacuated children in 1941. It was to remain the headquarters of the Stoke House Orphanage for four years until the balance of the children left were returned to the Astor Institute, Plymouth, in 1945.

The village school nestles in the tiny hamlet of Wrinkleberry (formerly Wrinklebury) still unchanged today except for building alterations which has brought it up to modern day standards and the loss of the older generation who are long gone. Clovelly School will always stay in the minds of the evacuees who were taught there by teachers from 1940 to 1945. From a normal class attendance of thirty children, Clovelly School suddenly found themselves responsible for more than two hundred children. What a nightmare it must have been for the teachers and the villagers to be invaded by so many children in such a short space of time. Teachers from different parts of the country who were sent to Clovelly found themselves teaching a vast array of evacuees transferred from London, Bristol and Plymouth. Schools were short of pencils, books and paper because so much had been destroyed in the bombing and with a world shortage of paper it was very difficult.

Clovelly School 1940. Many evacuees will remember their days at this school in the war years. Use of photo with kind permission Mr Harry Clement (BEM) former London evacuee & Clovelly. Now Bideford Devon.

The teachers and evacuees came from different walks of life and the pupils brought even stranger accents to the North Devon village. Mr Mark Hesketh was the Head Master, and his wife Mrs Hesketh was the sewing teacher. From Plymouth came Miss Pamela Williams who taught children from seven to nine years of age and Miss Marion Blann who taught the five and under fives. From Peckham and Deptford in London came teachers Mr Bamsey and Miss Plaice and from Bristol there was a Miss Howell. One of the Clovelly teachers was Miss Barbara Cruse who also taught the under fives. Subjects taught were religion, arithmetic, English, writing, geography, history, and the most favoured subject, (because we were outside) the nature lesson.

Clovelly School Class 1941-1945. Mixed Evacuees, Stoke House & Local Children. The Stoke House children were billeted at The New Inn. All rows read from the left. Front Row. 1. Kenneth Row (Clovelly) 2. Jackie Symons (Stoke House RIP). 3. Victor Frood (Stoke House RIP) 4. Eric Symons (Stoke House). Second Row. 1. Jean Scott (Plymouth) 2. (Unknown) 3. Mark Hesketh (Headmaster Clovelly School RIP) 4. Ruth Cruse (Clovelly). 5. (Unknown). Third Row. 1. (Unknown) 2. Pat Roberts (Stoke House RIP) 3. Betty Newham (Stoke House) 4. Rosemary Buckingham (Stoke House) Back Row. 1. (Unknown) 2. (Unknown) 3. Alan Johns (Clovelly) 4. Dick Richards (London RIP) 5. Ronnie Watts (London RIP).

Clovelly School opened in 1872 and the school bell still has that date inscribed on it, now owned by the Devon County Council the school has struggled to maintain its independence despite constant threats of closure. Clovelly School facing north east nestles at the top of Clovelly in the little hamlet of Wrinkleberry. The school looks out across Bideford Bay toward Morte Point along the Taw and Torridge Estuaries. On the distant horizon is Exmoor and South Wales.

There was a lady called Mrs Pengelly who lived in Wrinkleberry Cottage opposite the school, and during the war she used to stoke up the stoves with coke so the children could dry their wet coats after walking to the school. The coke was kept in the playground and often the children would jump up and down on the pile, and their clothes would be black from the coke dust. There were four heaters, one in each of the two classrooms, and two in the main hall, which was divided into four separate classrooms by huge curtains. Each heater had a large metal guard surrounding it and as the clothes were drying the smell was awful. Both teachers and pupils had to be resilient to tolerate the aroma.

Clovelly Transport from Picture Postcard courtesy of BA Sweetman & Son Tunbridge Wells 1934.

At the very top of the cobbled street is situated the Mount Pleasant Park and the war memorial remembering the sacrifice of precious sons during the First World War, it is now owned by the National Trust given to them as another gift from Christine Hamyln. Throughout the village pretty baskets and pots of flowers hung from many a cottage wall or window. Donkeys with their pannier-laden wares were used to transport luggage, provisions, coal and logs, up and down the steep cobbled streets, carrying their mauns or wooden harnesses across their backs. One donkey man that the Plymouth children still vividly remember is Roland Hortop. The postman or postwoman would collect the mail from the village and he or she with the donkey would haul it up the steep cobbled hill to the Turnpike Gate. Two men would roll full beer barrels down the village, the casks would be parbuckled into the cellar and a donkey would carry back the empty barrels on its wooden harness. Another form of transport was when the bread was delivered in the village it would be hauled down in a tea chest and handed to the little shop for the customers to buy. Wooden sledges were used to take the heavier loads, these were man-handled and the men had to be strong to heave them down and back again, a feat indeed, considering the steep cobbled street which descends four hundred feet to the sea.

Temple Bar circa 1898 before repair. Note the great wooden beams believed to be salvaged from wrecked sailing ships.

During the war years 1939-1945 the villagers discreetly hung their washing out only on a certain day and many a secret coded message was sent to a husband or lover on the boats fishing in the bay. Often a certain coloured garment would be hung to signal come - or stay away!

One of the oldest parts of Clovelly is known as Temple Bar or given its ancient name The Bow, it still retains its original character and it has been said that the lower roof beams were built from timber of a former wreck. For many years the Coxswain of the Lifeboat lived at Temple Bar. A favourite spot is the Look-Out, which gives a breathtaking view out to sea, and in the distance one can see Saunton and Braunton Sands.

At the bottom of the village is the well known 18th century Red Lion Inn steeped in folk lore encompassing the myths that surround the history of the famous smuggling haunts below the Hobby Drive to the west of Mouth Mill. Contraband exchanged hands and smuggling was proved when Revenue Officers frequently visited the famous Red Lion Inn, which was involved in running illegal goods. Fishermen and their wives were caught with contraband such as spirits, silk, tobacco, pepper, tea and lace. If the cellar walls of the Red Lion Inn could talk - what a tale they would have to tell. Alongside the beach lies a small natural harbour protected by a single harbour wall, and the bollards on the quay are said to be up-ended cannon from the ships of the Spanish Armada.

Plymouth children on Clovelly beach 1941. The Gardener of Stoke House Mr Arthur Scott was evacuated to Clovelly with his family who were billeted in Providence House. From the left. Barbara Scott (daughter) Muriel Gray (Cook's niece) Jean Scott (daughter) Betty Bennett (New Inn Stoke House) Jean McFadyen (Cook's niece) Look at all the children in the background! Photo courtesy of Mrs Jean Job (nee McFadyen) Plymouth.

The breakwater was built in 1885 and at the end of the pier in a niche cut into the granite wall, a small light was placed in memory of two fishermen drowned at sea in 1882. During the herring-fishing season this would be lit as a mark of respect, however, during the war years it was not allowed. Only a limited number of small boats now cull the sea for crab, lobster and fish, others who may beach their boats are usually visitors. Gales often lashed the shore and harbour wall and one could hear the roar of the wind and see the foam from the white horses spray pounding on the cobbled beach. Seeing its awesome power man knew his place. The pebbled beach in fine weather was a child's paradise and the New Inn children loved every minute playing there. During 1941-1945 every pebble must have been turned over to look for the crabs. Famous names spent holidays in Clovelly during the war years and two regular stars who were well known in the village were singers Ann Zeigler and Webster Booth, Nosmo King of the crazy gang was another well known visitor, he died at the age of 63 in January 1959.

The Lifeboat Station was commissioned in 1870 and the Clovelly lifeboatmen have a very proud record. The Plymouth children at the New Inn were to hold the lifeboatmen in very high esteem. They had adopted the waifs and strays and found many ways to give them treats and precious time to play in their boat and even take them out in the bay. What a thrill that was, God Bless them! The Clovelly Lifeboat at the time was called the City of Nottingham a motor boat lifeboat built by Saunders-Roe at East Cowes. It was provided by the City of Nottingham Lifeboat Fund granted by the Royal Naval Lifeboat Institution Headquarters in June 1936. Founded by Sir William Hillary in 1824, the Lifeboat Institution was to save many lives by its inception. Mr George Lamey (1894-1981) who was the Clovelly Lifeboat Coxswain (1935-1955) was a well-liked man. Rugged, strong and easygoing, he had come from the ancestry of the Huguenots La'May who as refugees had fled their homeland to settle in England. George Lamey lived in Appledore until the Great War (1914-1918) however in 1919 he moved to North Devon and in 1921 he married Mary Braund, and moved into the house called Temple Bar in Clovelly. He and his brave crew were called many times for rescue attempts at sea, and to assist ships on fire or search for aircrew who had crashed into the sea off Hartland Point. George Lamey had secret orders during the war, which even his crew and many well-informed villagers were

The Clovelly Lifeboat in the 1940's. Called City of Nottingham. Forever in the hearts of the children who stayed at the New Inn in the war years. In the Boat from the Left. Percy Shackson, Richard Cruse, Steven Headon and the Coxswain George Lamey. Standing from the Left. Jim Cruse, James Whitfield, Bert Braund, Charlie Shackson, Fred Shackson, John Moss & last Unknown. Photo courtesy of Miss Sheila Ellis Clovelly.

Coxswain George Lamey close to retirement taken about 1954 with colleagues at an unknown location after receiving the Bronze Medal. Photo courtesy of Mrs Christine Giddy Clovelly and Mr Fred Colwill Bideford Devon.

not aware of until the public records were released many years later. Naval despatch riders from Westward Ho! would go to Clovelly with sealed orders for the navy ships anchored in the bay and they would pass the instructions to the Lifeboat coxswain. He then informed the ship captains when they could leave. In 1954 George Lamey was awarded the Bronze Medal for gallantry.

Now in the year 2001 Clovelly still has its lifeboat, which was dedicated in 2000 as "The Spirit of Clovelly" a fitting and well-deserved name. Clovelly's history had its chapters of tragedy in the past by the tragic loss of fishermen and boats to the power of the sea. Twice the little village was torn apart. In 1821 a fierce gale claimed twenty-four fishing boats and thirty-one men, and in 1838 when twenty-one men were drowned. This disaster was to decimate the community of the tiny village. Two more were drowned in a storm in 1882 and again in 1998 the sea claimed another two of Clovelly's fishermen. What a terrible price to pay for fish "What is that saying?" For those who go down to the sea in ships… Apart from the fishing boats that are few now which fish for mackerel, sole and cod, the scene has changed little. In August 1943 in very bad weather conditions a bomber manned by an RAF crew whilst on Anti-Submarine Patrol crashed at Clovelly Cross and sadly all the crew were killed, one Canadian, one Scot and four Englishmen, they were all young men in their twenties. Harry Clement a former London evacuee at Clovelly from 1940 always remembered the tragic event and vowed one day he would ensure a memorial would be placed near the location of the crash so that the crew would never be forgotten. True to his word and having worked tirelessly in finding all records and building the memorial with the help of his son his dream was realised. In October 1993 on the fiftieth anniversary of the event the dedication took place.

Clovelly never experienced the dreadful outcome of a bomb on the village and it must have been very difficult for the villagers to understand what the bombing did to the evacuee children. The children of the New Inn spent many happy hours playing in the three mile Hobby Drive which had been constructed in 1829 by Sir James Hamlyn among a profusion of trees, heath, heather and wild flowers. We were safe from the horror of the bombings and we played happily with our school friends climbing the trees, picking the daisies to make daisy chains, playing conkers and marbles, skipping and hopscotch, and forming statues. There were some hilarious figure presentations, but our childish antics were the normal things that children do and the villagers understood. Then there were the streams and grassy meadows which in the spring were covered with bright yellow buttercups and the pale lilac Cuckoo Flowers (Lady's Smock), and the wonderful sound of the singing crickets. The Stoke House children will never forget the freedom we had to run free and to grow.

On the 30th April 1998 a group of Stoke House orphans formally of Plymouth returned to Clovelly for a four-day reunion, fifty-seven years from those memorable days in 1941. Many had come from very long distances, some of the former children had died and some have still not been traced. The group repeated history and stayed at the New Inn. The Honourable John Rous of the Clovelly Estate had been generous in letting the group stay at the New Inn with reduced prices and the Manager, Alan Cook, and his staff made us welcome. The reception received from the Clovelly villagers and the school was overwhelming. On the Friday we made our way slowly up the steep hill which did not seem so steep all those years ago (or was it because we had become slower?) to the school where we had been taught during the war years. The Clovelly school pupils and their helpers with the Head Teacher Chris Nicholls entertained the former evacuees with a lovely cooked dinner. This was followed by speeches from the Clovelly Head Teacher and our own former Teacher Mrs Pamela Pearce (nee Williams) who although in her eighties had travelled from Bristol to attend the nostalgic reunion.

The afternoon was spent singing the war songs with the little school choir who had practised for days to learn the words and the music. We were invited to look around the classrooms and compare the education facilities of today; many of our hosts were children of the people in the village during the war. Several photographs were taken and we made friends with the village children who were mesmerised by our history. It was truly a wonderful day! We spent the day on Saturday walking the three miles of the Hobby Drive. George Dymond, one of the villagers, drove us to Clovelly Lodge in a Land Rover and we strolled along reminiscing those childhood days. Stalwart villagers of Clovelly, Sheila Ellis, (Author of "Down a Cobbled Street" depicting photographs of Clovelly) Bessie May (nee Perkin) (who was a Land Army girl at Clovelly Court during the war) Margaret Braund (nee Tridgell) and Harry Clement (a former London evacuee, author of "No time to kiss Goodbye") organised a party at the village Parish Hall for Saturday evening. June Littlejohns of Bradworthy, (Author of a booklet "Down Wrinkleberry Lane" which consists of poems and memories of Clovelly school days), had kindly made and decorated two beautiful cakes celebrating the reunion.

Many local residents, former pupils and evacuees who had been friends turned out to make us welcome and what a spread of food they had so generously supplied. (No rationing here!) On the Sunday we made the long trek up the hill toward Slerra to a thanksgiving service at Clovelly's All Saints Church. We were much slower now and stiff limbs made it a laboured journey but we would not have missed it for the world. The Lord had been good to us by giving us four brilliant days of sunshine, making the reunion complete.

The BBC spotlight and Westcountry television reporters had covered our reunion and we hold a wonderful memory of a very special weekend. One could use so many superlatives to express how we felt about Clovelly and its villagers, but ours is simple, we remember it with love. Many years have past into history but for those of us still surviving we say now: Thank you for your kindness. For those people who still live and remember us we say: Deep in our hearts you will always remain, and for those who have left this world and to the relatives of those dear Clovelly villagers, this is our message; May all the Angels light your way!

Donkey Parade Clovelly taken outside number 98 High Street circa 1941-1943. From the Left. 1. Hands only visible with donkey. 2. Muriel Gray (Cook's niece) 3. Brian Scott (Gardener's son) 4. Ernest Beer Clovelly (in Trilby hat) 5. Jean McFadyen (Cook's niece) 6. Roland Hortop with donkey Sam.

Clovelly 1942. From the Left. Mrs Abbott (Villager) Mr Oscar Abbott (Fisherman) Edith Abbott (St John's or Red Cross?) Granny Coombes (Mother to Cook New Inn).

George Lamey as a young man on Clovelly Quay mending his fishing nets. Circa 1930's. Photo courtesy of Mr Fred Colwill Bideford Devon.

Clovelly 1941. Left. Cook at the New Inn Miss Beatrice Thompson. Middle. Granny Coombes (Cook's mother) Right Mr Arthur Headon (Clovelly Donkeyman) Photo courtesy Mrs Jean Job (nee McFadyen) Plymouth.

George Lamey's daughter Miss Nora Lamey in her Red Cross Uniform 1941-1945. Photo courtesy of Mr Fred Colwill Bideford Devon.

Clovelly School circa 1944 - 1945 Miss William's class. Mixed London, Bristol, Plymouth & Local pupils. All rows read from the left.

Front Row. 1. Pat Reid (London) 2. Mary Westlake (Clovelly) 3. Marlene Ayson (Stoke House) 4. Jill Gadd (London). 5. Gloria Pillman (Hartland) 6. Rosemary Bragg (Clovelly)

Second Row. 1. Kenneth Cook (Clovelly) 2. Jeannie Goulding (London) 3. June Prouse (Clovelly) 4. Miss Pamela Williams (Teacher Plymouth) 5. Margery Sanders (Clovelly) 6. Margaret Bragg (Clovelly)

Third Row. 1. Roy Cook (Clovelly) 2. Top of Head only, not known. 3. Not known. 4. Leslie Newham (Stoke House) 5. Not known.

Back Row. 1. John Goulding (London) 2. Reginald Colwill (Clovelly) 3. John Ellis (Clovelly) 4. Fred Robins (Clovelly) 5. Brian Taylor (Clovelly).

Junior Dancing Class September 1942 Clovelly. Mixed London, Bristol, Plymouth (Stoke House) & Clovelly children. Photo from private collection, Copyright approval courtesy Mr Harry Clement (Bideford formally Clovelly). All rows read from the left.

Front Row. 1. Margaret Ray. 2. Dorothy Sabine. 3. Jill Gadd (London) 4. Margaret Tridgell (Clovelly) 5. Not known. 6. Doreen Law (Peckham-London).

Middle Row. 1. Violet Ray. 2. Not known. 3. Allison Cavendish (Clovelly) 4. Ann Hutchinson (Clovelly) 5. Seager (London)? 6 Patricia Reid (London).

Back Row. 1. Gloria Pillman (Hartland) 2. Ruth Jewell (Clovelly) 3. Marion Mazonawitch (Clovelly) 4. Jeannie Goulding (London) 5. Elaine Waight (Plymouth-not Stoke House) 6. Joyce Axe (Bristol) 7. M. Baker (Plymouth). 8. Barbara Baker (Plymouth).

Some of the delicate children taking in the fresh air on Clovelly Beach 1942. Front Row little girl not known. Boy front right Douglas Scribley (Stoke House) Middle Row left Miss Holly Penna. Centre Miss Beatrice Thompson (Cook) Right Rosemary Buckingham (Stoke House). Back Row. Blond Boy left not known. Right Fernley Dawson (Stoke House)

From the Left. 1.Mrs Molly Abbott (Clovelly) 2. Granny Coombes (Plymouth) 3. Hilda Glover (New Inn) 4. Beattie Thompson (Cook New Inn) 5. Mr Bernard Abbott (Clovelly) 6. Mrs Marshall with kitten (Clovelly) 7. Miss Ruby Cutter (Cook's niece Plymouth) Photo taken in 1942 courtesy of Mrs Muriel Ellison (nee Gray) Plymouth.

Clovelly 1941. From the Left. Marian Blann (Teacher under fives Plymouth) on Donkey Barbara Goldstein (Stoke House New Inn) Right Roland Hortop (Clovelly Donkeyman).

Clovelly 1941-1942. Front Row Left Margaret Tridgell (Clovelly) Right Joyce Axe (Bristol). Back Row from left. Mr Tridgell (Clovelly) Mrs Tridgell (Clovelly) Soldiers on convalescent leave known only as "Mac" & "Tosh" Photo courtesy of Mrs Margaret Braund (neeTridgell).

Clovelly Villagers 1939 who was to become so much a part of the New Inn evacuated children's lives during the war years. From the left. Stanley Prince, Belle Whitfield, Steven Evans, Jim Whitfield, Harold Braund, Arthur Headon, George Lamey (Coxswain–Lifeboat) Roland Hortop (behind top of head only) & Charlie Shackson. Photo courtesy Mr Tom Cruse Bideford.

Bessie May (nee Perkin) who was a Land Army Girl at Clovelly Court Clovelly 1943-1945. Bessie married a local man and remained in Clovelly opening a Bed & Breakfast facility at Slerra Clovelly. Photo from private collection.

The Interior of the All Saint's Church Clovelly 1900. Postcard from the Francis Frith collection. Look at those lovely-hanging lamps.

During the war everyone had to double up on doing his or her bit for the war effort. The Cruse family were part of that era. Left is Barbara Cruse in Civil Defence Uniform by day a Teacher for the under fives in Clovelly. Right James Cruse in his Special Police uniform by day the Butcher who supplied meat to the New Inn children's home on contract to Plymouth City Treasury. Photo courtesy Mr Tom Cruse Bideford Devon.

How Clovelly Court looked flying the Red Cross-Flag before the fire totally destroyed the left wing in December 1943. It was being used as a convalescent home for the services. Photo copy courtesy of Mr Tom Cruse Bideford Devon.

Clovelly Court after the fire in December 1943. Photograph taken from the P.A. Ellis collection by kind permission Miss Sheila Ellis Clovelly.

Clovelly 1944. All rows read from the Left. Front Row. 1.Phyllis Cook (Clovelly) 2. Ellen Saul (Stoke House New Inn) 3. Bernice Waight (Plymouth) 4. Pat Roberts (Stoke House New Inn). Middle Row. 1. Lily Evans (RIP) (Stoke House New Inn) 2. Dorothy Saul (RIP) (Stoke House New Inn) 3. Rosemary Buckingham (Stoke House New Inn) 4. Eileen Law (London) 5. Pat Richards standing (Stoke House New Inn) Back Row. 1. Unknown. 2, Doris Dobbins (London) 3. Betty Newham (Stoke House New Inn) 4. Jean Rutley (Bristol). Photo by kind permission Eileen Law.

Outside Stables at Clovelly Court 1943-1944. All rows read from the Left. Front Row. 1. Beryl Wyles (London) 2. Eileen Law (London) 3. Phyllis Cook (Clovelly) 4. Unknown. 5. Betty Cook (RIP) (Clovelly). Middle Row. 1. Violet Holly (London) 2. Pearl Jones (Coventry) 3. Unknown. 4. Jean Rutley (Bristol). Back Row. 1. Mavis? 2. Pamela King (London) 3. Gwen Tyrell (Stoke House New Inn) 4. Unknown. 5. Freda Shackson (Clovelly) 6. Dorothy Saul (RIP) (Stoke House New Inn).

CHAPTER FOURTEEN

DAGGERS DRAWN

To the children from war torn Plymouth the village of Clovelly was a playground paradise but to officialdom in the Devon County Council it was a financial nightmare. A plan was formulated in March 1941 by taking into

consideration the special needs of evacuee children in institutions; a question was brought to the notice of the Devon Public Assistance Committee at Exeter. It had been suggested that an appointment of an experienced Almoner to assist them in making and retaining contact with relatives and friends had been considered by the Institutions Sub-Committee. The Minister of Health agreed that a salary of such an official would be allowed. However, the sub-committee questioned the heavy cost of the travelling expenses and their capability

The Girls! Summer Clovelly 1943. Look at those posh uniforms thanks to the British War Relief and Red Cross. Shortly after this photograph was taken some of the girls were boarded out with families they had never met. Returned to Plymouth without being told where they were going and ending up in yet another strange environment.

From the Left. 1. Not recognised. 2. Margaret Ray. 3. Violet Ray. 4. Barbara Goldstein (little one with bonnet). 5. Margaret Bailey. 6. Dorothy Sabine. 7. Betty Bennett. 8. Barbara Baker. 9. Pat Roberts. 10. Pat Richards. 11. Dorothy Saul. 12. Margaret Pester. 13. Rosemary Buckingham. 14. Betty Newham. 15. Miss Holly Penna.

Photo courtesy Mrs Pamela Pearce (nee Williams).

of covering the whole county, sadly, the appointment was not recommended. This explains why so many children lost contact with relations, once again financial expediency had won and the childrens' emotional needs lost. The institution sub-committee reported difficulty with nursing staff as staffs from institutions were looking for more highly paid posts and nurses were difficult to retain. Not many nurses applied for institution posts during the war years.

When the exhausted children and staff from bombed out Plymouth arrived at Clovelly in April 1941 the villagers were shocked at the disparate group that had suddenly been thrust upon them without warning. Already full of other evacuees the villagers had to endure an extreme change in their life style, it could not have been easy for them and we too viewed them with caution. The Plymouth City Council and the Social Welfare Committee paid periodic visits to Clovelly to monitor the staff and children at the New Inn. As early as June 1941 the Ministry of Health had submitted a letter to the Social Welfare Committee stating the childrens' home at the New Inn Clovelly was overcrowded and asking that steps be taken to relieve the congestion. Arrangements for the safety of the children in the event of fire had to be overhauled.

This led to a new policy that children in the New Inn were to be boarded out as soon as possible to alleviate the situation, the Ministry of Health did not raise any objection to such cases being reported as departures from the regulations. Here again the children were to be snatched away and fostered with people they had never met, indeed, a salient fact of moving the children like pawns for financial expediency. In June 1941 a letter from Secretary for Education was submitted stating that with regard to evacuated boarded-out children a Ministry of Health Inspector had suggested payment of clothing allowance, pocket money and retaining fees of 2/6 per week to foster mothers. The search for new premises to rehouse the orphans had already begun. It was clear that the City Council were forced to measure the needs of the children against the need to balance the budget as requested by the City Treasurer. The authorities considered the fees requested by the Clovelly Estate for the hire of the New Inn as excessive. Inevitably the children were the losers.

The Boys who lived in the Annexe of the New Inn circa 1941-1945.
From the Left. 1. David Dunbar. 3. James Ray. 4. Philip Ray. 6. Victor Frood. 10. Charles Ayson. 11. Leslie Newham. 12. Bernard Prout. 13. Peter Sabine. 14. Raymond Blatchford. 15. Ronald Stansbury. Number 2,5,7,8,9 not recognised. The boys were also boarded out with strangers in Plymouth or surrounding areas with families they had never met.

Photo courtesy Miss Sheila Ellis Clovelly.

The children settled in at the New Inn and an orderly regime was set in motion and all the children were registered for school. Breakfast was served at eight o'clock and then the children were dispersed to their school classes. A local doctor had been designated as temporary medical officer to look after the childrens' medical needs during their stay. Doctor Sawyer was a kind and well liked man and he treated many minor injuries that the children suffered. An Inspector's report in early 1942 again highlighted the fact that the New Inn was grossly overcrowded and recommendations were made to alleviate the situation. The policy undertaken was to board children out into foster care to relieve the numbers at the New Inn. Unfortunately, it did not take into consideration the feelings of the child and the transfer to an unknown foster family was initiated without any warning. The child was told to get dressed, have an early breakfast and then whisked away! Council minutes in 1942-1943 continued with the instruction to find new premises to rehome the children at the New Inn because the City Treasurer's report had concluded that the cost of the maintenance of the childrens' home in Clovelly was far too high.

In 1943 the City Treasurer of Plymouth had been approached to submit to the Social Welfare Finance and General Purposes sub-committee, a statement as to the cost of maintenance from the date of evacuation (April 1941) to the current year. Ongoing costs were reaching astronomical proportions and there was concern at the continued escalation, which was not acceptable to the public purse. It was agreed in principal that new premises should be sought. There was a very strong feeling about the high cost of maintenance for the rental of the Clovelly property for the evacuated children. The Town Clerk of Plymouth had stated that the annual compensation payment in respect of the occupancy of the New Inn was too costly and he requested that the Social Welfare Committee endeavour to find alternative cheaper accommodation.

In 1943-45 the Plymouth City Council were determined that alternative homes had to be found for the children at Clovelly. Older children were to be boarded out to families as soon as it could be arranged. More motherless children had arrived in 1943 as their fathers were in the services and were unable to look after them. All the rooms at the New Inn were overcrowded. Many of the original fifty had already been boarded out in 1941-1943 and the younger ones (approximately twenty-five) were to be found alternative accommodation as soon as possible. The Social Welfare Finance and General Purposes sub-committee expressed their desire for accommodation, which was not so expensive; subsequently they set up a sub committee with the express task of searching for new premises. Several houses were visited with the view to converting them into childrens' home. Houses considered were Hapstead House near Buckfastleigh, which was viewed by the lady members of the committee and reported back as to its suitability. Burleigh House, Peverell, Plymouth, Battisborough House, Holbeton, Alwyn House, Tamerton Foliot, Plymouth, Panflete House, near Holbeton, Woolston House, near Kingsbridge, and Warleigh House, Plymouth, (which had been formerly a nursery under the Public Health Committee).

The committee had visited various places with the view to purchase and the town clerk was asked if The Mount a large house at Lipson in Plymouth, could be released by the National Fire Service to convert into a children's home. The ding-dong battle between Plymouth City Council and the controlling estate for the New Inn at Clovelly had continued to rage for four years. Finally In May 1945 Social Welfare Committee Minutes indicated a letter received from the Ministry of Health suggesting that urgent steps should be taken to discontinue the use of the New Inn as a childrens' home. The final decision was referred for consideration to the Chairman of the committee at that time Councillor Ray. The situation was becoming difficult and the escalating cost not acceptable to the City Treasury, this forced the committee to even consider re-opening one of the scattered homes that had been closed down, particularly as the bombing raids had eased. A working committee suggested re-opening number 80 Mount Gould Road in Plymouth, however, it was not actioned, as the conversion would have been too costly, so it was leased to the Public Health Committee as temporary accommodation for the nurses from Mount Gould Hospital.

Meanwhile in order to save on cost, the decision was taken to reduce the staff at the New Inn and staff member Miss Foster was the first casualty. When Miss Beatrice Thompson the cook at the New Inn fell and broke her ankle in 1943 she was taken to Bideford Hospital. She never returned to her post as Cook and the position was not advertised. It was clear another cut

Miss Vera Foster as a young woman in Clovelly wearing the white overall worn by all Stoke House staff. Year unknown

139

back had been accepted, of course, this meant the kitchen assistant Miss Hilda Glover and the older girls and teachers had to help in preparation of the meals. Temporary gardeners were employed at the New Inn in place of Mr Arthur Scott who had been recalled to the RAF in 1943. There was quite a list of gardeners who applied for work and some even commuted to Clovelly in order to secure the job. Former applicants were Mr F.C. Parkyn, Mr J Renworth, and Mr Bushby from Stoke, Plymouth, and Mr. R.W. Wilson of Windy Ridge, Wheal Kitty, St Agnes, and Mr. S. A. Mills. In March 1943 Social Welfare (Liaison) and the Education Committee had suggested replacing the gardeners at the childrens' home Clovelly with an agricultural worker and handyman or alternatively a member of the Women's Land Army. The Plymouth City Treasury Department was always looking for ways to cut costs. The controversy surrounding this cost cutting exercise only succeeded in manipulating the children of Plymouth for financial expediency. It did not allow for the distress the children would have to endure at being uprooted from a happy environment.

Sadly relations on the official front between Plymouth and Clovelly had become strained and both protagonists could not agree on a financial compromise so in March 1945 the owner of the furniture contained in the New Inn (which had been hired out) insisted on early possession of his property. It was clear Plymouth City Council were recalling the children before the war had ceased. In July 1945 Plymouth City Council received six months notice from the owner of Providence Cottage, Clovelly, where Mr Arthur Scott the gardener's family had lived, to quit the premises. Clovelly estate insisted that the children of the New Inn should vacate the premises as soon as possible. A decision, which once again affected the happy times, the children had had in Clovelly. The home was officially closed just two months before the war had ended, the children still left at Clovelly were returned to their Devon City and re-homed at Astor Hall, Stoke, Plymouth.

CHAPTER FIFTEEN

SWEETS WE REMEMBER 1930 -1940s.

Every child loves a treat.
Make each day happy with a sweet!

Nearly all children love sweets and in the 1930's/1940's sweets were top of the list for children of the poor. Unemployment and low wages meant that not all children automatically got a weekly allowance, times were hard and money scarce. Watching the expertise of the shop assistant serving the sweets in greaseproof paper scoops and bags was a real novelty. When wartime came the sweets were rationed to two ounces each person and children of institutions often had to rely on good citizens giving up some of their ration coupons to enable them to have the joy of additional sweets. The rationing was a devastating law for sweet tooth enthusiasts bearing in mind that the United Kingdom had been enjoying sweets since the sixteenth century and Britons were amongst the world's biggest consumers of confectionery.

In the reign of Queen Elizabeth the first, sweet treats made with sugar were considered only an expensive luxury for the wealthy. Sugar prices went down in the eighteen hundreds and British confectionery began to boom. In the Victorian era sweets were still made by hand by many little localised firms, some traded in back rooms or even garden sheds. Setting up a confectionery business was relatively easy and reasonably cheap and staff were employed to roll the sweets out. By the turn of the twentieth century there were ten thousand sweet manufacturers in Britain. Small family concerns became established and from 1860 brand names became well known, there are still some small family businesses surviving which have been managed and owned by direct descendants right up to the present day.

The same basic method of making sweets is used today as it was in times past, although manufacturers have modern machinery to help with production. Sugar boilers were the lynchpin of the confectionery business and were a most important piece of equipment in the making of sweets to obtain the different sugar temperatures. On reaching a certain temperature the mixture would be tipped out on to a large cold slab and treated with lard, olive oil, petroleum jelly and then flavouring and colours would be added. The mixture would be thumped and kneaded into blends and shapes and finally rolled out and cut with scissors into the relevant pieces. The art of mixed colours was achieved by pressing two or three lumps of mixture together to obtain different patterns; it was indeed very hard work.

For the children of the poor sweets were a very precious source of comfort, the most favourite was of course the well-known liquorice! Liquorice has been enjoyed by the human race since well before the birth of Christ, it also found favour with Assyrian Kings and Greek physicians. Roman soldiers were issued with liquorice roots to chew as a means of quenching their thirst when on long route marches. After the fall of the Roman Empire monks kept the secrets of liquorice safe and when they came to England at the time of the Crusades they brought the liquorice plants with them. Many chose to settle near Pontefract, Yorkshire, (originally known as Pomfret) and they began to cultivate the plants in the gardens of their monastery. The liquorice plant looks like a small acacia shrub growing approximately four feet above ground. It is still grown at Pontefract in England as the composition of soil is not suitable elsewhere; further harvesting of the liquorice plant is from Iraq and Spain, and the Deep South of the United States.

No invitation for sweets went unnoticed by the wartime children and adults were reminded of their availability. Article from a private collection.

Wilkinson's seal of perfection is today part of Trebor Bassett Limited who still produces the famous liquorice, catherine wheels, whirls, twists, pipes, pencils, bootlaces, watches and liquorice allsorts, with dear "Bertie Bassett" the Company symbol taking his first steps in 1929 and bringing sweet joy to successive generations of children. Liquorice comfits had different coloured sugared icing which, if you picked the red coloured ones, girls could make their lips look as though they had lipstick on. Another favourite was the pontefract cakes (or, depending where you lived, Yorkshire pennies) which was a round flat liquorice sweet and not forgetting the very popular blackjack. Who can forget those famous Barratt Sherbet treats? The sherbet dip, lemon, fountain, pip, and sucker dab, with a hard stick of liquorice to suck out the sherbet, which had been available to all children since 1925. Children chewed the liquorice roots, which looked like wood twigs; they would last a long time.

Other well-known sweets were Kruger's whiskers, strands of coconut covered in sugared cocoa; available too was the delightful coconut squares and coconut ice, strings of arrowroot, and another special treat was the chocolate tobacco. Coconut button mushrooms were a novelty as were the bon boms covered with a white powder. Most children loved the little chocolate Rowntrees Smarties (released in 1937) and Rowntrees trio of fruit sweets (released 1935) consisting of soft juicy fruits, hard clear gums and sugar coated chewy fruit pastilles. These were sold for 2 old pennies a tube. Rowntrees manufactured clear gums from 1893 into the 1930's, but later they were renamed to become the popular fruit gums, as we know them today. Now Rowntrees is incorporated into the Nestles Company.

Remembered too are the Bassetts jelly babies (otherwise known as peace babies) which most children loved. How about the well known Mackintoshes Rolo and Quality Street? The latter being a new selection of toffees and chocolates in a tin, and were launched in 1936. One luxury was the deliciously expensive Parisian Creams not within range of most childrens pocket money. Barrett's Paradise Fruits at sixpence a quarter pound was a very popular sweet as were Maynards original wine gums and pastilles introduced in 1909 and the forerunner of today's wine gums now part of Trebor Bassett Limited.

Trebor was founded in 1907 as Robertson & Woodcock and now Trebor Bassett incorporates famous confectioners like Barratt, Pascall, Sharps, Maynards and Wilkinson. Walker Nonsuch (which takes its name from Henry V111's legendary "Nonsuch" palace) a well known independent company since 1922 were one of the toffee specialists making toffee in the 1930's with raw cane, brown sugar, glucose, full cream condensed milk, vegetable oil and butter. The modern toffee came about with a combination of hard British butterscotch and soft American style caramel crushed and mixed together making it the chewy substance it is today. Affectionately remembered are the trays of break up toffee issued with a toffee hammer which was every child's delight until the outbreak of war forced the company to restrict its output as the raw sources of materials dried up and they could not produce again until after the war. Popular also in that era was the Sonny Boy toffee bars, Devon cream toffee, Bluebird toffee and Sharps super kreem toffee. Sharps toffee tins were launched in 1934 at tuppence for four ounces, and were promoted with a picture of Mickey Mouse on the tin. Another famous toffee manufacturer was the firm called Walters who made Palm Slab Toffee and Fudge. Remember the Dainty Dinah Toffee made by Horner's at four pence a quarter pound? Their factory had been based at Durham but the toffee was distributed throughout the country and many children enjoyed the chew! Another was the delicious Watson's Toffee, which sold at two ounces for a penny. The children loved the tuppenny slabs which, could last for a long time succulently sucked in the mouth. There were Blue Boy toffee rolls comprising liquorice, fig, brazil, cream, rum and milk rolls.

How about the Sovereign Creamy Whirls and Banana Split Fruit Bars? There were pink and white coloured sugar mice with string tails, and the children's favourite sweet the gob stoppers! They were dyed in layers of bright colours and as each layer was sucked away our tongues would be multi-coloured. Children would buy the sugared sweets shaped as cigarettes in a packet and pretend to smoke them to make themselves appear grown up. Dolly mixtures were popular and could be bought loose, they were small and sweet tasting and had curious shapes like stars, hearts and cubes, and were a variety of colours, and the assistant would put our purchase into a little white triangular paper bag. Alternatively we could buy the alphabet letters and they had a sweet scented taste, and not to be forgotten the love sweets that girls would give to their sweetheart of the moment. Another treat was the milky Glo-Joys. Most sweet shops would have a halfpenny or penny box on their counters with a selection of various sweets for the children to choose from and always on the counter was the large bottle containing twisted barley sugar sticks.

Succulent Rainbow Crystals were popular with younger children and welcome too was the Barratts Jamboree Bag comprising sweets, nuts and popcorn. Cashew sweets were a favourite as one could have a roll of mixed colours or a complete roll of Parma violet perfumed sweets. Another favourite was buttered walnut. Many various types of sweets and chocolate were available before the war rationing. In the 1930's block chocolate was the most popular chocolate confectionery with adults and children. However, a new revolutionary chocolate bar made an appearance onto the market with the introduction of the Mars Bar in August 1932. The new chocolate bar offered a succulent taste of nougat and caramel covered in thick chocolate. Children soon became avid fans of this chocolate luxury.

The Milky Way chocolate bar arrived in 1935 and the little Milky Way candy bar for one penny proved popular with the children during the war years. Another success for Mars was

Maltesers launched in 1936 to a special recipe known only to the makers. The little round balls, of honeycombed biscuit covered in chocolate, are mouth watering and once a packet was opened all the maltesers were devoured in one go! The launch of these new brands were to be the foundation of a successful business for

A wartime advert for the Milky Way chocolate bar bought for one penny if one had enough coupons left. From a private collection.

Mars Confectionery Limited who through the years grew from a tiny workforce at a small rented factory to its now large work force employing thousands at the factory in Slough, Berkshire. New on the market and facing fierce competition were the Black Magic deco bar and the Nestles black magic box of chocolates launched in 1933.

The now famous Cadbury had a large selection of chocolates available such as the chocolate Dairy Box, and chocolate fruit creams, and the delicious dainty box of variety creams was a sweet joy. Many readers will remember

the Milk Tray assortment, (make the day with Cadbury's milk tray) which many a suitor bought to enhance a prospective romance. Cadbury dairy milk chocolate had been on the market since 1905. Their Crunchie Bar with the honeycombed centre had been available since 1920. During the war if one were lucky to buy a Crunchie Bar that would be one week's sweet ration. The milk chocolate bubbled Aero bar was launched in 1935

The popular bubbled Aero chocolate bar was launched in 1935 and the Polo Mint in 1948. Photo courtesy of the Rowntrees Company.

145

by Nestles which challenged the might of Cadburys who in the same year had produced the Cadbury dairy milk flake at tuppence a bar. This was followed in 1936 by their sixpenny nut and raisins milk chocolate bar. Cadbury's Roses were launched in 1938 with the eye-catching Dorothy blue carton packs and tins named after the 'Dorothy' evening bags, which were fashionable during the 1930's. The cartons became familiar with their distinctive embroidered red rose design; Cadbury Roses chocolates sold in half-pound boxes or in round tins at one shilling and sixpence a tin. Other known chocolates available were the red tulip chocolates, chocolate coconut bars, and the Five Boys milk chocolate by the famous Fry Company.

Other varieties were the Neapolitan and Masonic Boxes and all the various types of block chocolate. Children could buy the halfpenny, penny or tuppenny bars. Cadbury Brothers were synonymous with chocolate in many spheres since 1897 when they challenged the Swiss producers who were dominating the market, and in 1905 the company launched their new milk chocolate recipe, incorporating the Cocoa bean. As one of nature's finest food it was to be for them a great success. Cadbury's also dealt in loose cocoas, Bournvita, red label drinking chocolate, chocolate coatings, chocolate cup syrups and chocolate biscuits. In 1939 they had a huge collection of assorted chocolates in tied boxes known as Caskets and such a variety of well known selections with classic names like Carnival, Continental, Crystal, Queen Mary, Princess, King George V, State and Vogue. Nestles launched its chocolate crisp bar in 1935 and renamed it Kit-Kat Chocolate Biscuit Bar in 1937. Favourite brands of chocolate were eagerly sought, such as Cadburys Milk, Terry's, Tobler, Duncan's selection, Nestles, Rowntrees, Mayfair's Premiere Assortment. Another was Fry's chocolate cream bar, and not forgetting the lovely Tiffin Bar, a chocolate bar with a honeycombed biscuit. All most acceptable until the war when there was no full cream milk and the chocolate substitutes tasted bland after that.

During the war Rowntrees sold jars of full fruit apricot jam which used natural fruit in an effort to keep customers happy with something that tasted sweet, but it never could really replace sweets. Children were encouraged to have Fry's chocolate spread as an alternative. In 1940 the Plymouth Co-operative Society used to advertise pure loose cocoa at three pence a quarter pound. Mixed with some sugar (if you could get it) it would taste like

An advert from the newspaper Western Independent Plymouth 1932. Photo courtesy Sunday Independent.

substitute chocolate. Young children would take pleasure in their favourite sweets, and adults favoured Mackintosh's "Carnival" de-luxe assortment at sixpence per quarter pound. Family members who saved GP tea coupons could redeem them and on occasion exchange them for a box of George Payne's chocolates. Younger children loved the chocolate money wrapped in gold coloured paper; it was so good it really did look like real money! Many Plymouth children would revel at the choice of Lear's sweets and the special fruits, which were sold at fourpence a quarter by the Lear Brothers in their sweet shop.

Marsh's hard-boiled sweets were sought as they could be kept in the mouth for a long time. There were blackcurrant drops and raspberry drops, which looked like miniature raspberries and children,

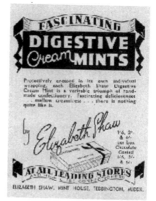

could buy their halfpenny worth of peardrops or gooseberry sweets affectionately known as "Goosegogs." Children loved the lucky dip bags with an array of sweets inside and in the bag there would be a little novelty gift. Other favourites were fruit salad sweets, lollipops, aniseed balls and peppermint bull's eyes, and not to be forgotten the mint humbugs, Old English bulls eyes and the Fox's glacier mints still going strong today.

Elizabeth Shaw's chocolate covered Digestive Cream Mints popular in the 1930's with children & adults alike. Article from a private collection.

Hot sweets were Victory V Lozenges and Imps, small black lozenges that most children avoided, as they were so strong although they were not rationed. Elizabeth Shaw's box of chocolate covered digestive cream mints at one shilling and sixpence was much sought after, as was the popular Murray mint (The too good to hurry mint) and after the war in 1948 the famous Polo mint was launched. Mint flavouring starts life as an oil extracted from the fragrant leaves of the Mentha plant. Spearmint and bubblegum were very popular, both peppermint and spearmint oils are used in the production of mint sweets.

There were individually wrapped penny chews consisting of various fruit flavours such as strawberry, raspberry and blackcurrant. Most children liked Wrigley's chewing gum and it proved to be very popular with adults too. The Ancient Greeks used a natural substance similar to chewing gum to clean their teeth, and the way they did this was by extracting gum from the bark of the mastic tree. Later in history a substance called 'chichle' was extracted from the sapodilla tree and utilised to make gum but today more modern ingredients are used and Wrigley's chewing gum is known world-wide.

Other favourites were Batger's Silmos Lollies a mixed fruit collection and Pascall Saturday assortment in a tin, comprising chocolate eclairs, butterscotch, caramels, nougat and fruit lollies. Although sweet rationing was lifted in April 1949 most children were still restricted because the prices of sweets and chocolate had escalated which still meant poorer families not being able to afford the extra costs. Time has proved that rationing was well controlled and did no harm to the children, indeed, we did not see so many overweight children as there are today. The Children of Stoke House and the Scattered Homes benefited from their transfer to Clovelly, North Devon in 1941 because, due to the generosity of villagers and billeted citizens from other areas, who willingly forfeited their ration, the New Inn children were never short of sweets.

This variety of Rowntrees was taken in 1952. However it incorporates all the children's favourite sweets and chocolate that we remember in our childhood. Photo courtesy of the Rowntrees Company Limited.

CHAPTER SIXTEEN

THE SOCIAL STIGMA OF AN UNMARRIED MOTHER

'In the family way.' Society in the 1920's/1930's was opposed to illegitimate children and even members of family turned against the expectant mother and often the parent would suggest going into a workhouse to have the child. My name is Eileen Hext (nee Dunbar) and I am the mother of David Dunbar.

My story begins when I was being very sick in the mornings at nineteen years old and my father took me to the doctor who confirmed I was pregnant. This was a result of a short passionate love affair with an RAF serviceman Victor Burnett. We were young and attracted to each other, and he was a nice looking man. In the 1930's it was a disgrace to be in this predicament and there was no Social Service as such to encourage pregnant mothers to keep their babies, and there was no financial help. My parents condemned my sin and our family life was very strained. It was arranged that I go to see two ladies at Portland Square Plymouth, one lady was called Miss Noyse and the other Miss Shaw. A few days later I was collected and taken by car with these two ladies to St Agnes in Cornwall, to a place called Rosemundy House which was a home for about twelve girls and where I had to stay for one year. My son David was duly born on the 31 March 1938.

The Matron in charge was a Miss McLeod a nice person and very kind, she did not look down on our misfortune and treated us with respect and dignity. Of course, we all had to take our turns to share with the daily chores, and in our leisure time, we were supplied with Viyella material and wool to make clothes for our babies. I remember it being a very pleasant place with good wholesome food. David was christened at the Chapel in the Home by the then vicar of St Michael's in St Agnes. Time came for me to leave and I was put on a train to Plymouth to return home to my father and stepmother. Things were so different! No potty to put the baby on, no bath, and oh how I missed Miss Mcleod's guiding hand, and her saying "How's my little manny today?" she called all the boys mannies. I loved my little tousle-haired baby boy he was so beautiful.

The next thing I remembered was being taken over the water by ferry where David was fostered with a nurse's family. I believe her name was Miss Searle and I had no say about him being taken away from me. It was about this time that I had a nervous breakdown and was put in a home run by the Sister of Charity nuns at Plympton, Plymouth, and I remained there for six months. From then on I had no connection with David at all. From here I got a job working at a private house in Colebrook, but I could not settle and walked out. I was determined to find my baby but all my efforts to find him were hopeless.

It was now September 1939 and war had broken out and I had to go to the Labour Exchange in Treville Street to get another job as all women of working age had to register for war work. I was sent to the Navy, Army & Air Force Institute (NAAFI) in Tidworth, near Aldershot. I remember being told you got a lot more money in a factory, so I asked to be released from the NAAFI so I could go to work in a factory. I felt my intelligence called for more than washing dishes! I was sent to Coventry to work at the Standard Motor Company and was billeted at Tile Hill, Coventry.

During this time, as I was never informed of my son's whereabouts, David had been put in Stoke House without my knowledge or approval. I lost touch completely and I have no recollection of this at all, as I totally blocked out the anguish of separation. Single mothers were made to feel submissive and were not considered as being worthwhile and punished emotionally for one mistake. I did not know until 1998, when the author of this book informed me, that David had been in Clovelly, North Devon. I have since ascertained that from Clovelly, he was fostered out again with a family at 2 Little Ash Road, Saltash Passage, Saint Budeaux, Plymouth. They wanted to adopt him and I only found this out because a note had been written on the back of his birth certificate. However, it appears that they changed their minds. Many things are still not clear in my mind as I experienced one problem after another and coming to terms with the loss of my son was sometimes just too much to bear.

However, my life was to take a turn for the better at last as I met my husband to be, he had been in the Army for eighteen years and on leaving the service he worked at the Morris Motor Works. We were married on 14 September 1946, in Coventry, and he already had three children of his own, Miriam,

Bob and Jennie, the latter is still in touch with me today. We moved from Coventry to Plymouth to my father's place in Rendle Street. It was not a very satisfactory move, so we applied for another home and were allocated a house at 35 Alcester Street, Stoke, and my son David came to join us there for a while.

It was wonderful having my son home with me, he was a lovely looking boy and one could understand someone wanting to adopt him. I still feel angry at the fact that the Social Services would allow my son to be put up for adoption without my knowing and no effort was made to inform me of this action. Again my nerves took a turn for the worse and life became very strained, I never really fully recovered from my earlier breakdown. In later years I was able to find out from a caring doctor that I was, and had been unknowingly for some time, suffering from agrophobia, afraid to go shopping, afraid of open spaces. So the children were never taken anywhere and they were missing out on so many things and my sense of guilt did not help. Eventually one day in frustration my husband took his three children away to his own city of Coventry. This left myself and my son David in the house on our own. Later my husband returned leaving his children in Coventry to come to Plymouth to sort out all the possessions, then on completion leaving David and myself to live on our own.

Months later my husband wrote to say would I like to go to Coventry but not to take David yet, so a neighbour offered to take care of David to enable me to sort our problems out, until such times as I could have him back. Time went on and my neighbour was not happy with the length of time I was taking, so she contacted Social Services who then took David away. David was taken into care again in July 1942. Later he was evacuated to Clovelly but I was never told. Finally I walked out on my husband and returned to Plymouth. By now my husband was missing me and thankfully our relationship was renewed and we settled in Plymouth and my son David joined me on 21 May 1947. David and I have become very close, although he lives in Birmingham he rings me every week and he visits me several times a year. My husband passed away in 1975. Since then I have married three times and lost two more husbands who have passed on. I am now happily married to Leonard Hext and as he is in his late seventies and I am now in my eighties. I can at last say I have found peace and contentment.

CHAPTER SEVENTEEN

GEORGE STUART- THE RUNAWAY BOY

I was born in 1922 at 39 Rendle Street, Plymouth, and named John Albert George Stuart. I never knew my parents as I was abandoned at twelve months old. My brother Jim who was sixteen years older than me carried me in his arms, and left me on the doorstep of Hill Park Crescent, Plymouth, a Scattered Home for children. I did not see my brother Jim again until I was a young man when I started work in the Dockyard, that is explained later in my story.

My mother was Louisa Maud (Nee James) and my father William Stuart. Throughout my life I have been called either George or John. Later, at the first reunion in 1997 at the Manadon Masonic Hall, Plymouth, of the Stoke House and Scattered Homes people, I got the address of the Social Services to obtain my records which had been subject to a seventy five year closure ban. I wrote to them and learned that I had another brother Arthur, who was seven years older than I, but I never saw him and found out he had been killed in a motor bike accident. I also learned that I had three sisters, Lily, Alice and Nellie, it was obvious they did not want to know Jim and I as they were older than us, and had made no attempt to contact us. I read all the information sent to me and I felt a deep inner anger at being denied the love of a family, and in frustration I burnt all the records I had. I could not come to terms with the heartache even after all those years. Thankfully though, my dear wife who suspected what my reaction would be had taken photocopies, so we still have some family history record.

I spent the whole of my childhood in care and I still remember the hurt and the cruelty I endured. I was twelve months old when I was fostered at this home at Old Laira Road, Laira, Plymouth which was a small local house designated as a Scattered Home. I can remember my first smack vividly; I was only seven years of age. I had been sitting at the table having my tea when I accidentally upset a cup of tea; my foster mother gave me a good hiding at the time. I did not know then in my childlike innocence that it was the onset of years of beatings. For many years I suffered the hammering for the most trivial of reasons. Of course I was mischievous at times like all

152

young lads growing up, but I did not deserve the beatings that occurred.

One of my tasks was to get up at six-o-clock in the morning to make the porridge, which was often lumpy as it was made with water, and I was not always able to get the right combination of water and oats. Another of my tasks would be to scrub the kitchen floor. Each time I took a beating I vowed I would get out as soon as it was possible, but where could I go? Who could I turn to? I had no family and I was too young to understand that if I had reported to someone in authority, something may have been done to stop it! I started running away very early, desperate to get away from the regime of the home. Each time I was brought back, my foster carer who was supposed to guide me and look after me, would shut me in a dark cupboard, I was afraid of the dark and the closed cramped area, and I was often terrified. One day in a temper my foster carer shoved me in the cupboard again and forgot to lock it! That was my cue! I got out and made my bid for freedom, alas it was short lived, in those days any child seen out unaccompanied by an adult was questioned, and all scattered homes children were immediately returned to their carers.

Every year children would have a fortnight's holiday at Maker Camp and how we would enjoy the trip on the ferry, and the open spaces at the camp to run around freely. When we returned to our foster home, I had resolved that Maker Camp is where I would like to stay, mindful that it would be lonely on one's own I teamed up with another boy called Jack Dawson in the same house as me, and we planned to escape. All children were given a money allowance of one shilling per week, (in those days twelve pence equalled one shilling) However, I only received sixpence, and my pal and I put twopence a week away until we had saved a shilling, and we kept our shilling wrapped in paper hidden in the drain.

Our trip to Maker Camp had been in the August 1934 when the summer was at it's best. On the day we returned to Plymouth from our camp holiday we were sad and reluctant to leave and it was then we decided we would run away for good. My pal and I had breakfast, as we would not be sure when we would eat again, gathered our shillings and made our dash for freedom, I was twelve years old. We found our way to the ferry and landed at Cawsand and made our way to Maker Camp. When we arrived at the camp it was closed and we had not thought of that, so we broke in and each acquired an iron bed to sleep in. So far so good! For a while we ate berries and dried bread, which we bought with our odd pennies, but hunger began to bite hard, and we knew we had to search for food to survive.

It was Sunday, and we assumed there would be day-trippers visiting Cawsand for the weekend and perhaps we could get some food. We made our way down to the beach and asked one or two people if they had any food to spare but they said no. We then decided that we would try and catch some fish, go back to camp, light a fire, and try somehow to cook it so we could have something hot. We managed this but by now our enthusiasm for freedom had cooled somewhat! We again made our way down toward Cawsand from the camp and then an unexpected incident happened. Little did we know that on that Sunday an official from Plymouth had been attending a function in Cawsand and was on his way back when his limousine car passed us by. Suddenly the car slowed and came to a stop, we were unsure of our next move as the car slowly reversed back and he wound down the window and said "Where are you two young lads going?" We replied "Cawsand Sir" He said "You are the two missing boys, and you have run away from the orphanage home haven't you?" Knowing the game was up we admitted our action and said "Yes Sir". I told him of our treatment at the home we had been placed in and our reason for absconding. He said, "Boys have to be punished when they have been naughty!"

The official made us get into the car and took us to a large house and gave us a lovely cooked breakfast before returning us to the Scattered Home. Shortly afterwards I was moved to a Scattered Home in Mount Gould, and I was transferred from Laira Green School to Mount Street School. Although I knew little of the outcome I do know it was the beginning of enquiries into how the homes were being run and investigations were underway. We heard later that my former carer was no longer allowed to foster children. Because of my harsh treatment in my first home I had become difficult and I was always fighting, why I do not know, but I soon learnt how to stand up for myself. I had hoped that my change of home would have brought me respite and loving care but it was not to be. The Superintendent of the home was as free with her hands as my former carer had been, and she carried a cane with her at all times. She would lay it on thick and no one would hear my cries or feel my pain. The only good times I can remember are the holiday trips to Maker Camp and Christmas, as we would have an apple and an orange on Christmas Day and some better food. When the jubilee mugs were handed out at school we thought we would have a nice keepsake, however, every orphanage child's mug was taken away and we never saw them again.

My happiest memory comes from a very nasty accident. I was on my way to school and I heard a motor car racing up the road and as I turned it hit me and I found myself in hospital, battered and bewildered. I stayed at the City Hospital for four weeks and what a super time I had! I lapped up every minute because I had lovely food, and the nurses would give me sweets, and they would put their arms around me and hug me. After a complete rest and recovery I was returned to my Scattered Home again. Pampered by the hospital I was discontented on my return to harsh reality and unsettled, so I did the obvious, I ran away again! The police did their usual rounding up of lost and runaway boys and once again found myself back in the home of misery.

At fourteen I left school to start work and my first job was at an Ironmongers shop on Mutley Plain run by a man called Mr Blake. I was employed as a plumber's apprentice; he had three plumbers and three boys, I settled in and was reasonably happy. My wages were six shillings a week, which I took back to the orphanage; they would keep five shillings and give me one shilling back. I was detailed other tasks and one of these was collecting the debts owed. Mr Blake sent me to Hartley to collect outstanding payments for work done, I was sent with ten envelopes to collect the money and he told me "For every debt you manage to collect I will give you a shilling," This gave me an added incentive. When I received my wages of six shillings there was an extra five shillings on top, which gave me eleven shillings. A princely sum in those days! Alas I did not have the money very long, the orphanage took nine shillings and gave me two shillings to keep.

Another task I was detailed to do was to take the scrap lead down to Union Street from Mutley Plain on a handcart. The scrap would be weighed and I would be given a chit stating the amount valued and Mr Blake would collect the money himself. Many times I did that journey and got leaking wet in the process. Eventually I got wet once too often and I was taken poorly with shingles and was off work for three weeks. As I had no payment because I was sick, I did not get any money, and the home I was in would not give me any pocket money until I went back to work. One day whilst working in the Hartley area of Plymouth, on trying to locate a burst pipe in the road (in those days they were lead pipes) the dig had taken quite some time, and naturally we stopped for a cup of hot tea as it was a bitter cold day. My plumber said to me,"George, have you signed a contract with Mr Blake?" I said, "No not yet, Why?" He said,"Well, there are three boys and he is only going to keep two." So I said, "Oh! That's his game is it?" And he said, "Well as far as I know." The next day when I went into the shop, I walked to the plumber's office at the back and I saw Mr Blake and told him, "I am not coming in tomorrow, I am going for a job in the Dockyard" he said, "You can't do that George you have got work here!" I said, "No, I am going to the Dockyard where I will have a secure job." I didn't go in the next day, instead I went down to the St Levan's Road entrance of the Dockyard and saw the policeman on the gate. He guided me to the offices and I applied for a job, I passed the examination and was told to come back on the Monday morning to start work in the Dockyard.

As I got older, although I was working, I was placed in different foster homes and one particular home I remember was with a lady who lived at 3 Ivy Cottages, Lower Compton, Plymouth. She was very strict, if I went out I had to be home by a certain time and the time did not allow me to have the pleasure I was entitled to. If I went to the pictures I could not see the end of the film because of the time I had to be back. One day I went to a lovely concert and forgot the time, dashing home as quick as I could I knew I was late for my cooked meal, but hoped my carer would understand and allow me this one indiscretion. When I arrived she took the meal out of the oven all dried up and I could not eat it. "You have got to eat it," she shouted, and I replied, "No thank you" She raised her hand to strike me and I thought, no not again! Angry and lost with no one to turn to I ran out, and that night I slept in Hartley Park in the shelter. I slept there again on the Sunday night and went to work on the Monday. My thoughts were "Where I am going to sleep tonight?" I knew nobody, I had nobody, so I was left on my own, but I did have my job.

Although always wary of the staff in the Orphanage there were one or two people who showed kindness to us, and the children soon knew which ones they could appeal to for a little understanding. One of the ladies who had been more receptive to me was called Mrs May Woods and she would relieve the foster mother on her day out, and it just so happened that this was the very lady I bumped into when I was going up Albert Road, Devonport. "Hello John," she said, "How are you keeping?" I said, "Well I am looking for somewhere to live." After telling her of my situation she said, "I have got a spare room in my house, you come back with me!" I took the offer gratefully, she had a lovely house at 3 Duckworth Street, Stoke, and I had been given a very nice bedroom, I was comfortable and contented. Then came a shock from the past!

It was 1937 and my brother Jim had found me, he was in the Dockyard on board a ship, he was in the Royal Navy and was to spend twenty-seven years in the service. He had learned of my whereabouts but had not bothered about me before although it had been fifteen years since we had been together. I thought did I really want to know him? But blood is thicker than water and as he was my real blood kin I felt he should not be denied, so I agreed to meet him. We were strangers and I did not know what to say, he was about to undertake, either a two and a half year or a five year commission at sea in HMS Gloucester. She was built at Devonport and was manned by Devonport and Plymouth seaman. He asked, "Where do you live? And I gave him my address. One evening he arrived at the house and asked to see Mrs Woods and me together. He said," I am taking over, I want him to come and live with me, as he is my brother." Jim had a home in Millbrook and in my heart I did not want to go, but he was my next of kin. Millbrook was across the water, which meant I had to get to work from there to Plymouth every working day. He saw that I was hesitant so he said, "Come with me and I will buy you a bicycle called The Golden Arrow." Oh Boy! I thought a bike of my own! He said,"You can cycle to the ferry, and then cycle into Devonport Dockyard from Stoke" I must admit the bicycle was the deciding factor, so I went with him. It was to be the biggest mistake I ever made! I had lost the routine I had been happy with at Mrs Woods, I felt isolated and I could not get on with my brother's wife.

157

Unhappy, I made the decision to leave and return to Plymouth. I could not go back to Mrs Woods because an influx of contractors had come to the town to undertake building work and Mrs Woods had let all her rooms to these men and they were now her lodgers. This time, determined to maintain my independence whatever the cost, I hunted around, looking for a flat or a room. I managed to obtain an attic in Morice Square, Devonport, in an old house that was in ruins but a couple of rooms and the attic were habitable. I paid the landlord half a crown (twelve and a halfpence today) per week. I lived on cakes and sandwiches but sometimes the lady in the tenement room would bring me a dinner on Sundays, not very often because times were hard in those days. I drifted along making the best of the situation then once more fate took a hand.

War was declared in 1939 and I volunteered for the Army, but I was turned down because I worked in the Dockyard! Unable to accept this logic I persisted, and kept turning up at the recruitment centre until finally they accepted me. I became a Gunner in the Artillery and I loved the Army as I had three square meals a day, a uniform supplied and good training. I did not mind the discipline. I did as I was told because I was used to being ordered around at the orphanage. It was a good life for me in the Army. On leave in Dover one day I was to meet a girl who later I was to marry.

Of course, the war brought heartache too, as I lost many good mates on Sword Beach where we landed at six-o-clock on the morning of June the Sixth, 1944. I survived the war, but was badly wounded and although a nightmare with which I still live, I served with pride and I can look at my medals and say,"I was there!" Sadly, I later learned that Jack Dawson the boy who I ran away from the home with was lost at sea in HMS Repulse.

I kept in touch with my brother Jim until he died at the age of eighty-six years. My wife is one of the best, there could not be a better wife, we have been married fifty-two years and I still think the world of her today. We have brought up four children and they have never been in trouble, they are lovely children and I have a lot to be thankful for. I made sure that they had all the love my wife and I could give them, and they were not kept short of anything, they would not be unwanted or unloved as I was! I would not wish to see any child put in an orphanage because once those doors close behind them nobody knows what goes on!

Recently I visited the house at Old Laira Road with my son. As we pulled up in his car the present owner was coming out of her gate and we asked permission to take photographs. I asked her if the cupboard was still inside the door, and it was! When I told her I had been locked in it many times she could not believe it, and did not know the house had been used as a Scattered Home for orphaned and unwanted children. Let my story tell that foster parents can make or break a child, nevertheless, nothing replaces the love of parents.

Postscript. Sadly, George's wife Doris passed away in July 2000. (RIP)

George Stuart 1998 proudly wearing some of his medals. He was awarded the Normandy Landing Medal, the War Medal 1939-1945, the Defence Medal and two Stars. The Atlantic Star & the France-Germany Star. He has no photograph of himself as a child.

CHAPTER EIGHTEEN

MEMORIES OF MY AUNTS

AUDREY RAY (NEE STACEY) NURSE PENNA'S NIECE

What a lovely surprise to be asked to write my memories of my Aunt Audrey the second oldest daughter and my Aunt Holly the third born. There were two more Aunts, sisters to Audrey and Holly, Gwendoline my mother the oldest and Valerie the youngest. I shall never forget Aunt Audrey as she was always there for us all; she looked after all the family in turn. I was only nine years old when the war started and a week after war was declared in 1939 I was put on a train with my brother Roy. Our mother was worried because we came from Greenford in Middlesex, which was very near Northholt the RAF Aerodrome, which meant it would be a likely target for bombing. Wrapped up warm and with labels pinned on our coats stating our names, off we went on the train to Plymouth. Aunt Audrey and my Granddad met us at the station and took us to Saltash, Cornwall. It was a big upheaval in our young lives our freedom much more restricted, however, we quickly settled in.

One of the highlights of my life in those days was to be with Aunt Audrey on her day off from Stoke House, the childrens' home at Devonport, Plymouth. First she would take me to Stoke House to show me around and I would help her with some cooking. She taught me a lot. There used to be a large kitchen with a big wooden table in the centre and also a scullery and larder room. Often we would go shopping in Old Plymouth, I also loved shopping and still do to this day. Aunt Audrey loved her food and she had a really good appetite, even in later years. She was a loving caring person, who would do anything for anybody, extremely generous especially to her friends and sometimes over generous. However, she was also very stubborn and liked to have her own way being quite bossy where her sisters Valerie and Holly were concerned. She did not have any hobbies except embroidery which she did on occasion. I never saw her read a book, but she loved visiting old friends so was always out and about, apart from that she lived only for her job, and loved the children. Whenever she went visiting she always brought a load of goodies to take with her.

BLITZ MEMORIES.

Standard Junior Gas Mask and the smaller childrens mask. Items courtesy of Mr Dick Eva Plymouth.

"Goodnight children – Everywhere"
Wartime children will remember this saying -
And the cups of oxo they were given to drink.

Incendiary Bomb (non-active) Item courtesy Mr Dick Eva Plymouth.

Stirrup Pump (which also had a metal bucket) as part of a Warden's Kit. Item courtesy of Mr Dick Eva Plymouth.

Keeping the spirits up! Postcard (circa 1915) courtesy of Mr & Mrs L Fisher. Torquay. Devon

C(LOVE)LY

Taken at the reunion at the Masonic Hall Manadon Plymouth in 1997. Left to Right. Eileen Law (London) Bernice Waight & sister Shirley Waight Plymouth. Bernice Waight was another regular playmate in Clovelly although they were not Stoke House children. We spent many happy hours playing in the Hobby Drive. Photo from private collection.

The Clovelly Cross Memorial to the RAF crew killed when returning from an Anti-Submarine Patrol over Clovelly in 1943. Memorial presented by Harry Clement (BEM).

The RAF Crew killed. Wing Cmdr R. Musson, Flying Officer F. Rodda, Flight Lt L. Burden (Canada), Flight Lt E. Carr, Flight Sgt I. Walker, Sgt E. Todd. Photo courtesy Mr & Mrs R Vittle Plymouth.

Class of 1936 Clovelly County School. From the sum total of this class attending the school to nearly two hundred pupils in 1941. It must have been quite a culture shock. All rows read from the left.

Front Row. Kenneth Cook, Reginald Colwill, Jeffery Simmons, Kenneth Rowe, John Wonnacott & Raymond Bale. Second Row. Caleb Jennings, Leslie Rowe, Jean Jennings, Phyllis Cook, Ruth Cruse, Norman Headon, John Westlake & Margery May (Teacher). Back Row. Tom Cruse, Beryl Wilson, Freda Shackson, Molly Beer & James Whitefield.

Photo courtesy Mr Tom Cruse Bideford Devon.

This happy picture was taken in the playground of Clovelly School May 1998. The pupils and staff had given us a scrumptious meal. The pupils entertained us with singing old wartime songs and we compared notes on standards of education. In this photo is the Clovelly Headteacher (centre back near tree) Mr Chris Nicholls and our former Teacher Mrs Pamela Pearce (nee Williams) (standing in front of Mr Nicholls) with formers pupils 1941-1945 and their husbands and the pupils of Clovelly School. Photo by Mr Tony Manley Hartland Times Bideford Devon.

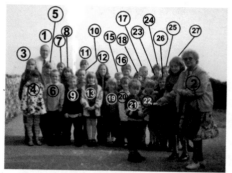

The Clovelly school pupils September 1998. We had a very happy day! Here I am presenting them with a Readers Digest Book for their library as a gift from the Stoke House children who stayed at the New Inn 1941-1945 called "Yesterday's Britain" which explains the history of the war years and the way we lived. Listed are their names so that in sixty years time they will not have to spend months of research to put names to faces. The names of the orphaned children in the New Inn 1941-1945 were not linked to the faces of their photographs.

1.Chris Nicholls Headteacher Clovelly County School. 2. Miss Veronica Norman (Plymouth) Clovelly Pupils. 3. Daisy Perham. 4. Kristy Watts. 5. Heidi Green. 6. Jack Perham. 7. Kirsty Johnson. 8. Felicity Cook. 9. Olive Vanstone. 10. Hethe Pearson. 11. Emmie Perham. 12. Jessica Pearson. 13. Coral Johnson. 14. Not used. 15. Taz Winchcombe. 16. Luke Grist. 17. Orry Winchcombe. 18. Karina Brockett. 19. Sarah Vanstone. 20. Samantha Gray. 21. Oiver Coulam. 22. Michael Brockett. 23. Bethan Vanstone. 24. Jenny Ward. 25. Kieren Vanstone. 26. Thomas Ellis. 27. Bysha King.

GAMES WE PLAYED.

All cigarette cards by courtesy of Imperial Publishing & Imperial Tobacco Company.

The Spitfire! Everyone's favourite.

Very popular with the boys.

Bird lovers had their favourite collection

The animal collectors favourite.

A Soldier in Tank Regiment Uniform. Collectors of Uniforms would have sets of these.

The Morris Eight Saloon.

How many girls swooned at handsome Errol Flynn?

Clark Gable. Remember "Gone with the Wind?"

163

LIFE IN THE NINETEEN THIRTIES.

A 1936 Austin Cambridge 10 Courtesy of Mr
& Mrs Toms, Kingsbridge, South Devon.

Philips 636 de-luxe
model super inductive
receiver long range
wireless circa 1933.
Photo courtesy Mr
Gerald Wells Wireless
Museum London.

The Film Annual was a Luxury Book in
the 1930's. Very popular with children
and adults alike. This 1935 front cover
courtesy of Miss Margery Pursell
Maids Moreton Buckingham Bucks.

Hardware Bargain prices
during a sale by JC Tozer
of Devonport circa late
1930's. Look at those
prices! Courtesy Miss Jean
Tozer Justice of the Peace
Plymouth. (Daughter of Sir
Clifford & Lady Tozer).

The Robertson Bramble
seedless Jelly popular with
children in the 1930's. Poster
published by kind permission
of James Robertson & Sons
Ltd.

Fashions in the 1930's. Buttoned
Jackets, contrast borders, slim
fittings, and bodices trimmed with
bows, side pleats, small collars and
pockets, and look at those hats!
Suits were priced at one shilling &
sixpence. Photo courtesy Pattern
Bureau, La Belle Sauvage, London
1939.

All cigarette packets by kind permission Imperial Tobacco Co.

The Woodbine The
working class cigarette.
Some were sold in
machines in packs of
five.

The Craven A packet
which children used to
collect for the Black Cat
said to be lucky if you
found an empty packet.

My folks were avid Park
Drive smokers it was
also a popular brand for
ladies.

Nearly everyone
will remember this
packet with the
famous seafarer's
face.

164

SWEETS WE REMEMBER

The distinctive blue Dorothy Carton Pack cover for Cadbury's Roses chocolate circa 1930's. Courtesy Cadbury Limited.

Every child loved to chew on a Rowntrees Fruit Gum later to be renamed Clear Gums. Courtesy Rowntrees Company.

Children loved the chocolate Alphabet box issued from 1931. Courtesy Nestles Vevey Switzerland.

Look at those prices! Even in the 1930's free gift coupons were available. Courtesy Nestles Vevey Switzerland.

Rowntrees Clear Gums the Smoker's favourite sweet circa 1935. Courtesy of Rowntrees Limited.

Sharps Super-Kreem Toffees were a lovely chew. From a private collection circa 1930's.

MORE SWEETS & CHOCOLATES

A lovely collection of chocolate bars. Happy memories! Courtesy Nestles Vevey Switzerland.

A lovely variety of Liquorice treats every child will remember. Courtesy of Trebor Bassetts Limited Archive.

Mars had their Mars Bar issued in August 1932 for the price of two pence. Ah! Those were the days! Courtesy of the Mars Company.

With the onset of war the quality of chocolate was to suffer, as milk for full cream was no longer available to the sweet manufacturers. Here is a selection of wartime rations. Courtesy Cadbury Limited.

The stand up chocolate mascots which could be bought singly in the Tuck Shop. Courtesy Nestles Vevey Switzerland.

Cadbury's Flake is still popular today. Not at this price though! Courtesy Cadbury Limited.

THE RATIONING

The Ration book did ensure that all citizens had their quota of meagre rations. Item courtesy of Mr Dick Eva Plymouth.

The Ministry of Food gave advice on how to stock the ARP larder. Item courtesy of Mr Dick Eva Plymouth.

The Clothing Book ration stamps, which every person was issued with. Some traded their stamps in exchange for black market items not normally available. Item courtesy of Mr Dick Eva Plymouth.

Children in the institutions rarely had toffee in the war years. Extract from a 1940's Picturegoer.

Some of the wartime recipes were good and others were horrid! From a private collection.

The nation was constantly reminded about not wasting food. The Ministry of Food issued leaflets throughout the country and fines would be imposed if anyone were caught wasting food. From a private collection.

RATIONING

Ministry of Food issued leaflets to advise the population on how to make puddings without eggs. Imagine Plum Pudding made with potatoes and carrots!

War cookery was an art in itself as housewives were instructed how to use their meagre ration of dried egg powder.

Food was the most important factor on the home front and everyone had to find methods of producing home-grown fare. Leaflet issued by the Minister of Food during the war years.

A wartime advert from a 1940's Picturegoer showing how many points was needed for the breakfast cereal.

Most children of the 1930's/1940's remember Golden Shred and the famous pictures of the Golliwogs. Poster courtesy James Robertson & Sons Limited incorporated into Centura Foods.

Wartime Kitchen waste had to be sorted and placed in separate bins for collection. Nothing was wasted! From a private collection.

I used to think how lovely it would be to live in Stoke House with all those children to play with, of course I was young and everything looks different, on the outside all seemed perfect. I remember once meeting the Matron a Miss Holden who seemed aloof and unfriendly to me. I can remember the lovely smells coming from the kitchen. The cooks were always fat ladies, and they always seemed to be cooking dozens of pasties and cakes. Aunt Holly worked there too, as she was an assistant to Aunt Audrey (who was a qualified childrens' nurse). Holly and Audrey were always having rows and were forever at loggerheads. I know Holly hated working there, she did not like her job or the children! She hated some of the things she had to do, and found it very difficult and embarrassing when she had to take some of the children to the Venereal Disease Clinic, poor little mites! Many children ran away from the home and stole food from shops to survive, only to be caught by the police. I myself did not hear of the abuse at the home, the staff were always careful not to speak whilst in earshot of a child. Holly was an avid reader and would shut herself off from everyone in her room napping and also reading. She was a very good strong walker, and would walk for miles, and she would soon tire me out. Poor Holly was the underdog and always seemed to be in the wrong, she was the odd one out in the family that is why she kept very much to herself. When Holly came and stayed with my family in her retirement years she was a different person, she chatted happily and was more relaxed.

I remember the Christmas Tree, at Stoke House, tall and beautifully decorated. Aunt Audrey would make scenes from crepe paper, dolls and toys; each year would be a different theme. There were regular holidays to a place called Maker Camp, Audrey loved it but Holly hated it! Poor Aunt Holly! She also dreaded the trip across the water to Cawsand for picnics on the beach. When the bombing started visits were less frequent and in April 1941 the home went up in flames. I remember the children were sent to Montpelier School, they walked in pairs all the way. Poor dears had only been there a little while when landmines were dropped and the school received a direct hit.

The children were in the shelter, which collapsed burying the children beneath it. Wardens, police, firemen, and servicemen dug out the children. Everyone in the area was asked to help in the rescue, in fact anyone, who could lend a hand rallied to the cause, it took some time to dig them out. Some children were badly bruised and some were very frightened, but thankfully no one was badly injured. Aunt Audrey was the only real casualty, she had a very deep cut in her upper leg and one other person had a minor cut. Aunt Audrey sent Aunt Holly home to tell their Mum and Dad that they were being moved to Clovelly, North Devon. Holly walked all the way home to Saltash that day; there was no transport. She bravely walked across the Railway Bridge, this she was allowed to do at her own risk, no trains were running, and everything had stopped. It must have been a worrying journey as you can look down and see the water between the sleepers. When she arrived home she had a quick cup of tea and a sandwich and then walked all the way back to Devonport again!

I stayed on with my Grandmother and a few days later her house was bomb blasted and the damage was so severe we could not stay there any longer. We moved temporarily to Truro, Cornwall, with relatives. Later we moved to Falmouth to be with Granddad's sister, who had a huge bungalow and we all lived there until the house in Saltash was repaired. I took my scholarship examination in the Education Office in Falmouth with five other girls. I am glad to say I did pass. Three months later we returned to Saltash and I was able to visit Aunts Audrey and Holly again, this time in Clovelly. I looked forward to seeing them especially Aunt Audrey, as I was very fond of her. Sadly my relationship with Aunt Holly was not the same, and she was very much the introvert. She was a very private person, hard to get close to. In fact I was a bit frightened of her, she was very strict and had a hard strong hand to smack with! You would never imagine her to be a very sickly child but she had been, she never had an easy life. It was only in later years that I really got to know her. As I got older she became more tolerant, and she would talk to me more openly.

When they came home to Saltash on their regular monthly pass from Clovelly they would bring home food parcels and extra goodies! I do remember the holdhall bags they used to carry and usually they would bring some tea, sugar, butter, sometimes a cake, some sweets and fruit. Of course one must realise they were bringing some of their own rations with them as their ration books would have been lodged together with the childrens' at the home, held by the authorities. Both Audrey and Holly's job included board and lodgings. Food was short at home with my grandmother as we only had our bare rations, so they had to bring their rations with them when they stayed with us as they would not have their ration books so would be unable to buy food in Saltash. It was the recognised practise that if a person visited another family something would always be taken to help out with the meals. Being a nosy child I always wanted to see what they had in their bags, I do not remember them bringing home excessive amounts of food, but no doubt they brought a little extra! The children in the home would receive extra food supplied by charities. Locals too had a great sympathy for the children. Some of the local farmers would supply extra, also the fishermen.

On one occasion when I was visiting I remember something happened that I have never forgotten. I often smile as I remember this particular local lad who had learning difficulties. He would on occasion throw open the kitchen door and throw in a lobster, flinging it across the room with peals of laughter shouting "Here's a lobster for you Misses". I think he was called Bertie Braund. Every one would jump away from the creature crawling around the kitchen; the staff were a bit squeamish especially when it came to boiling the poor thing alive. Bertie would also bring fish. Of course the children never had any lobster, the staff would have had that for their supper.

My two Aunts would often talk of a Mr Scott the gardener and handyman at Stoke House and Clovelly, everyone was fond of him and the children liked him, it was obvious he was a very helpful man. My Aunt Audrey made a life long friend in Clovelly called Mrs Abbott who lived in the cottage opposite the New Inn. She was very fond of antiques and I remember I used to be fascinated by her ornaments and china treasures. Audrey used to visit her for many years after she left Clovelly until sadly her friend died. Another of Aunt Audrey's friends from her nursing days was Mrs Gladys Janes. She lived in the village of Aveton Gifford and Aunt Audrey often took me to visit her. Mrs Janes had a daughter, Sheila, but sadly, I lost contact with here although I often wonder where she is now. Aunt Audrey had a man friend who was a big jolly policeman, I never knew his name as it was kept all very secret from me! Later I found out they were both going to keep on working until retirement, get their pensions, and eventually marry in their retirement years. Sadly he was killed on point duty in Plymouth and her dream died with him. Aunt Audrey retired in 1961 and Aunt Holly in 1963. When Audrey retired she often came to stay with me on holiday in Bourne,

Lincolnshire. All her life she had been a teetotaller, until she discovered "Cherry Brandy" we were so amused to see her go up the stairs every evening with her glass of tipple, saying it would make her sleep better! When they had retired, the three sisters, Audrey, Holly and Valerie started having caravan holidays in Devon and Cornwall; one favourite spot was Sandy Bay. I wish I could remember more of their time in Clovelly, I know that Audrey and Holly used to come home to Saltash with lots to tell us, causing peals of laughter. I think they were very happy to be in Clovelly and thoroughly enjoyed those times. My memory will not give up all the secrets, but remember I was only a child.

Audrey and Holly were born at Denmark House (it is now called Denmark Cottage) in Tamerton Foliot, Plymouth, Devon. Holly was born on 29 December 1903 and died on the 26 May 1987 she was the first to die. Her death was sudden. She had prepared the tea on that day and then gone into the garden to feed the birds. Suddenly, she collapsed and died. As she had not returned to the kitchen for her tea Audrey went looking for her and found her lying on the lawn, it was a great shock, but eighty-four years is a good age. Audrey was born 26 October 1901 and died 22 November 1989; she had achieved eighty-eight years. She suffered a severe stroke and was taken into Saint Barnabas Hospital, Saltash, Cornwall. As she was so ill I immediately raced to the hospital to be with her and held her hand as she passed quietly away.

Eldest sister Gwendoline was a teacher at Crownhill, Plymouth, and the mother of a little girl who was also called Audrey (me), and to avoid confusion they always called me "Little Audrey" My mother died at the younger age of fifty-eight years in 1959. Aunt Valerie was the last to pass away in 1990; As Valerie was the youngest she was kept at home all her working life to look after her Aunt, Mother and Father, when they died Valerie stayed with Audrey and Holly. Valerie was the last to pass on, at the age of seventy-nine, eight months after Audrey died, it is said she grieved for her sisters and lost the will to live. There are many more memories hidden deep in my mind, I could probably remember more, but with two marriages and two sons coupled with three score years of age, I find myself getting old and forgetful. Sometimes little things come back to my memory that I had forgotten about and I say to myself, "Whatever made me think about that!" I am happy knowing that they will not be forgotten, for this book will be a permanent reminder of them.

CHAPTER NINETEEN

MEMORIES OF STOKE HOUSE

Sybil Lillian Webb (Nee Bond)

This is photograph of me age 13 in 1938 it was taken at Stoke House and is the only one I have of me whilst in care. Photo courtesy Veronica (Vicky) Norman.

My memories of Stoke House are as vivid today as they were all those years ago. On my transfer from Hill Park Crescent I was twelve years old. My first recollections of Stoke House were the huge wrought iron front gates, and walking the gravel path leading up to the pillared entrance. The house itself was very large and had a glass dome on top of the roof, outside on the walls grew Virginia Creeper. I remember the Matron Miss Holden, as a miserable person who never smiled, and she wore dangling earrings and stooped as she walked, as she appeared to suffer with her feet. The only thing she loved was her little terrier dog Roger. When Miss Holden punished the children, such as smacking with a slipper, Roger used to bark and jump up to her and try and stop her. I hated Stoke House and the Matron in charge made the childrens' lives a misery. To me it was like a prison with no outside community life. When we had to sit outside the bathroom waiting our turn for a bath Miss Holden would come up the stairs and whilst walking to her bedroom she would pass by the girls sitting outside the bathroom, and if we were talking she would hit us on the head with a thimble on her finger (we called it thimble pie) it was very hurtful. When I grew older and became one of the senior girls I had to work and was allocated various jobs. There were times when I was treated as a slave and I would cry quietly in moments of despair. One of my duties was to take Miss Holden's supper tray to her bedroom; she used to have two Ryvita biscuits with butter and a little cheese. I remember one day she left a biscuit and as I had to bring her tray down and wash the dishes I ate the biscuit. Next evening I had to ask her for another packet and she said, "What have you done with the rest of the biscuits? There should be a number left!" I did not know she had been counting them, I was so scared that further punishment would be meted out! This time I escaped and I remained subdued for some time. Some evenings I had to go to Matron's bedroom and rub her neck and shoulders with wintergreen ointment. It had a horrible smell and even today it makes me feel sick at the thought of it.

Miss Henderson, who was well liked, looked after the boys at Stoke House, whilst I was there I helped mainly on the boys side of the house with Miss Henderson in charge. There were about twenty-five boys whose ages varied from three to ten years. One of my tasks was to clean the boots and shoes and I wore a hessian apron (called a wrapper apron) which reached right down to my ankles. If I got any black shoe polish on the floor I had to wash the floor until I removed every mark. On a Saturday morning Miss Henderson polished the dormitory floors, she used to have a large stone jar filled with floor polish and a stick in it, she would flop the polish onto the floor then one of the other girls and myself used to follow behind her and rub the polish into the oak floorboards. I often helped to clean Miss Henderson's bedroom for which she used to give me a sweet and sixpence, she was very kind to me. Often she would let me sneak out the back door to buy some sweets. I had to be careful in case Matron was around! Parents or other relatives would visit on a Saturday once a month at Stoke House, so I helped Miss Henderson bath the boys and get them ready for the visitors. The children that had no visitors were kept away from the dining room, and sent out to play on the lawn until the relatives had gone. Other girls and myself used to think the staff were afraid we would tell all about the nasty incidents at the home. I remember one day I came home from school and Miss Henderson told me there were some boys waiting for me up in the bathroom. I went up and found three boys had messed themselves and I had to bath them! Then I was to wash their dirty trousers out ready to be sent to the laundry. At night I had to help Miss Henderson pot the bed-wetters, I was only a child but I know how Cinderella felt! When it was Miss Henderson's day off I would help Miss Thompson (The Cook) see to the boys. She had this awful weird habit of switching on and off the light whilst waiting for the boys who were getting ready for bed. The switches were solid brass and I was standing at the door beside Miss Thompson and she had her hands, one resting on my shoulder, the other on the switch, doing the usual trick of on and off. All of a sudden I had an electric shock, it had gone right through her and then me and it has made me nervous of electricity ever since!

Miss Beatrice Thompson was the cook at Stoke House; she was a very large lady and had a very stern look and at times a temper to go with it. Being one of the older girls, when I got up in the mornings I had to put the kettle on, put the light under the Dixie filled with porridge, and give it a good stir. I used to make a pot of tea, take a cup to Miss Thompson then she would get up and come out to the kitchen and take over. One day I could not find the matches to light the gas under the porridge, but I found a taper and went into the staff sitting room adjoining the kitchen and lit the taper from the electric fire. I could smell burning so I went to Miss Thompson's bedroom and told her. She came out to the sitting room and found one of the staff had been ironing and had not disconnected it, hence the iron and fire were on at the same time. The iron was solid iron and the heat had gone through the ironing sheet and fire blanket and was burning the pine table. Cook said it was not my fault and did her best to cover things up as I could have been blamed, I was most surprised as just for once someone had stuck up for me whereas before any excuse to punish was the norm.

Miss Holly Penna was also another miserable person she grumbled about most things. Occasionally I helped clean her bedroom and ran errands to the Post Office and to the Chemist and once she gave me three pence, which was quite a rarity. For a while I was unsure whether to spend it or hold it in case she asked for it back. Nurse Audrey Penna, her sister, was totally different she was a very pleasant lady and it was obvious she loved children. I cannot remember anything unpleasant about Nurse Penna. My bedroom was situated right next to hers. I think she was aware of her sister's attitude toward the children and she kept a tight control on her and would often say "Leave the child alone". There was Miss Lavis who used to come and do the cleaning. One day Miss Lavis said she was going into Plymouth to do some Christmas shopping and suggested to Miss Holden that it would be nice to take myself and another girl with her as a treat. Miss Holden agreed to let us go. What a wonderful day! I have never forgotten that kind act.

I remember at times that I was given tokens to go on the tram, I caught the tram at Milehouse as the depot was just down the hill from Stoke House. Often it would be to run errands for the Staff. Occasionally Miss Holden sent me on errands to the Plymouth Education Offices; I had to put letters in the box at Cobourg Street and other addresses in Plymouth. Coming from the Plymouth Scattered Homes I used to run similar errands for Miss Bull who was the Matron at Hill Park Crescent when I was there, so I was quite used to doing these errands, she had been a lovely lady and my stay there was very happy in contrast to Stoke House! We were never allowed to mix with other children. I remember being taken on a walk to Marsh Mills and one of the staff giving us money to buy sweets at a quaint little shop. Away from Miss Holden, the staff were always much more relaxed and treated the children differently. They were afraid of her and we must remember during the 1930's unemployment was rife so everyone had to bite the bullet if they wanted to retain their posts. When important people or persons came to visit the home the children were all kept at a distance. The Lord and Lady Mayoress would visit at different times of the year. Christmas some visitors would come and see the decorations, the entrance hall at Stoke House was made like a garden scene with greenery and toys in front of a large furnished Doll's House. We were never allowed to play with it, after Christmas it was all put away. As far as I can remember the Doll's House was kept pushed back in the corner of the hall. One of the times I used to enjoy was Friday evening when Mrs Hitchcock used to come and talk to us about the evil of smoking and drinking and the importance of refraining from swearing. I was designated Chief Templar and we addressed the people as Sister and Brother. It was called the Temperance Society. Brother Stacey went out to Jerusalem and brought back a gavel made of olivewood and he presented it to me. I felt so proud! We used to sing different words to well-known tunes condemning the evil of drink. The pledge was said every week and the meeting ended with a prayer.

Sometimes in summer time, when I used to have my bath and wash my hair I was allowed to sit under the Mulberry Tree in the garden whilst my hair dried, for me this really was a treat. I often pinched a mulberry, as they were lovely and juicy. On Sundays whilst waiting for our tea the older girls were given permission to walk around the garden in twos and keep on the path. This was ideal as the borders had lovely flowers and at the bottom of the garden was a large pond, which had goldfish in it and beautiful water lilies. Mr Scott was the gardener and he kept the garden lovely. During the summer months he used to give us a jam jar for some of us to pick the caterpillars off the cabbages. When we filled it he gave us an apple which we thought was wonderful. Miss Crimp was the dressmaker, she was a lovely person, very quiet but caring. Miss Crimp was at Hill Park Crescent with me before our transfer to Stoke House. When I was measured for a dress she used to gently prick me (accidentally) then say "Sorry did I hurt you?" I used to say no and then she would say "Pride never feels the pinch" that saying has stayed with me throughout my life. At Stoke House we went out on our own only when we went to school or Sunday school, at other times we had one of the staff with us. When the younger children had all gone to bed, another treat for me early 1940, when the war was on, was to sit in the main dining room with one of the staff during Saturday evening and listen to the radio, the programmes coming from different places abroad. Favourite stars at the time were Gracie Fields, Vera Lynn and other entertainers singing to the troops, I enjoyed this immensely as it made me feel as though I was grown up like the adults.

I left Stoke House when I was fourteen years old to go to my first employment as an apprentice to be a tailoress in Plymouth, Devon, unfortunately the bombing put paid to that and the Youth Employment Department sent me to Exeter, Devon, to be an assistant Nanny. I did like this job but little did I realise then that I was to spend the rest of my life in Exeter. Every child who spent their lives in Scattered Homes or Stoke House had to live with the stigma of being different. We were labelled for life as maladjusted children when in fact all we craved was love! We would always be wary and feel guilty of our background, yet we were children and how could we help the unhappy dilemma in which we had been placed. I would cry for many hours and longed for the missing love I had been denied. On the other hand all the tasks of cleaning, sewing, ironing and looking after little ones stood me in good stead for the years ahead.

One of the saddest episodes in my life came just as I was courting a young man who had asked me to marry him. I thought I had found happiness. It was to be short lived! When he made enquiries into my background and found out I had spent my life in Stoke House Childrens' Home he challenged my parentage, and as I could not tell him all the facts as I did not know myself, he changed his mind and I never saw him again. Now at last I am obtaining all my records from the Social Services despite the fact a seventy-five year closure period on records of children taken into care was confirmed. However the Government White Paper on "Your rights to know" has eased that restriction, so now I am in my seventies I can at last find out the truth. I have been a widow now for twenty years but I do not crave for any expensive luxury. I am quite content with life; there is nothing I want only to go on as I am, as long as I am able to pay the bills I am content at making do with what I have. I have very happy memories of thirty-one years of marriage to my husband Maitland; he was a driver on British Rail Southern Region, and was a very good husband and father. We have a daughter Celia who is a teacher, and a son Robin who is a Trade Sales Manager. Between them have given me five lovely grandchildren and I am very happy at being surrounded by a loving family.

CHAPTER TWENTY

INTERIOR STOKE HOUSE.

As I remember by Sybil Webb (nee Bond)

The former childrens' home Stoke House was a large residence with its walls covered by Virginia Creeper and surmounted by a glass dome. I did not mind going up to the glass house on the top of the building as there were beautiful views and for a few minutes I would imagine myself out there roaming around and free! The house was approached through wrought iron gates and along a gravelled path to the pillared facade. Stoke House was quite a big house and very cold. It must have belonged to wealthy people in its history.

One entered into a large hall, decorated with two floor to ceiling pillars, from which a lovely wide oak staircase rose, illuminated halfway up by a window, and with a beautiful polished bannister in a wood resembling mahogany. Although the girls' dormitories were situated at the top of these stairs, only matron was allowed to use them, the children using the back staircase. Of course, we children used to have a sneak slide down on the banister if Matron was not to be seen. Sometimes we would be apprehended and we were hauled over the coals when caught.

To the right of the entrance hall was Miss Beatrice Thompson the Cook's bedroom. Facing the main entrance was the main dining room, as one entered the room to the right there were double doors leading to a smaller dining room, in which the older girls had their meals. The main dining room had a French window leading out into the garden onto the back lawn with a path around. Outside the French window several wide steps approached the lawn, and at each side of the steps there was a sculptured stone lion.

Matron's office was along the hallway, on the left near the oak staircase, and a little further along, the girls' lobby which was equipped with a row of wash basins, pegs on which to hang outdoor clothes, and below these pegs, lockers to hold shoes. Immediately opposite this lobby was a door leading to the cellar where the coal was kept (When I was sent to the cellar I was

179

very frightened of spiders and cobwebs) Near the lobby door was the back staircase made of pinewood and very shabby compared to the front stairs.

Next was the kitchen, a quite large room with the usual furniture, a long pine table and chairs and, in a recess, a large gas cooker. A scullery was reached through an archway and here the food was prepared and dishes washed. The boiler was in this scullery and had to be kept stoked as it provided all the hot water. Off the kitchen was the staff sitting room cum dining room. Further along this side of the corridor was the boys' lobby, similarly equipped to the girls' and beyond this, the back door leading to the yard. Miss Holly Penna's bedroom was on the other side of the corridor, opposite the boys lobby.

The oak staircase at the front of the house led to a long corridor. Nurse Audrey Penna's bedroom was the first room on the left, adjoining the first of the girls' dormitories. A glass-panelled door allowed access, beyond which were the three dormitories each with their own door. Beyond the furthest bedroom was located a fire escape. To the right of the corridor was the girls' bathroom containing two baths and next came the linen cupboard. Further along was Miss Holden the matron's bathroom with right at the far end, facing toward the stairs, matron's bedroom.

At the back of the house the second staircase led to the boys' dormitories. On a small landing, a door on the right led to a toilet. The boys' bathroom had only one bath and their dormitory, similar in design to the girls' but lacking the individual doors, were entered through a door to the right of which was Miss Henderson's bedroom. A fire escape was also provided, leading from the last bedroom.

The glass dome at the very top of the house was a room composed mainly of windows and having lovely views. It was used as a repository for unwanted items. The garden at Stoke House was lovely and the gardener kept it beautiful, there were colourful flowers and bushes. There were trees, a mulberry, a monkey-puzzle and a chestnut. Often we children would be caught knocking down the chestnuts. The large lawn was edged with flowerbeds and a path along which we were allowed to walk on Sundays. There was a goldfish pond at the lower edge of the lawn with goldfish and water lilies and to the side of this a long greenhouse.

There was a very large vegetable garden with many apple and pear trees, with climbing pear foliage trained up the walls. In the summer Mr Scott, the gardener, would reward us with a windfall in return for picking caterpillars from the cabbages. Adjoining the vegetable garden was the play area for children called 'The Lawn' it consisted of a few swings at the top end and at the bottom end, a climbing frame and sandpit. Also in this area was the air raid shelter, the older girls use to go in there and hold a little talent concert singing to our hearts content until one of the Nurses came and turfed us out!

The back door to Stoke House led to a cobbled yard where outhouses were used as garages and for storage. Nearby was the cottage where the dressmaker worked and the store of shoes was kept. The main back doors were large and wooden and painted dark green. They were heavy to open and exited to the main Tavistock Road. Yes! I remember Stoke House as though it was yesterday, I spent my whole childhood in the Scattered Homes at 13, Hill Park Crescent, Greenbank, and Stoke House in the village of Stoke, and I have never forgotten those years.

CHAPTER TWENTY-ONE

HAPPY MEMORIES AT HILL PARK CRESCENT

Sybil Lillian Webb (nee Bond)

I was four years old when I and my brother Frank were taken into care in October 1929, I was illegitimate and my Mother did not want to care for me, my Father who was unemployed was unable to take care of us. He could not obtain full employment and at the same time look after us. I was to spend the rest of my childhood under the auspices of the scattered homes. Various staff I remember at 13 Hill Park Crescent, were Miss Alice Bull, (Matron) Mrs Jefferies, Miss Cartwright, Miss Wyatt, Miss Saunders and Miss Crimp (Dressmaker).

My memories of the years I spent at 13 Hill Park Crescent were very happy, it was one of the many children's homes scattered around Plymouth, hence the name Scattered Homes. The home was a double fronted terraced house consisting of three large bedrooms and two attic rooms, one of which was used as a stock and storage room, the other attic being used as a bedroom for the four oldest girls. Miss Crimp the dressmaker had a room next door to Matron's bedroom. Downstairs there was the entrance hall and to the left of it was a front sitting room with double doors leading into an office, these two rooms were Matron's. To the right of the hallway was a door leading into the main dining room, beyond was another door into the kitchen. Just outside this door was a small walk in larder, and beyond this was the scullery leading out into the walled garden, in which there was an outside toilet. Although the garden was not very large we had many summer teatimes in it. On one side was a pear tree and on the opposite wall an apple tree. The fruit from these trees was stored upstairs in the attic on shelves and during the winter evenings we were often given an apple or pear. I think some of the fruit stored came from some of the other scattered homes as there was much more fruit than came from the two trees in our garden.

To me my years at Hill Park were very happy. The Matron was quite tall with white hair and with an upright way of walking. Her manner was strict but very kind and most important scrupulously fair. I was very fond of her. She had two sisters who ran the children's orphanage in Falmouth, Cornwall, and on occasion one sister called Miss Nellie Bull came up to stand in as relief Matron while our Matron went on leave. If we misbehaved we were punished, not by beatings but given little jobs to do that we did not like, such as washing the childrens' hair brushes and combs, or taking a meat skewer with a string of thread to push it through ripped newspapers for use as toilet paper. Another little task was to be given a pile of string, which had come from parcels to Matron and told to untie the knots. I find that little job has trained me to have patience, to this day my closest friend often gives me her knotted items to unravel. On a Saturday morning Matron used to send me to the bank on Mutley Plain. I had to ask for £1 of pennies, £1 of sixpences and £1 of threepenny pieces, I was told to hurry and not to speak to anybody. The money I carried in a rather large handbag belonging to Miss Bull, it was tan in colour and had a large wide bone clasp, and I used to fold it over and put it inside my coat because I felt silly carrying such a big bag, but the money I fetched was part of the children's pocket money. The older girls had sixpence a week, younger ones threepence and the very little ones a penny.

After dinner times on Saturday Miss Bull would come out to the dining room and give us our pocket money. The older girls were allowed to go to the pictures and the children who did not have enough money were sent to the park to play. Miss Bull was very good to us, and if the older girls went to the pictures and saw in the film trailers that a good film was coming in a few week's time, we would tell Miss Bull and she would save our pocket money for us as it cost sixpence to go in for a category A Film. Her only stipulation was that we left the house together and arrived back together. I remember once one of the girls was not outside the cinema when the film was over. We began to panic so the usherette looked everywhere for her. We did not dare to go home without her, so once again she checked the cinema to find our lost girl curled up and fast asleep in the far corner of the back row. At Hill Park Crescent each older girl had to be responsible for a younger girl, which meant I had to do that girl's darning and mending. I had a girl who was always getting big holes in her socks and rips in her clothes. I cried many a tear as by the time I had done my homework and all the darning it was too late for me to go to the park. Sometimes I cobbled the holes in the socks but when Miss Bull inspected them she would cut the darn out and make me do it again.

Christmas time at Hill Park Crescent was lovely, we would hang up our stockings on Christmas Eve, and on Christmas Day we all had one main present such as a doll, paints, or a game, with a few sweets, an orange and some nuts. Christmas dinner was turkey or chicken followed by Christmas pudding and Miss Bull always had threepenny pieces put in it. Tea-time we had mince pies and Christmas cake followed by the pulling of Christmas crackers. Everyone loved wearing the paper hats, and we would all read the mottoes contained in the crackers to each other with peals of laughter and in the evening we played games. A trip to the pantomime was another enjoyable time, we sat at the top of the Palace Theatre in the seats they called "The Gods" but we managed to see alright. Tessie O'Shea was my favourite star she used to come to Plymouth often. When Bertram Mills Circus came to town we were taken to see the show. Miss Bull gave the children some very enjoyable times.

There was one unhappy incident however which I remember to this day, the memory is clear and still hurts when I look back, and that was when I was taken to a party from Hill Park Crescent and presented with a dolls pram with a large doll and pretty covers. At bedtime I had a tantrum because I wanted the pram and doll beside my bed. Because of my outburst it was taken away and I never saw the doll or pram again until many years later when I and another girl were told to go upstairs at Stoke House and clean out the glass house on the roof of the building. This was a room where all the junk was kept, it had glass windows all the way around with beautiful views. There I found the pram, stored away all those years and my heart fluttered as I remember the heartache of its loss.

During school terms Miss Bull used to go to the schools to see how we were progressing with our schoolwork. Often she would be walking back home the same time as we left school to go home for dinner. Being children going home we would be dawdling about to play marbles or skipping up and down the curb of the pavement. Miss Bull did not acknowledge us then, however, after we had our dinner, she would come out to the dining room and act how she saw us behaving on the way home. This taught us right from wrong, Miss Bull was a wonderful lady and she never showed us up in the street. After school hours and when we had finished our school homework we were allowed to go to Freedom Park to play. During the winter months we had to come home from the park when the lamp lighter came around to light the lamps, which was usually five o'clock.

In the summer the younger children had to be home at seven-thirty and the older girls went home at eight o'clock. Sometimes we used to go down to Beaumont Park because there were swings and seesaws there, which Freedom Park never had. I also remember a gentleman called Mr Pickles who lived opposite our scattered home, he was a NSPCC officer and he wore a peaked cap on his head. He was very proud of his big waxed moustache and we children were amused as we watched him twirling the ends. Another person I remember was Mr Ken May who used to practice on his musical instrument and we would often listen to him playing, I think he belonged to a band. Then there was the gentleman who owned the Hill Park Crescent Pub he was a widower with twins, one girl and one boy. One day his little girl invited me upstairs to see her bedroom, it was so nice to see the pretty curtains and frilly covers on her bed a far cry from our red blankets with PSH (Plymouth Scattered Homes) in black sewed on each one.

Miss Crimp was the dressmaker at Hill Park Crescent; she also did the job of taking any of us to the optician and dentist. In the spring some bales of dress material were delivered to the home, Miss Crimp called each of us in turn to the workroom, we would look at the materials and she let us decide which we would like for our Sunday dress. She made lovely dresses; my favourite was a royal blue bolero over a dress with puff sleeves and flared skirt with floral print and a royal blue background that matched the bolero. We had a selection of straw hats and the older girls wore white Panama hats, the younger girls had coloured straw hats with fancy coloured floral print tucked up inside the brim. We were always nicely dressed, ankle socks in the summer with brown sandals and in the winter we wore black stockings, on school days and on Sundays we wore beige lyle stockings. The only thing I did not like was wearing the combinations, they were warm for winter but when spring arrived it was most uncomfortable. When we did physical training at school the other school children used to laugh at us because we had to roll up the legs and put them inside our knickers and at the top of the combinations there was a pleated shape to put one's bust in which at that time we did not have!

One day there was excitement as a Reddifusion speaker was installed on the wall in the dining room and this we thought was wonderful. At teatime we listened to the childrens' hour programme with Larry the Lamb, Uncle Mac Stephens King Hall, and in the evening we would settle down and listen to Henry Hall and his dance band. Sid Walker, who was a rag and bone man, told some lovely stories as he travelled around collecting rags and bones. The radio was a great source of entertainment for the children who did not have the love of a family but Miss Bull, bless her, made our lives as pleasant as she was allowed to and she was indeed one of the gems of the scattered homes.

Saturday we would have our comics to read. Popular at the time was Bubbles; Chick's Own and the Children's Newspaper. My experience of life in the Plymouth Scattered Homes has stood me in good stead. Now today when I look around and see all that is happening to family life I think I was very lucky to have so many happy times at 13 Hill Park Crescent. I do not regret having been brought up in children's home; my life was better than a lot of children of the 1920's/1930's when there was no much unemployment and poverty. Sadly Miss Bull had a severe stroke and due to her illness she decided to retire. She moved to Ermington to be with her family until her death. The children lost a wonderful foster mother and it was the end of an era as the home was closed and all the children were transferred to Stoke House. Life was never the same. Other children of Scattered Homes had not been so fortunate as we had been; there were many rumours of ill treatment as not all foster mothers were so kind. The quality of my life changed when I moved to Stoke House, where there was a different regime in control - so began my unhappy years!

CHAPTER TWENTY-TWO

DAVE'S TORMENT (as told by David Dunbar)

Note by the Author. David Dunbar spent all his childhood in care, either fostered, or in a Scattered Home, on being moved like a pawn on a chessboard on fifteen occasions, he must have suffered a dreadful feeling of rejection. His mother's story is told in the chapter "The Social Stigma of an unmarried mother" He was a nice boy and nearly all the girls remember David because he was good looking! Now read his story and wonder how he coped with such trauma.

I was born in March 1938 at Rosemundy House, a home in Saint Agnes, Cornwall, where my mother had been sent in preparation for my birth, as I was a baby born out of wedlock. At last I have been able to sit down and start to write my account of my childhood life that I can remember. I must say it has been very hard for me to begin, especially after reading and sifting through my past records, which I obtained from the Social Welfare in 1998, but there are still a few gaps here and there.

My earliest recollection starts at Clovelly as this is as far back as I can go, although I do remember during the war years the sound of sirens going off and having to rush off with everyone to take shelter from a bombing raid.

David Dunbar with Margaret Bailey and the Cat taken at Stoke House 1940. Photo from Author's collection by kind permission Dr Robert Crowte Worcestershire.

How I came to arrive at Clovelly in the first place I have no idea. However, I do remember Clovelly quite well. I suppose this was because I was happy there and you always seem to recall your happy moments in life. I remember walking up the cobbled road towards the top of Clovelly on my way to school and walking along a wooded lane. Although I am not too sure of walking, as I have a recollection of riding in the rear of a pony or horse driven carriage with some other children. I do not remember much about my schooling but I do remember one of the parents coming to the school and having an argument with one of the teachers whereby they had a set to on the local green. I do not know to this day what the final outcome was as we were on our way back to the village. It is funny how totally irrelevant matters seem to come to mind. I also remember going down to the harbour, which was quite small, and did winkle fishing by paddling in the shallow water. I used to cringe when the others used to fish the winkles out with a pin and eat them, (after they were cooked of course). I must admit my stomach would react to these sort of things and still does today!

David Dunbar (first left) at Clovelly 1943 after returning from Nethway Kingswear Nursery Home Dartmouth Devon. Photo from Author's collection.

The Lifeboat House was another attraction for us and we liked to play up and down the slipway which was used for launching the lifeboat and we were often told by the lifeboat men to keep off. The only two children I can remember vaguely are a boy called Leslie Newham and a girl called Dorothy Sabine. Leslie and I used to go conkering together and when ever we were found to be missing, the word got around, "Look up the nearest conker tree - they will be up there!" There was a time in Clovelly that I was playing in the wash area and I began to swing on the sink basin, whereby I caught my left leg on the drain plug underneath and gashed my leg open. It must have been quite a nasty wound as I still have the scar to this day. Most afternoons we had to take a lie down and try to sleep, I really hated this time, as like most boys I would have preferred to be playing outside. I accept that the carers had to have their breaks as well and it must have been an arduous task looking after us all, (Bless Them!) One of the carers would take us for a walk to the top of the village and on one occasion we came across these huge armoured tanks. One of the soldiers asked if I would like to get up on the top of tank and I readily agreed. Gosh! Was I excited! In fact I did not want to get off again and when the driver started the engine it gave me an experience I have never forgotten.

I remember leaving Clovelly quite well, it was in an ambulance with a few other children, I think Leslie was one of these. The reason I can recall this journey is that it seemed a long way and somebody was laying across my tummy and I felt quite sick. That somebody I have since found out was Dorothy Sabine. During the journey the ambulance stopped here and there to let certain children off until only Dorothy and I were left. On the next stop Dorothy got off and I was the last left on board, that was the last time I saw her or any of the others, particularly Leslie who had seemed like a brother to me. I eventually arrived at my destination, which was to become my new home.

My foster carers were called Mr. & Mrs. Banks at 2, Little Ash Road, Saltash Passage, Plymouth. They had a daughter aged thirteen called Rosemary. I seemed to settle down quite well at first, mainly because of all the different animals that were around me. The Banks' family had dogs, cats, rabbits, chickens and other varieties of different birds in an aviary, so I had plenty of things to take my mind off past experiences, with the exception of Clovelly of course. Mr Banks worked in the Dockyard at Devonport and he cycled to and from work everyday.

He was also a rabbit breeder and specialised in Chinchillas for their furs. He would kill the rabbit by holding it by its back legs upside down and giving it a sharp blow to the back of the neck with his hand which seemed to kill it instantly. Then the rabbit was skinned for its fur and the fur was pinned out on a board to dry out and the carcass was butchered for the stew pot. Meat being rationed was scarce in those days and this was one of the ways to keep a steady supply of food with rabbit, chicken, eggs and home-grown vegetables. I grew up to hate those rabbits as Mr Banks used to give me a big sack and tell me he wanted it filled with dandelions which was a favourite rabbit food. I had to scour the surrounding meadows or hedgerows looking for this rabbit food which was a very tedious job. The worse was yet to come, if the dreaded sack was not full he used to rant and rave at me for not trying and if there was any dockweed (poisonous for rabbits) mixed in with the dandelions I used to get a belting with his leather belt. I suppose I was a mischievous little lad at times always getting up to something.

There was a time, however, when one or two three-penny pieces (Mr Banks saved these) went missing and he swore blind that I had had them, although I swore my innocence, it was to no avail, off would come the belt and I got another lashing. It seemed Mr Banks had to take it out on someone and I was the appointed scapegoat each time. Oh how I hated that man, he was so evil.

Mr and Mrs Banks fostered another boy by the name of Donald who in my eyes turned out to be the favourite out of the two of us. I remember on one occasion when Mr Banks said to us "My old bike in the shed, If you can ride it, you can have it to practice on." Well I tried my best but I just could not get the hang of keeping my balance. Donald being a little older than myself got on the bike and rode it straight away and how I envied him! For some reason I never took to Donald, instead I played with my friend who lived near the top of the road. In his back garden his parents had a shed which overlooked the River Tamar whereby you could see the ships sailing along. We would watch the Saltash Ferry going from one side of the river to the other conveying passengers and vehicles across, sometimes we used to go down to the river's edge and play dare! We would jump on the ferry as it was moving off and jump off again, quite often we got our feet wet because we left it too late. Nearby was the Royal Albert Railway Bridge.

My friend and I spent some wonderful hours playing together in that shed, and there were others things we did together, exploring the beach and cave hunting on the embankment. We were too scared to go into the cave as it was so dark and our courage ran out, but I have often wondered what it was really like inside. It was not long after Donald arrived that I can recall my Mother visiting us at Little Ash Road in 1947. The reason for the visit was that she wanted me back and had applied to the official channels for my release into her care, thus another traumatic period in my young life was about to begin.

Mother had since remarried to a man called Mister Pringle who had three children of his own, one son and two daughters who were to become my stepbrother and sisters, but even at my tender age of nine I soon realised that I was the odd one out. I can recall running away and finding my way back to Little Ash Road, too frightened to go direct to the house in case I was confronted by Mister Banks, at that moment the front door opened and Rosemary (Mrs Bank's daughter) came out. I ran down the hill and hid in one of the gardens, but Rosemary spotted me and took me home to Mrs Banks who I remembered welcomed me with open arms, that was a wonderful feeling of being wanted.

Unfortunately, the experience was short lived as my mother found out where I was and took me back to her home at Alcester Street, Stoke, Plymouth. I began to hate living there as my mother and stepfather were constantly arguing and fighting. I remember when we had to take a bath, down in the cellar and it was so cold down there, in the middle of the cellar floor was a galvanised tin bath, which had to be filled by hand. Mother was always giving me Epson Salts to keep my bowels in order and I used to throw the horrible stuff away at the back of the fireplace. Mother had to scrimp and scrape to make ends meet, I remember her boiling the milk and skimming the top off to retain the cream. I would visit a lady across the road by the name of Mrs Redman, and she started to teach me how to play the piano, of course I soon tinkered the tune 'Three Blind Mice' but my Mother found out and stopped me from going over there. The arguing continued at home until one day Mister Pringle and my stepsisters and brother left home.

Memories during this period are a little sketchy, but I do remember my Mother taking up digs at a wheelchair bound man's house. The place was infested with mice and when I was in bed trying to sleep I could feel them running across the blankets or scratching somewhere in a corner. He was a horrid old man and he made me push the wheelchair around, and I was very unhappy. Eventually my Mother traced her former husband and stepchildren to Birmingham, she decided to go there to clear private matters up. I was left at a foster home under the care of Mrs Prince at Alcester Street, Stoke, the arrangement was for one week only so Mrs Prince readily agreed to look after me until her return. My mother never returned and I was again taken into care and was once more fostered with strangers, this time a Mrs Marshall of Roseberry Avenue, Lipson, Plymouth. I took some time to settle down in my new environment and my mind is a complete blank for the first few months of my time there. Meanwhile the Welfare Authorities had traced my mother in Birmingham and from time to time she would write to me.

With patience and understanding from Mrs Marshall I began to settle down into an orderly life and I was happy there, but I was only with her for eight months. Out of the blue my mother once again laid claim for me and I was whisked away to Birmingham where we were in and out of digs in different parts of the city. Finally mother returned to her estranged husband and his children and I too was taken along. Life was the same there as it had been in Plymouth with the constant bickering, I felt I was the main cause being the blacksheep of the family, and I wished that I had been left in Plymouth with Mrs Marshall. I attended the Secondary Modern School at Lea Road, which was approximately one-mile walk from home. I left school at fifteen and obtained a job in a bakery earning twenty-five shillings a week, I gave my Mother twenty shillings toward my keep and clothing and I kept five shillings as spending money.

I had this urge to move on and to improve and make something of myself so at the age of seventeen joined the Army and served with the Royal Corp of Signals. The basic training was hard at first but anything was better than the nightmare of constant bickering at home. On my first leave I went home in my battledress uniform as proud as punch. I boarded a bus in the City and offered to pay my fare, the Conductress would not take my money and said, "You keep it and have a drink on me." I felt elated and she certainly made my day and made me think I was somebody at last! I arrived at my destination and began the short walk up the road to my home. I did not tell my mother I was on my way home as I thought I would surprise her, so I knocked on the front door and waited. My mother answered the door and I will always remember this for the rest of my life as her first words were "Oh its you! You'd best come in!" In one moment I had gone from cloud nine to being down in the dumps, I felt angry and thought about turning round and walking away, what a welcome home and the hurt is still with me. I finished my service in 1958 but found it hard to settle again in Civvy Street. During my service I had learnt to drive lorries so I managed to get a job with Birmingham City Transport as a conductor and then as a Driver. During my employment with the company I met Joan who was a conductress, we had a short romance and married in April 1960.

At first everything was rosy, but living with Joan's parents and bedding down in the living room we seemed to get in everybody's way and petty arguments started to happen. Joan and I looked around for a place of our own and found digs not too far away. By this time we had our first child David to look after so we searched to find accommodation with the Council but were unsuccessful. We were unsettled and problems began to emerge that led me to the decision to go back into the Army knowing that after a short spell of basic training again I could apply for a Married Quarter. The

Army would supply everything we needed right down to the last knife, fork and spoon. My wife was a little reluctant at first but after talking it over she finally agreed. I re-enlisted in the Royal Signals and shortly afterwards was allocated a house in Catterick Camp whereby I spent the first two years furthering my education and trade. I was promoted to Corporal and took up the position of Drill Instructor and Physical Training Instructor. We stayed there for four years and I ended up as a Drill Instructor, then I was posted to Aden and later Northern Ireland, finally I left the Army in 1970.

Joan and I raised four children, three sons and one daughter of which all are now grown up and have families of their own, however, I do have five lovely grandchildren. Eventually we moved back to Birmingham into a Council house and once again I found a steady job as a Mechanic with Birmingham City Transport (now West Midlands Travel) I was promoted to Garage Foreman and later promoted to Garage Engineer. Unfortunately in 1988 I was made redundant and my life took another twist as I found myself suddenly in love with another woman who was younger than me. To this day I do not know how it happened, as I was not the type to chase after other women. This was something that just came out of the blue. Nothing could deter the feeling of love between myself and Tina, it was something I had never experienced in my whole life. The inevitable happened, my wife and I divorced in 1990 and Tina and I moved in together to start a new life, and we still lived near to my former wife. It took a long time for my ex-wife's family to accept what had happened, Joan suffered terribly and her family rallied around her. I have no axe to grind, as Joan was a fantastic mother in everyway. By the grace of God we are now on talking terms with one another and I visit her from time to time but her hatred toward Tina is conclusive.

As to my childhood I feel as though I was cheated of love and the experience of a normal family environment, to have a mother only at a distance and seeing her now and again made me feel rejected. The number of foster parents I had in my short years as a child left me loveless and alone, however, it did make me stand up for myself to survive. In later years I questioned my mother many times asking "Who and where is my Father?" When I was in my late forties she finally confirmed that my father was called Victor Burnett and he had been a sailor in the Royal Navy and at the time of their brief romance had been serving on HMS Ark Royal.

Receiving my records from Social Services gave me mixed feelings, elation at finding out the truth at last, anger at not being told before to allow me to set in motion the search for my father. I remember being angry with my Mother but realise now that circumstances and the life styles of the nineteen thirties did much to create the world of unwanted and abandoned babies. A new task is yet to be done and that is, living or dead, I must trace my father to link together the family history. God how I wish the past information had been made available to me thirty years sooner. I am sure I could have traced my father and who knows things might have turned out a lot differently. If my father were still living he would be in his eighties, what a wonderful ending it would be if I could be re-united with him after an absence of sixty years.

CHAPTER TWENTY-THREE

HEARTACHE HERITAGE Margaret Miller (Nee Bailey)

I was born in June 1936 to an unmarried woman in the Plymouth City Hospital. Unknown to me my biological mother already had three other children born out of wedlock, one of whom died at birth. I remained in the City Hospital until I was three years old. In July 1940 I was transferred to Ford House to be assessed and then moved to Stoke House at Devonport which was a Home for unwanted or orphaned children. I do not remember much about my stay at Stoke House as I was so young and as no person came to see me, one day was the same as another. When the war started I can remember the bombs falling and the constant interruption to my sleep as we were always running to the air raid shelters.

Margaret Bailey in the grounds of Stoke House 1940 age 3 years and 10 months.

On 30 April 1941 I was transferred to Clovelly, North Devon, with all the other Stoke House children, we were taken by bus, I was four and a half years old then. I remember the New Inn and when I went to school we would hold hands in pairs to the Wendy House at the top of the building, as the infants did not go to the County School in Clovelly. Riding the donkeys on the beach was lovely and searching for cockles was a delight. We would gather them in and spend hours winkling the cockles out of their shells with a pin. One day I found a sweet on the cobbles on the beach and I promptly ate it, I shudder now at the thought, but in 1941 sweets for us were rare. The village paths consisted of cobbles from the beach right to the very top and it was a very steep climb even for our young legs.

Sundays, all the children went to church and at Easter time we would all wear our bonnets, Sunday tea would be special as we had a soft bread roll with jam and cream! One Christmas I was given a black doll called a golliwog, (Polliwog). I treasured this doll and I clung to it every bit of the day and I would not allow my other friends to hold it, it was mine! Imagine my distress when night fell it was taken away, I cried and begged Miss Holden to let me keep it, but to no avail, I never saw the doll again.

Margaret Bailey in school uniform Clovelly North Devon 1943.

Birthdays did not mean anything to me, as we did not have a cake or card, it was just another normal day. The cook who worked in the New Inn kitchen would on occasion take me on the bus to Bideford, this was a real treat and I really loved those moments. In my own way I was happy because I knew no other life and not having a mother or father I was not able to compare the different lifestyle.

I knew little about life until I left the New Inn when I was eight and a half years of age. Suddenly I was fostered out to an elderly couple; it all seemed so strange, actually sleeping in my own room. To begin with I was very frightened and it scared the living daylights out of me. No other children to play with, I could not understand. What was going on, what was I doing there? I had not lived in a family environment before and it was so unreal. I went to school as normal like everyone else but I could not settle. My Guardians the Plymouth City Council Welfare Department kept in touch with the foster parents to monitor my progress and from the information given them were aware that they could not cope with me, so the decision to move me was agreed and I found myself fostered with

Margaret Bailey with Miss Joan Henderson & David Dunbar taken in the grounds of Stoke House early 1941. Photo from Author's collection.

another family. This time I was with a very old lady who was a widow and I was to be her companion as by now I was ten years old. The house was very large, cold and stark! But it looked like a palace to me, She was a loveable old lady and I called her Aunt Hetty, she was very kind to me and I really loved her, a very special lady. Aunt Hetty had a married daughter of her own who at the time lived with her husband who was a Royal Naval Officer in Fareham, Hampshire, where he was based. There was also another foster daughter living with Aunt Hetty and me with her husband and two sons. They had the downstairs flat and the boys looked on me as their big sister as one was four years old and the other only eighteen months old. For some reason the foster daughter did not like me and deeply resented me being there, and on reflection she did not appear to like her own children either, or have time for them. It was made clear that children of all ages should be seen and not heard! Aunt Hetty, bless her, was a dear. In 1948 there was no television so the wireless provided for our recreation time. When a dance orchestra would play on the wireless Aunt

196

Hetty would teach me how to dance, she also taught me how to sew and knit.

In the mornings I would fetch the coal, clean the fireplace and prepare the coal fire for Aunt Hetty and light it before going to school, I would make sure there was enough coal to last until I returned home. I would often do the shopping for her, as I knew she could not manage all these tasks herself, I did not mind as I enjoyed doing things for her. The foster daughter who disliked me would often make trouble for me and I was always on tenterhooks. On Sundays after we had our roast dinner, we would sit by the fire. One particular Sunday the foster daughter appeared and seeing me sitting by the fire demanded that I go at once to help her in the kitchen, this meant I would end up doing all her pots and pans. Aunt Hetty never said very much as she hated arguments and preferred a quiet life. This happened weekly and I deeply resented being used as a dog's body but kept my peace for Aunt Hetty's sake. She would often visit her own daughter in Fareham from time to time and stay for a short while; I would dread these times as the foster daughter took full advantage of her absence.

With the foster daughter in charge life changed! When home from school I would do all the chores, polish floor lino on my hands and knees, clean the runners on the staircase, dust and polish the furniture. Once she promised me that if I did the work for her she would buy me a bicycle, of course I did the work with more enthusiasm! However in my childish innocence I was not to know it was a false promise, I never did get the bike and to this day I have not ridden one. Meal times were very strict as she would have a boiling stick (used to take out clothes from the hot water in the clothes boiler) on the table, and should we speak or make a noise, or I started the giggles, bang! Down would come the stick on the table to frighten us, and I would have to pick up my meal, leave the table and go outside to the outhouse to finish my food, and should her own two children cry she would stuff a dish cloth in their mouths so no one would hear them crying. I would sit on the stairs and often felt the urge to commit suicide as I felt nobody wanted me. Even when the foster daughter made buns she would pass a couple to Aunt Hetty and said "Eat them yourself and don't give that little pig any." Aunt Hetty saw this happening so she would make a pot of tea and tell me we will have a bun each but I would say no, you have it, but bless her she never did, she believed in sharing. When her own daughter visited on holiday I found her to be a lovely person and I immediately took to her. Her visit was to have a pleasant surprise for me, as on the Sunday as I went to clean upstairs as I normally did, she enquired as to what I was doing and when she saw me actually doing the work asked me to explain why. I told her it was my duties set out by the foster daughter, this angered her and she immediately accosted the foster daughter and I was sent upstairs out of the way so I knew a heated argument was in the air. She admonished the foster daughter and I heard her say "How dare you use Margaret as a skivvy, in future you will clean your own part of the house." Furthermore she stated "It's time for you to find somewhere else to live". Aunt Hetty's son-in-law was retiring from the Royal Navy and that meant that they both intended to live in the house, which rightfully belonged to her mother.

At last the foster daughter who had been a martinet in the home, and her family, moved out. Now I was approaching the age of fifteen and my life became more pleasant as it was wonderful living with Aunt Hetty, with no one else to dictate to me. My thoughts turned to what job I would like to do when I started work, as my age meant that I would leave school at sixteen. I wanted to be a shop assistant but Aunt Hetty would have none of it, you will learn a trade she stated, so I became a seamstress. My wages were £2.50 a week out of which I paid Aunt Hetty my keep, and also each week I would buy her a little present.

Content with my lot I was settled and orderly then suddenly without warning my biological mother entered my life. She wanted to see me and asked the Social Services to arrange a visit. My mind was in a turmoil. Why, I asked myself, when she had not even bothered with my existence before. I often asked Aunt Hetty why she had not adopted me and she would say I was not allowed to do so dear because you have a biological mother so adoption was not possible, so for a while the matter was temporarily laid to rest. Eventually a social worker contacted Aunt Hetty with the news that my real mother had married and wished to see me.

I was now sixteen and had commenced work so I pleaded with Aunt Hetty saying, "Please, I do not want to meet her or know her." However, I arrived home from work one day to find my biological mother and her husband waiting for me in the sitting room. My heart missed a beat as I was so happy working and my life was good, now because I was earning a little wage my real mother was suddenly interested in my welfare even though there had been no contact all those years before. The upshot of their visit was that I left Aunt Hetty's and went to live with my mother and stepfather as you did as you were told in those days and respected your elders. In fairness my mother tried to make me comfortable but as it was only a small flat there was not much room and I was not very happy about the move. The flat was also situated in a run down area that was not very nice. Everyone who knew me noticed my unrest as I could not adapt to my new life and in an attempt to pacify me my mother introduced me to a male cousin who was a few years older than me, he took a shine to me and began to come to my mother's home for meals. He became my only friend so we started to date and walk out together, he would take me to the pictures and all seemed well.

As we drew closer my mother became angry and upset and gave me a very hard time; it had not been intended for us to become a courting couple. Angry words would be exchanged, as she became frustrated at our friendship that she resorted to tactics that were unpleasant. She would search my handbag, go through my personal drawers, and try to stop me from seeing my cousin, I was now seventeen years old and I wanted my own life. I made the decision to leave her and the flat where I was unhappy, I knew I could not go back to Aunt Hetty as her daughter and son-in-law were living with her now that he had retired from the Royal Navy. Making the bold move I took up residence in the Young Christian Association Hostel. My cousin asked me to marry him which I did and we managed to get a flat and settled to married life together. Alas this never worked out as I would come home from work and give him my wages when he came home thinking this is what I had to do, and he in turn would give me back a little money to pay my bus fare and to buy my meals. His hobby was the Territorial Army of which he was a member. When he came home he would expect me to be in bed waiting for him and if not he would beat me with his fists and he would rape me, it was not love, for him it was a marriage of convenience.

I felt trapped as he was not the same man who courted me and my world rapidly became a nightmare, what could I do? One day I plucked up courage and went to see Aunt Hetty as she was the only person I could turn to. Straight away she could see from my appearance that something was wrong and I blurted out the whole sorry story. Dear Aunt Hetty told me to pack my bags and come back to live with her, her daughter and son-in-law said they would manage somehow. So here I was back again in the house where I was happiest! Eventually I obtained my divorce on the ground of desertion after living in hell with him for two years. Once more I was with the people I understood and loved and whom I know loved me. I lost Aunt Hetty in 1958 and it was a very sad time, but I continued to live there with her daughter and husband and I now called them Mum and Dad, and as far as anyone else was concerned were my Mum and Dad! And that is how I looked upon them for the rest of my life.

I met my present husband forty years ago back in the late 1950's; he was a sailor in the Royal Navy. When we married we lived upstairs in the same house as my surrogate Mum and Dad. I had my first child there, a lovely son, and Mum and Dad adored him so he naturally called them Nanny and Granddad and I was so proud, at least my son would have all the love and not be unwanted. When my second son was born my husband and I decided that it was best to set up house ourselves, so we bought a small house within walking distance of Mum and Dad's home. My third son came along and I was now very happy and contented as we were a real family. With three children we knew we needed a larger house so invested in a new home with plenty of room, again in the same road as my surrogate family. Now my life was complete, a loving husband, three lovely children and my Mum and Dad had three wonderful grandchildren! I thank the lord for changing my luck from childhood misery to happiness and for the second marriage after the cruel first failure. Sadly my Mum and Dad died and for a while it left me with an empty feeling, I wish they were still alive today, however, life must go on.

Our children have long since moved out to lead their own lives, spread out far and wide. Now we have three lovely grandchildren and I give them all the love and affection I can lavish on them. Each one is treated the same and I will always be there for them. I will not let them be denied the love that I never had: to this day I remain deeply hurt by the rejection of my blood kin. To say it is forgotten is wrong because it is always there deep in my heart, but I have cast out the bitterness and have learned to live for today with my very loving family.

CHAPTER TWENTY-FOUR

ONE OF THE LITTLE SINNERS by Pat Roberts (Nee Richards)

My name was Pat Richards and I was born on the 15 March 1930. I had a brother David and a stepsister Eunice Webb. On May 15 1933 my father asked to appear before the Public Assistance Committee with a view to having his three children admitted into care under the Scattered Homes. This included myself aged three, my brother David who was five and my stepsister Eunice who was eight. His offer of 12 shillings per week towards our keep was accepted. My father had been in the Army during the First World War and had been heavily gassed which made him an invalid and he was unable to work, and as our mother was seriously ill he could not cope with three children and a sick wife.

The order to admit the three of us was given on 16 May and on the 18 May we entered Ford House. I was immediately transferred to the City Hospital and my mother was taken to Mount Gould Hospital suffering from tuberculosis where she died on 15 July 1933 aged 31 years. David and Eunice were transferred to the Scattered Homes and on June 15 1933 I was admitted into Stoke House. My father had tried to have us transferred to a Church of England School in London but there was a mix up between the Education Department and the Public Assistance Board so it never materialised. In January 1939 I was in 13 Hill Park Crescent, North Hill, Plymouth which was a Scattered Home for girls and David was in 80 Mount Gould Road, Plymouth, Scattered Home for boys. In April 1939 I was again transferred back to Stoke House. My stepsister Eunice, who had reached the age of fourteen, was boarded out under a charity trustees beneficiary. Both David and myself were evacuated to the New Inn, Clovelly, North Devon in April 1941.

My brother David did not stay long in Clovelly, as he had to leave at the age of fourteen to start work, and I did not get to see him again until he was a man and even then only briefly. Before the bad raids on Plymouth in March/April 1941 a group of girls decided to abscond from Stoke House because of the awful treatment we were receiving at the hands of the staff.

201

Our punishment was often unpleasant, with the bombings naturally we were scared, and sometimes children wet the bed. If a child did this he/she was made to stand up with their wet sheets around them in front of everyone and so they were shamed. Some children who were alone or abandoned and who felt so rejected reacted in this way, and if the bed wetting continued their mattress would be taken away and they would have to sleep on the bed springs. One girl who constantly wet the bed suffered with a weak bladder and she could not help her weakness, poor girl, and was always being punished! Any child unfortunate to soil themselves were stood in a bath of Jeyes disinfectant and water and scrubbed down with a very hard brush until their bottoms were blood red. The Matron had a nasty habit of wearing a metal thimble on her finger and if for some reason she caught you talking when you shouldn't be, there would be a painful flick behind your ear. There was often periods of time when we would have to have a "Vow of Silence" no matter what you were doing, from cleaning, to waiting for the meal, or even sitting on the bathroom floor waiting for your turn to be bathed. Seen and not heard was Miss Holden's motto; she was the Superintendent of all the Scattered Homes and Stoke House.

Sometimes, like all children, there was food that was not particularly liked, and if a child refused the food they would pinch your nose and force the food into the mouth, shovelling it in until the child urged or cried out. Children could never have an opinion and no matter how polite they tried to be, if they disputed an instruction or retorted a very soapy flannel was pushed into the mouth or mustard was spread on the tongue. We were always spoken of as the little sinners! I actually witnessed a girl having a pillow placed over her face with a member of staff sitting on it to stop her from screaming. I was so upset, but I could do nothing, as self-preservation was the order of the day. Two girls were taken down to the dreaded cellars when they had been naughty, and cold water was then thrown over them while still in their night-clothes. Of course children were naughty sometimes and discipline is a matter of course when growing up, but this was downright cruelty.

We never knew about nice food like pasties, biscuits, buns and cakes, even though the cook would bake plenty for the staff. One of the tricks played with our food was to melt the margarine (we never saw butter) to spread on our bread, this would leave ample for the staff to take home to their families.

The milk used to be slowly scalded and set overnight so that in the morning beautiful fresh cream settled on the top, this was then eaten by the staff. The food we were given was often very stodgy but filling, we would scoff any food because we were always hungry. In those days eating between meals was not allowed. Mealtimes were 8 am for breakfast, 12-noon dinner, and 4 o'clock tea. If a child was punished by being sent to bed early, without tea, this meant going without food for 16 hours, a long time and sheer agony for a child.

Regularly we would be given Epson Salts in a cup of tea to keep our bowels clear. Iodine was freely applied to all cuts and grazes, which made one grip tight with the awful stinging. If a child complained of not feeling well the staff would say "You have got the devil on your shoulder" this used to frighten me into submission, and with that you were left to cope with it! At the end of the day when it was bedtime we used to pray, I deeply resented it when they asked me to include them in my prayers! Especially when they had been cruel to us. We all used to chant in unison whilst we knelt by our dormitory beds "God Bless Miss Holden, Nurse Penna, Miss Penna and the cook Miss Beatrice Thompson. Now in my later years, I do realise that everyone is entitled to be blessed, but at the same time they should be willing to repent. At the time they did not understand the meaning of the word. They had missed an important quote in the bible "Suffer little children to come unto me"!

My worst experience was in 1937 when I fell over and broke my leg, the pain was terrible. Naturally I screamed and screamed and one of the staff came out saying, "Stop that screaming girl! Get up and stop playing around!" Meanwhile my leg had started to swell and a member of staff suggested that I put it in cold water, so I did so in a desperate attempt to ease the pain, then they suggested I try hot water. They did not seem to grasp the seriousness of the situation, and I again cried out in sheer pain. The Matron demanded to see the child creating so much noise with the intention of chastising me, but by then I did not care because no one understood the pain I was in. I was only seven years old and a child wants love and comforting in that situation. Still nothing was done, and I had to hop around as best as I could, you can imagine how awful I felt. I would cry out at every hop and in anger the Matron sent me to bed immediately for punishment for not keeping quiet. I could not believe it when she said to me "If you are still limping around in the morning, I shall see to it that you will have something to limp for!" During the night the pain was so bad I just cried begging for help, this resulted in me waking the other girls in the dormitory and the senior girl went to fetch Nurse Penna.

At first she was angry at being disturbed in the night, but when she saw the state of my leg she realised something was terribly wrong. Thank God she notified the doctor without informing Matron so I could get it seen to properly. Even then the doctor would not come until the morning and every minute was excruciating. On examination he did not hesitate, I was immediately taken to hospital to have my leg set in plaster, I think they were worried about a possible deformity with the delay in treatment, but by the grace of God and time my leg healed. To this day I have not forgiven Miss Holden.

There would be the annual Lord Mayor's visit to the Childrens' Home at Stoke House when the staff would all put on their starched uniforms. We were all well rehearsed in our replies to any question raised by the Lord Mayor, and clear instructions received as to what the outcome would be if we failed to reply in the manner expected! The Lord Mayor spoke, "Hello children are you happy?" "Yes Lord Mayor" in chorus was the reply. He would then note the lovely spread of food on the table (so did we!) and he said "Children you will enjoy eating this". "Yes Lord Mayor" we again replied in unison. As soon as he said goodbye and had left the building all the children were ushered out into the garden to walk around the massive lawn. Meanwhile the staff had cleared away all the food; it had been equally divided between the staff! You can imagine how we children felt, once again we had been punished for being a nobody's child. As for entertainment we had to make our own as we had no toys. We would read, cut out paper dolls, or act out little plays amongst ourselves.

The older girls were detailed duties such as cleaning the younger children's shoes, woe betide anyone forgetting the heels! Once I was detailed to clean all the shoes, about 25 pairs. I wanted to do them quickly as I had been reading a book and I wanted to get back to it. Unfortunately, I skipped some of the heels and I had them all thrown at me and made to clean them all again and my book was confiscated. Cleaning all the fireplaces in the staff rooms and polishing the dormitories was another task we undertook. It was a very hard life! The older girls completed all their tasks before they were allowed to retire for the night. Other duties included putting the hot water bottles in the staff beds late in the evening. The children were also responsible for washing all the dishes including the staff dishes. It has often made me think why did they need the staff? Stoke House employed cleaners but I am still not sure what their duties were. We always had to take up the morning cup of tea to the staff in their bedrooms. Fed up with the treatment I decided to run away with some of the other girls. Most of the girls knew of our planned escape and saved their slice of bread and margarine so that we would have something to eat on our journey. A couple of girls took some clean pillowslips from the linen cupboard, unfortunately they opted to take them to the pawnshop to sell in exchange for money. The oldest girl Gwen Tyrell told the pawnbroker that she was the mother of the other three girls, how about that for enterprise? Of course he did not believe her, so the girls quickly left the shop.

Meanwhile the Stoke House Staff now aware of their absence were in a state of panic, already under suspicion of cruelty and abuse they did not want the authorities to know, so in hope they ordered the gardener to search for them on his bicycle. Any enquiry into the girls running away would have been an embarrassment for the Matron and Staff. It is to be said not all the staff were cruel, but it is to be noted that employment in the 1930's and early 1940's was precious and staff who wished to retain their posts kept a still tongue. Children in those days were seen but not heard! The children were missing for four hours, it was the gardener Mr Scott who found them, he was a very nice man and kind to the children in many ways. He found them on Stonehouse Bridge feeding the swans with the bread that the other girls had saved for them! One of the girls Betty Newham was so afraid of a beating she told the staff that she would tell her relative on the next visiting day. In fact she did inform her aunt about the constant beatings and the running away episode, and the aunt immediately went to the authorities. However the raids became so severe that the inquiry was shelved and the terrible firebombing occurred in April 1941 which finally led to the children being evacuated to the little fishing village of Clovelly, North Devon.

At the start of the early raids on Plymouth we had been trained to take up our positions in the air raid shelters and we would amuse ourselves by singing or crocheting odd balls of wool into a big square and then unravelling it to start again. The one thing we all looked forward to without letting the staff see, was when the candles in the shelter melted down to overspill the remnants of wax, we would pop this into our mouths to chew like gum. There was a time when there was a really bad air raid and you could hear the constant whistling of the bombs as they hurtled down from the German planes. The Matron Miss M Holden, shared our shelter cubicle and each time the whistling started she would bow her head and clasp her hands together saying "Our Father, which art in heaven," and to me this seemed as far as she could recite, so when the next bomb fell and she repeated the performance of only quoting the first line of the Lord's Prayer about a dozen times, I thought that perhaps she did not know the rest and I wondered if she would appreciate a reminder. I leaned over and said, "Hallowed be thy name" which made her very angry and she gave me a stinging slap across the face and told me not to be so rude! It was only through my later years that I realised what was happening. Miss Holden was I think on the verge of another nervous breakdown. Many times since those childhood days when I have had occasion to quote the Lord's Prayer, I have been tempted to hesitate at the end of the first line.

March/April1941 was the start of the severe raids on Plymouth and during one of these terrible raids in April 1941 some incendiaries fell on the childrens' home setting alight the top floor. We were already assembled in the stairwell passage in case of just such an emergency. The local fireman advised the staff to take the children and leave. The fireman escorted the little band of frightened children down the road to the Royal Dockyard Orphanage in Albert Road, Stoke, to sleep on the floors until the next morning. The next day we walked to the Devonport High School for Girls at Montpelier, Peverell, Plymouth, where we were temporarily billeted. On the 28 April 1941 the school took four direct hits from parachute landmines and part of the building collapsed. Some children were buried under the rubble and frantic efforts by civil defence workers and servicemen on leave to dig them out alive succeeded.

By now the order at last had been issued by Winston Churchill to evacuate as many children as possible because Plymouth was now designated as a dangerous area. Lady Nancy Astor was a great friend of the Hon Betty Asquith who lived at Clovelly Court; Lady Astor would frequently visit Clovelly to work quietly on her parliamentary notes and to play tennis. A telephone call to her friend asking for help with the Stoke House children resulted in the evacuation on 30 April 1941 to the New Inn, Clovelly, North Devon, and needless to say Lady Astor is forever in our hearts. The girls were billeted in the New Inn itself under the care of Nurse Penna and Miss Holly Penna. Miss Holden was the Superintendent in charge, and Miss B J Henderson looked after the boys in the annexe. All the children attended either the infants' school under Marian Blann or Barbara Cruse, and the older children went to the Clovelly County School in Wrinkleberry Lane. The Clovelly village and its close community lifestyle proved for us to be a blessing from heaven. The discipline was still very strict to begin with, and as the villagers became aware of our strict routine, a few dropped hints to staff by villagers and teachers brought a rapid response, and our restriction was alleviated, Every person attended church regularly; this meant all children and staff. Our favourite walks were the Gallantry Bower, the cornfields and collecting kindling wood and logs from the Hobby Drive; these were for the huge fireplaces in the New Inn.

One of the highlights was the visit to the cottage of the famous reader of stage monologues Nosmo King; he and his wife very kindly invited some of us for tea with them. Also the visit of Lady Astor from Plymouth whom we entertained with our singing and attempts at drama. After the war the orphanage returned to Plymouth and took up residency at the Astor Hall, Trafalgar Road, in Stoke. When we finally went to Clovelly, which to me was a place of my dreams, it was the beginning of a new era and I shall only ever relive my childhood there and push the Dickensian life of Stoke House forever to the back of my mind! Every thing about Clovelly was made perfect in comparison to our life in Stoke House with the kindness shown to us all by the villagers. This was the first time we had experienced freedom and being allowed to mix with the public and to walk freely to and from school. The teaching staff were firm but caring and my favourite teacher was Miss Pamela Williams (now Mrs P Pearce) bless her heart. I can remember her giving me a couple of her dresses and I felt like a queen. Goodness knows what they looked like on me because I was a very skinny girl, but I did not care because this was the best thing that had ever happened to me. This has been in my memory all those years, as I remember the bad things I can also remember the special ones. Let me say now, thank you Miss Williams! To end my recollections I must confess to some naughtiness I indulged in. One particularly comes to mind, when I became one of the senior girls and had to take my turn at early morning and late night duties with another girl this is what we did. We would go to the pantry where the cream was kept and fill a cup with it and sneak into the hallowed room belonging to the matron, (she was home in Plymouth on leave) sit in her arm chairs and gorge without any thought of being caught! We would then pour ourselves a cup of tea with spoonfuls of sugar, (we hardly saw sugar) and revelled in the luxury! Lovely Grub!

The most daring thing I ever undertook was to climb out of a window in the New Inn one evening to meet and kiss my childhood sweetheart goodbye, as he was leaving being a London evacuee and was returning home. I had a crush on him and I had to say goodbye so I would have taken any risk to do so. On reflection, I dread to think what my punishment would have been if I were caught, the kiss was innocent and lasted only a few seconds. His name was Dick Richards and he was a handsome looking lad. Sadly I heard that Dick had died at a very early age of 35 years. Ah! Those halcyon days of long ago. I arrived in Clovelly in 1941 and left in 1944 at the age of fourteen to start work. When I left the Childrens' Home I was told if you say anything about your life in the Orphanage you will be brought back! They knew this was wrong but whom could I turn to? I was so pleased to be free I was only too glad to keep quiet. I had always wanted to work with children so my first job was in the Doctor's Barnardo home at Kingsbridge in South Devon as a nursery nurse. This was a receiving home for children with medical problems. The main illness was rickets, and there were some very sad cases, it was fairly well known in that period of time. However, I was waiting for the first nursery-nursing course to start in Plymouth in which I was lucky enough to be accepted.

On successfully doing the two-year course and passing the examination I then went on to become a nanny with the National Nursery Examination Board qualification. I was so proud! I married Harry Roberts in 1954 when he was in the Air Force and we had eight children, four sons and four daughters, we both loved children. However, the memories of Stoke House were always in my mind, and I made Harry promise me if ever anything happened to me when each baby was due, on no account would he put them in a childrens' home, this was my worst fear. Thank goodness by the grace of God we survived to be good parents. I was deeply saddened to lose my stepsister Eunice in 1996. I was excited to see photographs of myself outside Stoke House and in Clovelly, these photographs had never been seen by the children, and it took fifty-seven years to bring them to light, and I have the author of this book to thank for that thrill.

CHAPTER TWENTY-FIVE

THE LAUGHING BOY by Ronald Stansbury

I am the lad laughing standing on the very end of the row right taken in Clovelly 1943. Photo courtesy of Miss Veronica Norman Plymouth.

My name is Ron Stansbury and I was orphaned at a very early age. I was born in Greenbank Nursing Home on 11 August 1929 where I stayed until I was three years old. My mother was called Rose Stansbury, and through the Author who did my research for me I have since found out that I had a brother David Stansbury but I have never met him. I wish I knew many years ago that I had a brother, as it would have been so nice to have other kin living. I was informed by the welfare in 1998 that he too had been in the Scattered Homes.

When I reached the age of three I was put into Stoke House and remained under their care for the whole of my childhood. I remembered being punished frequently, sometimes for no reason at all, depending on the mood of the disciplinarian. Trying to knock the spirit out of us no doubt. I took comfort in coping with it by laughing, so they would put me in a dark cupboard on bread and water. At times I was so hungry! I remember the bombing air raids on Stoke House Plymouth, seeing it on fire and bombs still dropping all around. There were fifty girls and boys and as we had nowhere to sleep it was decided to send us to other accommodation for that night. The next day we walked to Montpelier School, Peverell, which had been converted temporarily into an emergency rest centre.

We were only there two nights when we were bombed again and there were casualties from this. Terrified children were wondering what was happening and next we found ourselves being transported away from Plymouth. All we knew was that we were going to a village for safety. The bus drivers faced a fearful journey to begin with, for as they were taking us through Plymouth to join the road to North Devon, bombs were still falling around us and the two buses, one with the girls and one with the boys. The drivers ran the gauntlet of fire, shrapnel and bombs, and one bomb burst in an area close by our bus, the driver was slightly wounded. He refused to stop and continued the journey; those bus drivers were heroes to get us through that nightmare!

When we arrived in Clovelly, the girls were billeted in the New Inn and the boys in the Annexe, it was awfully crowded, and we were packed like sardines in a tin. I remember the school at the top of Wrinkleberry Lane; life was much more relaxed than at Stoke House, we still had to be careful though as Mr Hesketh the Head Master of the school was a tartar with the cane! I do not dispute that I was a mischievous boy so I was often on the carpet. We would work hard in helping on the gardens and allotments, as digging for victory meant Clovelly had to grow a lot more vegetables now there were so many children to feed. We would help out on the farm as well and I used to help to deliver coal and logs on the wooden sledges, they used to slide down the cobbled stones in the village. I did not mind as I would receive a little tip and for me that was super, I would get sixpence or if I was really lucky one shilling! Another task I assisted in was helping the old chap who used to stoke the boilers in the New Inn Hotel.

I left school at 14 years old but still stayed in Clovelly doing whatever job I was detailed to do. Then, when I was fifteen I was sent back to Plymouth to find work, I had no idea what to do as the people in charge of me had not taught me about life and kept us ignorant of the outside world, my goodness I soon learnt though, I knew I had to survive somehow! I took up accommodation with two elderly sisters at Peverell, Plymouth, then when I was sixteen started an apprentice course with Pearn Brothers in Gibbon Street, Plymouth. My work was soon to be interrupted with the advent of National Service 1947-1949. I was stationed with the 1st Battalion Royal Hampshire Regiment and reported to Devizes Basic Training Camp for six weeks training then moved down to Bulford Camp, Salisbury Plain.

When I had completed my basic training I was sent to a transit camp in Austria, then on to Hamburg Docks on the "Blue Sleeper from Trieste", and onward to the Hook of Holland. I found myself caught up with the cold war and was posted where International "Zone" Guards operated. There were

British, American, and French, and we were constantly on border patrol where Russian and German servicemen was stationed. I completed my National Service in 1949 and was demobbed, but was told to hold myself in reserve if required. I returned to my trade and everything was fine.

I courted a young lady called Jean and quite soon we were married. Just as I had settled again, the Army recalled me for emergency training service with the 1st Battalion the Devonshire Regiment, and I found myself stationed at Topsham Barracks, Exeter, Devon. This time I had to undertake training in tropical gear and was packed off to Nairobi, Africa, as there was trouble with the Mau-Mau in Kenya. Civilians were being slaughtered and the Devons were given the task of bringing it under control. I served fifteen months there, had four weeks leave, then back to England. I was so pleased when we landed and my wife was glad I was home again. I returned to my post again after leave, but this time I was sent to Germany, I completed my time and left the Army in 1956. I carried on with my trade as painter and decorator and did thirty-five years before retiring in 1985.

I never forgot Clovelly, and in the late 1950's I took my wife there as we were visiting friends nearby, she loved it and understood my love for the village. I promised myself I would go again but life does not always allow the best-laid plans to happen. I lost my wife in 1980 with liver cancer and missed her very much. The old house where I live was empty without her but I have kept it going with my son Ron who lives with me as he was made redundant, and between us we do the decorating. I also have a married daughter and three lovely grandchildren, who have me wrapped around their fingers, so I look on the bright side of life to compensate for the love I missed out on not having a normal childhood. In April 1998 I was privileged to return to Clovelly on a reunion with some of the ex-Stoke House folk who were by now as elderly as myself, and it was indeed an unforgettable experience.

Taken in 1998 outside my family's home in Plymouth Devon. Photo from private collection.

Having my cup of tea at Clovelly School 1998. We had had a lovely dinner with the school pupils.

At the reunion in Clovelly 1998 tucking in to the lovely buffet given by the Clovelly villagers and ex-evacuees. Photo courtesy of Miss Veronica Norman Plymouth.

CHAPTER TWENTY-SIX

THE INFANT TEACHER STOKE HOUSE
Marian Godden (Nee Blann)

I was known as Marian Blann and was born in Plymouth in 1916 during the First World War, and spent all my childhood in Plymouth. I lived at Garden Street, Devonport. My mother was always at home in her full time job as a housewife and my father worked in the Dockyard. I had always wanted to be a teacher so I studied hard and did my teacher's training at St Mary's College, Cheltenham. After qualifying I did supply work, filling in for teachers who were sick or on leave. My posts were mainly in Devonport, Plymouth. When the Second World War broke out, all the schools were closed and I was immediately sent to Stoke House Childrens' home in view of the number of children living there, to teach in the nursery class which was for infants between the ages of three and five. I taught the under fives before they went to a proper school; my nursery class consisted of a dozen of them, boys and girls. The youngest ones attended College Road School, near St Levan's Road, which is where I taught them; the Headmistress at the time was a Miss Gilbert. The older children went to Somerset Place School.

Stoke House was a very big house in a large garden in which there stood a large mulberry tree. I remember gathering the mulberries so that my mother could make a fruit pie. During a visit of the King to Plymouth I remember asking the Matron of the Home, Miss Holden, if she would allow me to take the children to see him when he was passing through Devonport as I thought it would be a nice treat for children who were not normally allowed to mix with the outside world. Permission was given provided I accepted full responsibility; with little ones this would be quite a task. However, I remember sitting on the garden wall at Stoke House with the children on either side, tied to me with skipping ropes, holding them with a firm grip in case

Marion Blann on the beach Clovelly summertime 1941. Note how busy the knitters are. Left to Right. Margaret Ray (obscured) David Dunbar (blond curly hair boy) Marion Blann (Infant Teacher) Barbara Goldstein (baby girl) & last girl Violet Ray.

they fell off the wall. Although it was so many years ago I can still remember some of their names. I recall a Margaret Bailey, Barbara Goldstein, Betty Bennett, Violet Ray, Jean McFadyen, Muriel Gray, Douglas Scribley, David Dunbar, and the brothers Jimmy and Phillip Ray. On occasion, with permission, I would take six or seven of the older girls on a boat trip to Turnchapel and we would walk along the cliffs. They were thrilled, as they did not get out very often at Stoke House. After the walk I used to take them to my Aunt and Uncle who lived on the Barbican for tea; my Aunt was a dear lady to entertain six or seven orphans. I wonder if any of the girls still remember!

After the destruction of the home from the terrible fire bombing in April 1941 I was transferred to Clovelly, a little village in North Devon. I lived on the famous cobbles at Providence House joining Mr and Mrs Scott; he had been the gardener at Stoke House. Shortly afterwards Pamela Williams, another teacher from Plymouth, arrived. Teaching the infants in Clovelly took place in the "Wendy House" at the top of the New Inn. The Plymouth Authorities had commandeered the Inn, although the bar remained open. One memory is still strong in my mind: I recall Mr Scott presenting me with a couple of rabbits (unskinned and unwrapped) when I made my first visit to my future in-laws on Merseyside. How he laughed at my squeamish response! My time in Clovelly was very happy and I often look back with nostalgia remembering those far off years. An occasional highlight would be a local "hop" at which members of the RAF from Hartland Point would attend. Local dances were a very welcome source of entertainment during the war years. Having acquired a puppy I used to spend a lot of time walking along the cliffs to Mouth Mills and along the Hobby Drive. I used to take the children down to the beach to play in my spare time, where they would spend happy hours playing with the pebbles and searching under each stone for crabs. I would often take my knitting with me, as I had to teach the girls how to knit. (Insert photo here of Marion on the beach with children) The other teacher from Plymouth Pam Williams, and I would also spend a lot of time on the beach or walking the coastline depending on the weather.

I was recalled to Plymouth, at Easter 1942, to ease the teacher shortage, as the worst of the bombing raids were then over. Although my stay was short those years bring fond memories to the fore. Upon recall to Plymouth I lived

Married to Arthur Godden this photo was taken at Formby in August 1944. Photo from Authors collection by kind permission Mr & Mrs A Godden (nee Blann) Grange-Over- Sands Cumbria.

in a flat in Beaumont Road with my parents. They had moved there following the destruction of their home in Devonport during the awful blitz. All the local schools were full to capacity and the Education Authority took over space in the Community Centre in Lanhydrock Park: this was quite close to my parents' flat. I taught there until my marriage in August 1944 when the Education Authority stopped half a day's pay when I had time off to get married! I married Arthur Godden a Merseyside man who was serving in the Royal Navy. It was love at first sight and we have been happily married for many years. We had one son and one daughter and now we have one grandchild. At the end of the war we moved north to Formby, near Liverpool, where Arthur resumed his post in a major insurance office. I took up teaching at a private school for a short while before going on to teach in Liverpool until my retirement in 1980, after which I undertook voluntary work at a local hospital for mentally handicapped children. In the end we retired to Cumbria.

The war years were very traumatic; however, it did unite the people in one common cause and taught us the importance of trust and peace. It brought together citizens of every class and changed the whole structure of life for all time, I trust there will never be another World War.

Marion Godden (nee Blann) & Arthur Godden 1998. Photo courtesy Mr Arthur Godden Grange-Over- Sands Cumbria.

Marion Blann with her son and Grandaughter 1998. Photo courtesy Mr Arthur Godden Grange-Over- Sands Cumbria.

CHAPTER TWENTY-SEVEN

MEMORIES OF CLOVELLY 1941-1945
Pamela Pearce (nee Williams)

THE JUNIOR CLASS TEACHER

Spring 1941 was the period of the heaviest air raids on Plymouth and an eventful time in my life. The raids were almost nightly in February and my Mother died after three months illness. In March our house was so severely damaged that we were forced to leave it, and in the same week the school, St Stephen's in Devonport, where I had recently started my teaching career, was partially destroyed by high explosives and incendiary bombs, and the children dispersed to other schools. Up to this time Plymouth had no evacuation plans as it was thought an "unlikely target!" However plans were quickly drawn up and put into effect in April with thousands of children being moved into the relative safety of Devon and Cornwall. Meanwhile I had been allocated to duties at an emergency feeding centre in Ker Street, Devonport. This was an unforgettable experience offering initial food, shelter and some comfort day after day to distressed men, women and children, survivors of a night's bombing during which many lost not only their homes, but also friends and family. With our house uninhabitable my Father, sister and I found temporary accommodation on a farm at Bere Alston, so I made the daily journey between the devastation of the city, and the primrose covered fields and hedges at the farm.

Then in May I was directed to go to Clovelly as the teacher in charge of junior children from Stoke House Childrens' home which had been destroyed by fire. I arrived in Clovelly in the late afternoon of a beautiful day and shall never forget the incredible view from the top of the village, the trees of the Hobby Drive, the roofs of the steeply sloping village and the expanse of shining blue sea, stretching across to the golden sands of Saunton. Accommodation had been arranged for me and the accompanying Infant Teacher, Marian Blann, at Providence Cottage a few doors down from The New Inn where the children were installed. Marian and I were well taken care of by Mr and Mrs Scott who were part of the Stoke House staff.

Taken in Clovelly 1941. On the left with dog Miss Pamela Williams, a popular schoolteacher from Plymouth. On the right Miss Joan Henderson who was the nurse in charge of all the Stoke House boys in the annexe of the New Inn. Miss Henderson was well liked by the boys of Stoke House. Photo courtesy of Doctor Robert Crowte MBA PhD Barnt Green Worcestershire. (Joan Henderson's son).

I remember meeting the Matron, Miss Holden, Nurse Penna, Joan Henderson and others, whose names escape me, at the New Inn. And, of course, the children, who struck me as extraordinarily resilient considering the terrifying experiences they had just come through, plus total bewilderment at their new surroundings. Yet they soon coped well and cheerfully with this huge change in their lives - helped as well by the warmth and kindness of the Clovelly people, accepting yet another influx of evacuees. As I grew to know them all, I got the impression, that while discipline was strict, there was also kindness and affection between staff and children.

School was a bit of a shock, such a small building to accommodate so many children, evacuees from London and Bristol as well us from Plymouth. The London and Bristol children were all billeted in residents' homes around the village, some more happily than others. Clovelly School, Wrinkleberry, high above the village, reached by a steep and winding footpath, or a long detour round the road, was now being asked to accommodate over two hundred children - in contrast to the twenty-five or thirty normally on the roll. One hundred and sixty had come from London in 1940, forty from Bristol in February 1941 and now fifty from Plymouth. The youngest group was now using St Peter's Chapel down in the village, and some of the eldest were taught in a converted coach house in the Rectory grounds. The school building itself consisted of two small classrooms and the hall. By the use of curtains strung on wires across the hall, three classes were taught side by side - very closely, with the other two lucky classes having a very overcrowded room each. Mr R K Hesketh was the Headmaster, the other teachers being: Barbara Cruse, the only Clovelly teacher, she was young, jolly and musical, we got on really well, Mr Bamsey (Peckham); Miss Plaice (Peckham or Deptford); Miss Howell (Bristol); Marian Blann (Plymouth) and myself. Naturally there was a constant hum (at least!) and movement, and the strain of trying to hold the attention of one's own group of thirty to forty children in a confined space within hearing and touching distance of two other classes, was tremendous, making a quiet atmosphere almost impossible to attain. Great patience and tolerance was required and amply demonstrated on both sides and generally worked well. Added to which there was a constant shortage of books, writing materials, paper etc, let alone any facilities for art or craft. Try as we all did, there were undoubtedly periods of much frustration and almost despair. And yes - caning did occur, much as I am sure we afterwards regretted. I know that personally I felt, and after all these years, still do feel a sense of shame and sadness that I share the responsibility for inflicting pain on more than one child in this way and now, for that, however belatedly, I ask forgiveness.

Miss Pamela Williams Teacher from Plymouth enjoying the company of a dog on the Quay Clovelly 1941. Photo courtesy Miss Veronica Norman.

There were good times too, of release from the overcrowded schoolrooms, when we enjoyed after school and weekend walks in the countryside, through the Hobby Drive, through the Park to Gallantry Bower and Mouth Mill beach. To help in the war effort we collected waste paper and scrap metal, knitted balaclavas, wove strips of hessian into camouflage netting, dug for Victory in the school gardens, adults took their turn of duty at the Red Cross post. I had soon found myself in charge of girls' games, which I enjoyed very much, and remember some very energetic and bruising games of shinty, played sometimes on the lawn at Clovelly Court and at other times even more exciting on the loose gravel on the car park. Once or twice a month there would be a whist and 'euchre' drive or social in the school hall. This involved a massive move out of desks etc to clear space for tables and chairs.

At Christmas we went carol singing, again for the Red Cross. I remember one brilliant moonlit night, very cold and still, with the full moon shining a path across the sea, and no other lights showing. We started down on the quay and worked our way up through the village. We were told how lovely the voices sounded to those high up in the village, even the regulars in the Red Lion Pub came out to listen.

In 1941 a wing of Clovelly Court was turned into a Red Cross convalescent home for service men, most of who seemed to be very convalescent. There were many evenings of games, quizzes and entertainments sometimes by the ENSA groups, sometimes by our resident celebrity, Mr Watson, better known as Nosmo King who, with his wife was living in Clovelly. Jack Watson, his son, later a well-known actor on stage and television was a frequent visitor when on leave from the Navy. Sadly in December 1943 a fire seriously damaged the Red Cross wing in Clovelly Court which ended its use. No more convalescent soldiers came after the fire so our social life slumped badly!

After a spell of ill health in the winter of 1942-1943 I was invited to move into 104 High Street Clovelly, the home of Mr and Mrs Lyddon and their daughter Marie. At home at Christmas I had developed measles of all things, and then in the spring had some weeks off with severe anaemia. The doctor advised a move further up the street as the lower houses suffered a lot of damp and complete lack of sun during the winter months. After a very happy stay at 104 where Marie Coote became, and remained, a close friend, I finally moved up to Wrinkleberry and lodged with the Robins family, and regained my usual good health.

Pam Pearce (nee Williams) Teacher from Plymouth tobogganing in the snow Clovelly 1945. Photo courtesy Miss Sheila Ellis Clovelly.

War came closer again when groups of Commandos, some Canadian, were billeted in and near Clovelly, practising cliff climbing in preparation for assaults on the French coast. They were a lively lot who after a days climbing on the cliffs round Gallantry Bower would come rushing down the street, their iron shod boots striking sparks from the cobbles. The training completed, they disappeared. Sadly many of them did not return from the Dieppe raid. United States troops had also begun to make themselves known, one group in particular had a certain Sergeant called 'Art' who seemed able to convince his officer that a fitting end for a route march was near Clovelly school! In August 1944 Barbara Cruse and I put on a combined Physical Exercise and Maypole dancing display on the Clovelly Court lawn.

Then the last winter of my stay provided heavy snow and Sheila Ellis (a Clovelly villager) and I had many a hair-raising sledge ride down from the car park and over Mount Pleasant. A long time ago! So many people I recall, Miss Scott, Miss Woodall, the Cavendish family with whom I kept in touch for many years, Mr and Mrs Ellis with their kindness and their wonderful shop; Mr and Mrs 'J.C.'; The Lameys; The Braunds; Stan Squire; Mrs Burrows; Mrs Jewell at Burscott Farm and of course Mr and Mrs Robins, Freddy and Granny Robins with whom I lodged so happily during the last year of my stay.

By 1944 numbers of evacuees had dwindled considerably, but those of us remaining felt quite settled and war seemed remote. Not all that remote though, when one dark night of rain and thick mist, an RAF Wellington bomber having taken off from Braunton, failed to clear the high ground above the village and crashed in a field not far from the local police station. The noise of impact was incredible, the crater enormous, but security was quickly in place, and few details emerged though plenty of rumours. The winter of 1944-45 was exceptionally cold and Clovelly had its first major fall of snow for many years. Sheila Ellis and I laid our hands on a sledge and had some hair-raising descents on the footpath down from the car park and also in the steep field by the war memorial, great fun! Clovelly! A wonderful

Pam Williams (Plymouth Teacher) and Beatrice Thompson (Cook New Inn for Stoke House children) taken at the Mount Pleasant Peace Park Clovelly 1941. Copy of photograph courtesy Miss Veronica Norman from an original supplied with grateful thanks from Mrs Jean Job (Nee McFadyen) Plymouth. (Niece to Cook).

place - wonderful people! Not least Mrs Betty Asquith who was so kind and generous to us all, I am glad I got to know this North Devon area so well. With the Cavendish family, Marie Coote and Sheila Ellis we cycled many times to Spekes Bay, Hartland Quay and occasionally to Bideford. Looking back on those years I am glad, strangely enough, to have experienced the Plymouth blitz, which brought an end to the first part of my life, and also the contrast of almost four years in such a unique place as Clovelly. I remember the good times we had. I know I grew fond of many of the children and I have learned a lot. I am only sorry I can not remember enough names and faces. I hope some of them too, have happy memories of those very special years.

On my return to Plymouth I taught at Egg Buckland School until my marriage in 1948. My husband was a Civil Servant. We lived at East Portlemouth, near Salcombe and in South Pool for seven years, where my three children were born. Strangely, the two older ones started school in a small village very similar to Clovelly School in Wrinkleberry, two classes, totalling twenty-eight children. What a contrast! In 1959 my husband was promoted in the Civil Service and we moved to Bristol, Avon, and I have spent forty years of my life there. Sadly my husband died in 1987 and my two sons and daughter are settled in different parts of the country, Berkshire, East Anglia and Birmingham. I keep in touch with school affairs thanks to my five wonderful grandchildren.

CHAPTER TWENTY-EIGHT

SOME OF MY WARTIME MEMORIES - Sheila Ellis.

The Ellis & Lyddon Family of Clovelly outside the New Inn Clovelly 1943. From the Left. (Back) John Ellis, (Front) Mrs Gladys Ellis, Sheila Ellis, (Behind Sheila) Mr Paul Ellis, Marie Lyddon, Mrs Florence Lyddon, Mr Albert Lyddon holding "Chips" the Airedale dog. Look at the old blackout curtain in the background! Photo courtesy Miss Sheila Ellis.

When war broke out on 3 September 1939 I was twelve years old and my brother John was aged five. We were standing in the sitting room with my parents and grandmother listening to the news on a small wireless. We heard Mr Neville Chamberlain say, " We are at war with Germany". We were living in the beautiful little village of Clovelly in North Devon, miles away from Germany so we thought how could it affect us? We were to learn - very soon! Preparations for war were under way and we were trained to use gas masks, instructed on the rationing of clothing, food and petrol. All these items could no longer be bought unless you had a ration book with the coupons required. It was the beginning of a new era of change that was going to have a dramatic affect on all our lives. Suddenly we were faced with a terminology that was new to us, black out curtains or blinds, ARP Wardens, Home Guards, Land Army Girls and servicemen; the village began to organise.

The men went away to fight and a Searchlight Battery settled in Higher Clovelly and Commandos practised climbing our steep cliffs prior to the D-Day landings. In those days the radio was the main source of entertainment and communications for the average citizen, so we would listen frequently for the latest news and updates of the war. We would hear the German bombers flying over our coastline on their way to bomb the cities. The devastation was terrible and we counted ourselves lucky that we were in a quiet (so we thought) fishing village. Soon word came, and our bombing was to be of a different nature, the arrival of over two hundred children who had been subjected to continuous bombing in London, Bristol and Plymouth. The decision had been taken to evacuate them to Clovelly.

Coachloads of boys and girls with teachers arrived from South East Peckham and Deptford in London, and later from Bristol.

Cottages and farms were filled as each household was expected to take a child, some of these evacuees stayed the whole war in Clovelly and some who were homesick and could not settle returned home when they could, willing to stick out the bombing rather than live in a strange environment. Then came news that Plymouth was being devastated with the continual bombing night after night and the city was being totally destroyed. A group of fifty orphaned children arrived from a childrens' home in Plymouth with the staff who took care of them. As all the farms and cottages were already full it was decided to put them in the New Inn. The girls were in the main building and the boys were billeted in the Annexe on the opposite side.

The New Inn Hotel was empty as with the declaration of war daily holiday makers and other visitors would not be coming to Clovelly again, so the hotel was closed and local citizens would go to the Red Lion Hotel down near the beach for their evening tipple. The large rooms downstairs in the New Inn were converted into a sitting room, dining room and playroom.

The Ellis Family Clovelly late 1940's. From the Left. Sheila Ellis, John Ellis, Mrs Gladys Ellis & Mr Paul Ellis. Mrs Ellis was known as "Auntie Glad" to the orphans in the New Inn during the Second World War years. Photo courtesy Miss Sheila Ellis Clovelly.

Clovelly residents became aware that these were orphaned children, and felt so sorry for what they had been through that the villagers made them welcome, and everyone turned out or made childrens' clothing, as when they arrived all they had left was what they were wearing. By now the parish of Clovelly was overflowing, the village school had two classrooms and a hall, which suddenly had to accommodate two hundred children. The hall was converted to three classrooms by means of stringing curtains across. A spare room in the village (now known as Saint Peter's Chapel) and another small room over the old lifeboat house were used to teach the under fives and smaller infants. If the weather was nice they would be taken on a nature walk or they would help to "Dig for Victory" in the gardens, anything to keep them occupied, as it was impossible with the number of children to teach them all at the same time, there was just not enough room! Senior girls learned to sew and cook in a dwelling known as the "Rectory Room," meals were prepared by a cook and a helper in the kitchen for all who could afford to stay to dinner.

My brother and I were at school with the evacuees and we learnt a lot of their games and songs. The teachers told us of far away places and helped us to grow up together, not an easy task as villagers and city folk are not alike. Before the war years we had learnt the most important things, to read, write and to add sums. We were also taught about the stories in the bible. With the evacuees we soon learnt new songs, played different games but on the whole my school memories were happy ones.

The Ellis Family Shop Clovelly right opposite the New Inn where the children made a beeline for their sweet rations when the pocket money was issued. Year of photograph unknown. Photo courtesy of Miss Sheila Ellis.

Our mother and father owned a small shop then, and the village shop was the hubbub of conversation and latest rumours, a place where villagers could meet and chat whilst buying their wares. The shop sold souvenirs of Clovelly, postcards, films, chemist goods, household items, wool, sewing cottons and other haberdashery. A square white table stood just inside the front door and the shelves held tea, coffee and biscuits, sweets in glass jars, and small bars of chocolate, nearby were the scales we would use to weigh the sweets. Coupons were needed for sweets and chocolate and villagers, ever aware of the orphans, would pass in their extra sweet coupons. My mother would let the evacuees have a few extra each, especially the Plymouth children in the New Inn as they lived next door. She had a heart of gold and several have returned in later years and told me of her kindness.

The Plymouth children from the New Inn always went up and down the cobbled street holding hands in a double formation, sometimes with a helper in front or behind. This was a strict arrangement and the same would happen as we saw them go to the parish church of All Saints on Sundays, some children would sit in the choir seats. The Rector then was the Reverend R P Cavendish who with his wife and children lived in the Rectory next door to

the Rectory Room. Clovelly Court lies next to the parish church; here lived the Hon Mrs Betty Asquith and her family. One of her friends was Lady Nancy Astor who was then a Member of Parliament for Plymouth. From time to time, Lady Astor visited Clovelly and I can remember seeing her walk up and down the village dressed entirely in black!

Sheila Ellis Clovelly 1939 as a young schoolgirl.

Sports and dancing displays were held on the lawn of Clovelly Court to give pleasure on special days in summertime. Some of the girls who once lived in the New Inn during the war years have called on me to talk and re-live their wartime years in Clovelly. Not all told happy stories, some made me feel sad and angry. I wish that we had known about the unhappy times, maybe - just maybe, someone would have stepped in and tried to improve their lives. One girl said, "No one would have believed us!" I love to meet the returning evacuees and feel so grateful that I was happy in my beloved village, how lucky I was with my family and friends around me throughout the wicked war years! I hope and pray that no future generation will have to listen again to those words "We are at War!"

CHAPTER TWENTY-NINE

MIXED FEELINGS - JOHN ELLIS

John Ellis Clovelly North Devon circa 1940's.

I was born in 1934 and lived with my parents, my sister Sheila and my Grandmother in Clovelly North Devon during the 1939-1945 war. My parents had a shop opposite the New Inn about half way down the cobbled High Street. I was five years old in 1939 when the war started and left Clovelly School just after the end of the war in 1945 when I was eleven years old. This means that all my memories of children and events associated with Clovelly School must date from the war years. I have vivid personal memories of many of the events and people, and also recall clearly things that I must have heard discussed in my parents shop, where most of the villagers called in for a chat, or I learned from the wireless and the papers at the time. In adult life I have discovered the reasons and often the truth behind some of the things I remember from the war years. I apologise in advance if anyone feels libelled or forgotten but these are the things I remember. I remember evacuees in Clovelly, adults with their children and unaccompanied children. I remember the Naylor family and a boy called Douglas, who I believe has now passed on, he lived with Gordon Perham and his wife higher up the street than the New Inn, I think Douglas's family was related to Mrs Perham and that they came from the Portsmouth area, possibly Gosport. I remember that Raymond Squires, who lived about fifty yards below the New Inn and still lives in the Clovelly area, had his Grandfather from London staying with them. He was "Pop Butcher" to us children. There were children from Deptford and Peckham in London, from Bristol, and from a home in Plymouth Devon; they took over the New Inn.

Clear in my mind is the arrival of the London and Bristol children, and how they were billeted with people in Clovelly and the reactions from the villagers. One party arrived late at night and Mary Cruse wore her ARP uniform complete with tin helmet, as evacuees and hosts milled around the High Street while accommodation was sorted out. I have never learnt what arrangements the government of the day made, nor, for example, how much compulsion was used to make parents in the cities being bombed give up their children, or to make people accept these children into their homes. Looking back I assume the people on whom these children were billeted must have received some payment for their food, clothes and accommodation as well as the childrens' ration cards. I do not know whether the parents alone contributed or whether the government also made payments.

A census was carried out in the village to find out who had spare bedrooms, there were five of us living in our house, and also the shop and storerooms, so we did not have an evacuee billeted on us. The census was carried out by a Mr Eddie Hutchingson, from the top of the High Street above the New Inn. He also measured the children for gas masks and was responsible for placing the evacuees with people whose homes were without children. I do not know if any selection took place or if any preferences say for people to look after a girl or boy, was considered. I believe that brothers and sisters were generally kept together. As in any community there were some kind people who made the children welcome and part of their family, and close relationships were formed, some of which lasted many years after the war until the old people died. There must have been a majority of houses where the evacuees and local people simply lived together and after the war quickly lost touch. I was not aware of any of this as a child. Incidents were discussed where evacuees and their unwilling hosts could not live together amicably. Nobody ever analysed the problems for me at the time, but now I can understand and make a good guess at the reasons. Many of the people with spare bedrooms were elderly, who either had never had children of their own, or had grown up children who had left home, and they did not want to be responsible for somebody else's child. Some of the villagers had their own ideas about the way children should behave that were different from the way the children had behaved at home, and imposed their own standards and discipline on what they considered to be rebellious children. Perhaps some of the blame can also be placed with the children. Today the excuse would be made that the children had been traumatised by their experiences, which was true, but all the children had had similar experiences and only a very small number caused problems. Some of the problem children were simply undisciplined or "street wise" youngsters from the "Big City" who could not, or made little effort, to fit into the life of a small village in the country. Clashes of personalities or cultures were inevitable and I do not suppose

Clovelly was any different from anywhere else in those days.

There was the occasion when I overheard in my parents' shop the various incidents of evacuees assaulting their hosts. My own Aunt had her dentures broke by being punched by a child which caused much comment in our family. Seen as the last straw the child who punched my Aunt in the mouth was taken away and she was reallocated another child who lived with her happily until the end of the war. There were incidents of spectacles being broken and wilful damage being done, sometimes to precious family heirlooms. There were no cases of theft only assault. My memory may be selective because it was so shocking for me that the elderly respectable ladies I knew could be attacked so violently by a child. I do not know what happened to the children whose behaviour was unacceptable or who were desperately unhappy and unable to settle. Presumably these latter children returned to their homes in the cities being bombed.

However, there were some happy times, we learned to play new games and playground chants. We learnt new songs, hiding and skipping, it was a great period of widening of horizons for us all. I have memories of black and white films being shown somewhere, probably at the school, these films must have been training films, newsreels or blatant propaganda since they always showed our brave boys beating the Germans on land, sea, and in the air. We loved those films and spent hours playing soldiers around the school playground and in the street, and up in the Hobby Woods surrounding Clovelly. There always seemed to be plenty of boys ready to join in. We were certainly prepared to "Fight them on the beaches etc". "Dig for Victory" was a wartime slogan and I remember whole classes of us being taken down Wrinkleberry lane to where Mr Hesketh the Headmaster had his garden. This certainly got us out into the fresh air away from the overcrowded school, but, an excellent example of too many cooks, with dozens of small boys running wild with garden forks, spades and rakes, not achieving very much. At the right time of year farmers were allowed to keep their sons and evacuees billeted on the farms away from school to help with the harvest. All the rest of us clamoured to be allowed time off to go picking potatoes for which the princely sum of six pence (2.5p today) was paid per day, Children from Clovelly village were rarely chosen but we did not know how back-breaking the work could be.

My memories of the school playground which was segregated between boys and girls, is of overcrowding, boys from the farm in Higher Clovelly wearing enormous dubbined leather hob-nailed boots striking fire at each step and everyone playing soldiers making all the explosive noises or taking part in the latest jumping or sliding game. Today the most played game is football but none of us had footballs during the war, no one had a football at the school, perhaps they were banned. The girls seem to spend a lot of time holding bits of rope for high jumping practice or for complicated skipping with other girls joining and leaving to a lot of chanting. The ground was covered in chalk marks for hopping games. The Headmaster at Clovelly School during the war was Mr Hesketh, he had been in the Guards Regiment during the first world war and had seen a lot of good men killed. I vividly remember the stories he would tell of that war. I can calculate now that he would have been in his forties when I was at school. He was very fit and active and able to outsprint any of us. He and his wife and son Jack, until he joined the forces, lived in a splendid house with carvings on the front down the High Street near the Look-Out. Sadly Mr Hesketh has been dead for several years, however, we all owe him a great deal but few of us realise our debts to our teachers until it is too late to tell them.

The New Inn still occupies both sides of Clovelly High Street, at the beginning of the war the entire hotel was closed except the bar. Presumably the fuel and food rationing and the demands of the forces for manpower ended the tourist trade. The New Inn was occupied by children from a home in Plymouth just before I reached my sixth birthday, I cannot truthfully say I remember their arrival, one day they were just there! They continued to live together in a community as they had in Plymouth and have often wondered where in the city their home was, and whether today any of them are still here and remember their days in Clovelly, thanks to Vicky Norman the author of this book I now know part of the story.

They were known to us as the New Inn children and they fitted in perfectly well with the village, I do not remember any problems or unpleasantness caused by them. By today's standards they were closely supervised "marched" around two abreast at times and summoned to meals by the hotel dinner gong! I recall playing with some of them outside the New Inn only to be interrupted by that gong being struck by Nurse Penna, who I can still picture in her uniform standing at the top of the New Inn steps, she struck me as a very formidable lady!

The influx of children from London, Bristol and Plymouth into a small village naturally had a profound effect. The local children were outnumbered and almost swamped. The school could not accommodate all the children and I can remember being taught in a variety of semi public buildings and even a chapel. I clearly remember attending classes in the open air down at the quay avoiding the climb up to the school at Wrinkleberry. I am not sure if these classes down on the quay were just for the children of the village or included children from Higher Clovelly who would have passed the school to get down to the quay. Multiple classes at the school were held in the same room (the old assembly hall) with children sat back-to-back facing different teachers. What chaos would ensue today! Yet I do not remember too many difficulties from these arrangements. At lunch time (we called it dinner-time) cooked meals were available in a building near the rectory, thus a day at school involved walking from the village up Wrinkleberry Lane to school, then at lunch time out to the main road and down Slerra Hill to the "Canteen" in the rectory buildings and the return journey, this was several miles with only a little way on the flat. I remember Mrs Burrows was among those cooking the school dinners which always seemed to have included thick brown gravy and roast potatoes with leather-like skins, I do not know whether ration coupons were needed or cash had to be paid. As far as the war itself is concerned Clovelly was passed by. I remember Mr Cruse the butcher had corn planted in the Deer Park. Italian prisoners of war relieved to be somewhere safer than facing Monty's Eighth Army in North Africa, were sent to help with the harvest, they were friendly chaps in brown uniforms with bright patches sewn on their backs. They always made a fuss of the children, offering sweets presumably supplied by the Red Cross; they too were missing their own families and struggled to communicate. Mrs Silo who had married an Italian before the war acted as an interpreter to explain what was required of them.

The Clovelly Lifeboat was launched with Mr George Lamey as Coxswain to rescue three Luftwaffe airmen and brought them back to the harbour wet, cold, and shocked at having been shot down. A Clovelly woman recently widowed by the war had to be restrained as she vented her anger at the

Germans. One of the three airmen who was shot down in those years returned to Clovelly many years after the war to meet and thank Mr Lamey then an old man for the kindness and courtesy shown to him and his crew. Our shop was a centre for the exchange of news and I expect of gossip. My mother kept a big map of Europe on the wall and updated the position of the advancing Red Army by pinning little Russian flags on the towns in the BBC news. She named one of our cats after a Russian General, Timoshenko, who was apparently making spectacular advances against Hitler's Wehrmacht. I have never heard of him since the war so perhaps political changes forced him into retirement. I remember a variety of visiting troops, often American so it must have been in the later years of the war before D-Day 1944. Several called into our shop to enquire where they could start to trace their families and any relatives who still lived in Clovelly. Branches of my family have been in Clovelly since records began in the 1500s, and it was found that these visiting troops were related to us. My sister still exchanges Christmas cards with the sons and daughters of these men who called into Clovelly during a break in the war.

Clovelly looks out across the Bristol Channel to South Wales and I clearly remember being carried across the square to where we could see Swansea, Wales, being bombed and the resulting fires lighting up the sky in the distance, the searchlight were clearly visible. On another occasion we were visiting Dyke Green, there was a blackout and all the countryside was dark except for the glow in the sky to the south over Dartmoor, which was caused by fires in Plymouth, Devon. I can remember walking with my parents in the Deer Park around Christmas, photographs were taken and I can now identify the date as December 1943 because the photos show parts of the Mulberry Harbour, which was to be towed to the beaches of Normandy, no one knew what they were at the time. The Lifeboat crew with Coxswain in command, Mr Lamey, rescued a number of men from the Mulberry Harbour. It had broken adrift and Mr Lamey was awarded a medal for this action because the Mulberry, as big as a block of flats, was pitching and rolling in the rough sea, and could have smashed the tiny lifeboat to matchwood.

Among other things my parents sold sweets, which were rationed during the war. They could only order new stock if they could produce the ration coupons. My parents and the people of Clovelly worked out a scheme to provide sweets for the large number of children in the village. Elderly people who either did not want their sweet ration or did not want the wartime sweets available were persuaded to give my parents their sweet ration coupons, which were then used to order new stock. My mother gave sweets to the New Inn for the orphan children from Plymouth, and she always had sweets available for the children who called into her shop with their pennies. I do not like to think of the dental problems she may have caused, but she thought she was doing the right thing. I remember Mr Hesketh the Headmaster who passed over his entire sweet ration during the war telling my Dad that he particularly missed Quality Street chocolates. When the war and sweet rationing ended my Dad gave him a big seven-pound tin in weight of these and he was so pleased.

Another village resident I remember well was Mr Lyddon who lived opposite us dreaming of the hot toast "dripping with butter" he wanted after the war in return for giving his sweet ration coupons to order sweets for the evacuee children in the village, sadly he did not live long enough to enjoy his toast. Cod Liver Oil and Malt seem to have been freely available but not always appreciated by us children who were forced to swallow this unpleasant stuff. Another vivid memory I have is of Syrup of Figs which had to be taken every Friday night whether needed or not to ensure one was "free" to go to church on the following Sunday. How thinking has changed since those days! One night I heard a broadcast on the wireless that the success of an RAF Ace in finding and destroying German Aircraft at night was because he ate large quantities of carrots which helped him to see in the dark, his nick-name was "Cat's Eyes" Cunningham. You can still hear this idea repeated today and the result was that we too were fed an abundance of carrots to help us to see in the blackout, the whole carrot story was, however, simply an exercise in misinformation. Later in life I joined the RAF and learnt that Cunningham's success in finding the enemy aircraft at night was because his fighter plane was equipped with new RADAR, which was being kept secret from the Germans. For a long time RAF aircraft equipped with the new RADAR were not allowed to fly outside the coast of the United Kingdom to prevent the secret falling into German hands. I ate all those carrots for nothing!

During the "Dark Days" of the war when ships were being sunk in large numbers, boxes of food used to be washed up on the beach, although all these items were supposed to have been handed to the Customs Officer, Mr Picket I believe, there was occasionally enough dried fruit in the village for a splendid cake. The older boys, Bernard Abbott among them, patrolled the coast down as far as Mouth Mill to find any goodies before the Customs and Excise man.

Can you remember? Ernest Beer, a deaf and dumb man who looked after the donkeys belonging to the New Inn. Jack Foley, a white bearded man who ran the New Inn bar and rolled full beer barrels diagonally down across the steep cobbled street. The donkeys carried the empty barrels back up the street. Stanley Squires, the Clovelly Carrier and Taxi and a regular at the New Inn bar. Fred Shackson, who lived on the Square next to the New Inn and had a built-up boot, he was a fisherman. Oscar Abbott, was also a fisherman, and always wore navy blue jerseys and lived opposite the New Inn. George Lamey, the Coxswain of the Lifeboat. My Mum and Dad who kept the shop opposite the New Inn. My Dad was tall and thin with dark hair and carried a walking stick and my mum was short with fair hair. Donald Hambley, who was a Plymouth evacuee in the New Inn annexe and a good friend, I wish I knew what became of him. Some of the names of Clovelly children are, John Ellis, Sheila Ellis, June and Hilary Prouse, Freda Shackson, Bernard Abbott, Douglas Naylor, Anne Hutchinson, Barry Perham and Raymond Squires. All these lived within one hundred yards of the New Inn during the war.

CHAPTER THIRTY

MOUNT STREET SCHOOL

Mount Street School was built in 1876, and for teaching methods what a lovely school it was. The teaching staff was very good and they had infinite patience with the children. If a child was punished it was usually a short sharp rap across the knuckles with a ruler. It was a quaint stone grey building with one wooden staircase and very draughty corridors. There was a long, low, roofed tunnel called the lower section which infants would go through to reach their class, there were several passage rooms. Often the staircase became congested with staff and pupils and would have been a safety risk if an emergency arose. The school was inundated with damp and poor conditions, nevertheless I was very happy there. One has to admire the teachers in those days as they struggled to teach children in conditions not suited to their needs.

Mount Street School senior side taken in the 1950's. The Infants lower tunnel is not shown in this photo. From Plymouth Reference Library Archives.

Mount Street school was a junior mixed and infant's school and they taught nearly six hundred pupils, the standards were high and good behaviour was a must. The Headmaster was a Mister W. Crocker with fourteen assistant teachers. My first unpleasant memory was when the school nurse and doctor gave all the infants an immunisation injection against Diphtheria. There was panic in 1937 when suddenly children were being taken ill with chicken pox, scarlet fever and measles. In 1938 it was the dreaded influenza. There was a sad incident with a young popular teacher called George Stoneman who died after one week's sudden illness. The staff and pupils held him with affection and several staff attended his funeral. German measles and mumps were rampant at the school in 1939-1940.

In May 1937 to celebrate the coronation of King George the sixth each child was presented with a souvenir beaker (I broke mine on the way home and cried all evening and never had a replacement) and the infant class was provided with a sumptuous tea. The schoolroom had been gaily decorated and the tables were covered in white tablecloths. A waitress attended each table from selected senior girls from other classes; they looked so smart in their red, white and blue aprons, which had been chosen for them. They served us with food and drink, (which parents and teachers alike had taken of lot of time and effort to supply) and very good they were too! The councillor Mr Strachan visiting for the occasion spoke to each child and made us feel very special.

In 1939 Miss N Green became our visiting needlework teacher replacing Miss Grierson who had died on Christmas Day that year. As a junior pupil I remember on Empire Day in the school assembly hall the Head Teacher giving a talk on "Our Inheritance" and we would sing the Hymn "Recessional" and at the end everyone sang "God save the King" and a half day's holiday would be declared. June and July in 1939 was a happy time as Miss Winifred Viggers would take about twenty junior girls for swimming instructions to the Hoe swimming pool. Usually it was on a Friday between ten o'clock and ten-thirty in the morning, we were only allowed thirty minutes as time was taken into consideration of getting to and from the school. One afternoon a teacher took our class to Cawsand to do seashore research work in connection with our nature study. That was super! Another morning we would have secular instruction followed by scripture lessons, one would be on the Old Testament and one on the New Testament, and senior girls would enter and compete for the Peek Prize for Scripture.

Every child had to be registered.

Mount Street School received War Emergency orders on the first September 1939 and all the children were sent home. The school closed on the second of September 1939 on the outbreak of hostilities with Germany. On Sunday the third of September adults and children listened to a speech, broadcast on the wireless, given by Neville Chamberlain stating that, "A State of War exists between Great Britain and Germany." As children, we did not fully understand the enormity of the situation and the dreadful consequences that were to follow. Children who had reached the age of seven years were allowed to return to the school on the twenty-fifth September, but, the infants did not go back until much later.

Visiting Air Raid Precaution Wardens would come to the school to test our gas masks and to ensure we knew how to put them on. Fire drill and how to disperse to the shelters quickly would follow this, and every child's name was recorded and each child under sixteen was issued with an Identity Card.

In late July there was a sad incident when a popular young boy from Mount Street Boys School was found drowned in Sutton Pool on the Barbican. His death was quite a shock, as the tragic accident had not been connected to the war. Also in July 1940 the bombing raids began and several times schools would be closed because of unexploded bombs in the vicinity, which meant clearing the school until safe to return. The night bombing raids constantly interrupted our sleep and as the enemy raids increased the children's education was adversely affected. This was the beginning of six years of war and the seeds of disruption in the children's education had been sown. Several raids forced the children and teaching staff to run for the shelters during school lessons and it got so bad that some mothers refused to send their children to school, so absenteeism was rife. Some parents voluntary sent their children to safer districts.

The strain on the teachers and pupils alike was beginning to take effect, the fabric of normal school life was undermined and school attendance dropped dramatically. A notice was issued to the school staff informing all the teachers that all conscientious objectors in the employ of the Plymouth City Council shall be dismissed, this was met with some disquiet, but the order had to be obeyed for the sake of national security. One particular bombing raid in late August 1940 lasted from nine-thirty in the evening until four-thirty the following morning, everyone was so tired and edgy and shattered nerves began to take its toll as tempers frayed.

By January 1941 terrible raids continued to batter our beleaguered city and untold damage caused, it was at this time that Charles Senior School was badly damaged and some of the pupils doubled up with Mount Street School to continue with their education. Ironically in February 1941, as if we had not suffered enough, the weather decided to take its turn at making our lives a misery. There was a fierce snowstorm and the school was freezing cold. Of course we children when we got outside couldn't resist playing snowballs, but I ended up going home crying because I had taken off my woollen mittens to throw the snowballs and my hands had frozen! This bad weather also reduced the school attendance and that week only twenty-five per cent of pupils attended classes. March/April 1941 saw fearful raids over Plymouth, and the district of Greenbank suffered untold damage and loss of life. It was a terrible time and even the children who had been resilient up to this time were afraid and tired, the fun had worn off and death and destruction was all they could see. What was happening to us? The authorities under constant pressure from parents and teachers finally declared the whole City an evacuation area. The official date was set for May 1941 but I had gone in April. Most of the public and children went to Camborne and other outlying districts of Cornwall and to villages in Devon, Dorset and Buckinghamshire.

· WITHDRAWAL.

NAME OF PARENT OR GUARDIAN.	NAME OF LAST SCHOOL.	Date of Last Attendance.			CAUSE OF LEAVING.	NOTES re MEDICAL EXAMINATIONS. ETC.	REMARKS (Character, etc.)
		D.	M.	Year			
William	Prince Rock	8	4	36	S. James. Less.		
Edward	None	8	8	41	Plymouth High		
Ernest.	"	25	4	41	Stoke House		
Frederick	"	14	2	39	North, Prospect.		
William	"	21	7	36	Billacombe		

My withdrawal date from Mount Street School 25th April 1941 my last day at this school. Note the cause of leaving (third from the top) those dreaded words to Stoke House. (Ernest was my real father's name) Grateful thanks to Mrs Maureen Selley and Mount Street School.

CHAPTER THIRTY-ONE

MY INFANT YEARS

Those we love remain with us – for love itself lives on!

This photograph was taken on the 20th January 1935 when I was two years and six months old on a day out from the City Hospital. Aunt Muriel & Uncle Bert bought my first outfit and the mittens were too large for me. I was quite bewildered as to what was happening, look at that face!

I was born on Sunday the 3 July 1932 in the Greenbank Nursing Home known as the City Hospital and baptised in the Parish of St Jude by the vicar, W.R.Scott, in August 1932 and my Aunt Violet Foster was my Godmother. I remained at the City Hospital until I was three years old because my mother had post natal problems and had suffered ill health. I was the fourth daughter and the baby of the family. It was a tough time 60-70 years ago for a baby who did not fit into the system. Right from my birth it was clear I was to be a physically undeveloped child. When my mother married my father in February 1922, he was twenty-three years old and my mother nineteen. He was a private in the Devon Regiment (otherwise known as the West Devons.) He had lived at 6 North Street, and mother had lived at 8 Mainstone Avenue, both addresses in Plymouth.

My father Ernest Norman died in December 1934 at the age of thirty-five with cardiac failure and bronchitis, I was two years old. He lived at 22 Green Street, Plymouth, and when he left the Army, had been a fisherman and a general labourer and in the depression years of unemployment took any job available. One was even as a rag and bone buyer. My sisters were called Violet, (Born October 1922) Connie (Born July 1926) and Valerie Jean (Born April 1930). My mother Ida Norman died in January 1936 at the age of thirty-four, from pneumonia and cardiac failure when I was three years and six months old. On the death of my father she had moved to 18 Moon Street, Plymouth and with four girls and no wage earner, times were hard. In the 1930's the breadwinner was always treated with deference before the onset of feminism. Women left without a wage earner and children to feed were to suffer terribly.

Sixty years ago people had different values and priorities. Home life and family usually came first, often kith and kin would argue and disrupt family life, however, families always closed ranks when threatened by an outsider. Poverty was rife and overcrowding endemic. When earnings were lost there was only parish relief, which would not support a family, and often that would not be granted. Instead families were told to sell their furniture, which may already have been bought second hand, or they would have to pawn items before any financial assistance could be given. Sometimes poor people had to sell bags of clothes or rags to the ragman to obtain a few pennies.

I never knew my mother and father, but I am fiercely proud of them and no one will make me feel ashamed of my time of birth or how they lived. It was not their fault they were so poor. They paid the price with their lives because of poor housing, and lack of medical care. Unemployment in those days meant hunger and scraping to survive and in the 1930's there was no such thing as free dole money!

My very first memory was of standing on a large wooden kitchen table and being strip- washed. There was a sense of urgency and I could feel a heavy atmosphere in the air and became frightened and began to cry because I could not understand. The person washing me was also distressed (I later learned it was my sister Connie) and I quickly sensed something was very wrong. It was!

My real Mother. Ida Emily Florence Evelyn Norman (Nee Foster) (1903-1936)

My mother had died and had left four orphan girls. My Grandparents and Aunt Violet (her other daughter) my other Aunt, Muriel, and Uncle Bert, had struggled to keep us without any help. It was decided to have all four of us taken into care under the Public Assistance Board and my sisters and I were being prepared for submission and inspection by welfare authorities. It was August 1936 and I was four years old. By having all four of us taken into care financial support would then be provided, without which it would have been impossible for our kind relatives to care for us.

Whilst my mother was so desperately ill in hospital my Grandmother, Harriet Helen Beatrice Foster (nee Parsonage) and Grandfather, Albert Edward Foster, (who I may add were in their early sixties then, and there was no old age pension as the qualifying age was sixty-five) took care of my sisters Violet aged twelve, Connie aged ten, and Valerie aged five. My Aunt, Violet Foster, who was my mother's sister, had tried to help with her meagre wages of fifteen shillings per week to support all of us. She was employed as a Weigher at Reckitts Blue Starch Works at Coxside in 1936 but she was single and had her own life to live, and could not be expected to support us. Meanwhile my Aunt Muriel and Uncle Bert, who was my mother's brother, had taken me in their care in January 1936 and I was immediately registered on the 6th January 1936 in the infant class at Mount Street School. I was three years and six months old. When they took me out of the hospital I had not been taught to speak correctly and Aunt Muriel and Uncle Bert had to teach me. It would appear that they were quite successful, as later they would tell me that they could not stop me from chattering and I quickly received my first label "The Chatterbox!" I had no clothes so for the time being they had to buy some second hand ones for me. Unsure of my size my first real outfit is the one you see taken in the photograph.

The Welfare authorities had approached other family members to take me. If nobody would have me I would have to be placed in the orphanage. Children could not stay at the hospital once they had reached the age of three. Only the Foster family was approached, as my Grandmother would not let my father's relatives, the Norman family, have me. There was a hidden animosity between the families; I was never to see anyone from the Norman family again until my adulthood when I searched for them to find out why they did not look for me, only to find that my Grandmother had blocked their efforts.

My Grandparents had no financial assistance at that time and it must have been a desperate struggle. Grandmother was a Non Conformist and deeply resented my mother marrying Ernest Norman, so she refused to let any of the Norman family have her grandchildren. Family feuds can often result in changing completely the outcome of a child's life. My Grandmother and Grandfather could not cope with four orphan girls. My Aunt and Uncle, Albert and Muriel Foster (nee Burch) made a formal application to the

Welfare to foster me. Aunt Muriel was aged thirty-three and Uncle Bert thirty-six and secretly my Aunt Muriel had always wanted to have a little girl. She had one son Ernest who was aged twelve in 1936. It must have been difficult for my cousin Ern to suddenly have to accept a baby sister, which meant a complete reshuffling of home life. Aunt Muriel was unable to have any more children, so a boy and a girl would be just right! I think they wanted to adopt me but Grandmother was fiercely adamant that her grandchildren would not be taken completely away. Uncle Bert was a fireman on the Great Western Railway; and had taken Aunt Muriel and Ern and moved home to Pontypool in the early 1930's to enhance his possibility of gaining promotion as an Engine Driver. They returned to Plymouth in 1935 and rented the rooms at Clifton Street. Later he gained his promotion as an Engine Driver and had completed forty-five years service when he finally retired. Aunt Muriel had been the manageress of a Plymouth Co-operative Society Store, unfortunately she had to leave when she married, as in those days female married personnel were not allowed to stay on.

My Aunt and Godmother Violet Pargeter (nee Foster) (1903-2000) and her nephew (my cousin whom I called my brother) Ernest Foster (1924-1976) taken circa late 1930's.

In August 1936 I was officially taken into care under the control of the Welfare Authorities together with my three sisters. Formal approval had been given for me to be fostered with Aunt Muriel and Uncle Bert. I was the little girl they chose to care for, despite my having ginger hair, freckles and blue eyes and the fiery temperament that went with most such children. Now she was entitled to receive a pension and maintenance allowance to help pay for my keep. The Public Assistance Board granted them eight shillings and sixpence a week and seventeen shillings and sixpence per quarter for clothing. On officially being taken into care, my two sisters Violet and Connie were given back to Grandmother and Grandfather. My little sister Valerie Jean was fostered with a family called Collins in 12 Kirkby Place, near North Road, Plymouth, who wanted to adopt my sister but my Grandparents refused. The Collins also received maintenance allowances for Valerie, coupled with the orphan's pension, which was seven shillings and sixpence. These were decisions, which were to have a marked affect on my life in later years, as I was never to see my sisters Connie and Valerie again.

My Grandfather (Pop) Albert Edward Foster and two of my sisters Violet Norman (left) and Connie Norman (right) taken in 1935 when I was still at the City Hospital.

Mr & Mrs Albert Foster (Aunt Muriel and Uncle Bert) my second Mum & Dad. Taken in the 1950's on holiday in Scotland.

	Date of Admission			Date of Re-admission			ADMISSION. NAME IN FULL (Enter Surname first)		Date of Birth			Whether Exempt from Religious Instruction	Address
Admission Number	D.	M.	Year	D.	M.	Year			D.	M.	Year		
521	6	1	36				Mortimore	Cyril	16	11	29	R.C.	33 Providence St.
522	·	·					Gist	Joyce	14	12	30	R.C.	20 Mill Park Cres
523	·	·					Norman	Veronica	2	4	32	R.C.	18 Clifton St.
524	·	·					Corry	Derek	24	10	31	R.C.	14 Wellington St
525	·	·					Thorn	Derek	30	11	31	R.C.	14 Camden St

My Admission to Mount Street School at the age of 3 years six months. With grateful thanks to Mrs Maureen Selley and Mount Street School Plymouth.

This is my real father with two of my sisters Violet & Connie and I think the baby is myself taken in 1932. For many years I had badgered my Aunt Violet for photos of my family and when she went into a nursing home in 1996 among her private papers was this photo which she sent me.

My real Father. Ernest Harold Norman. (1899-1934) The uniform is that of the Devon Regiment (known as the West Devons) I saw this photograph for the first time in 1998 with grateful thanks to my newly found cousin Mrs Eda Rowe (nee Norman) Plymouth.

242

CHAPTER THIRTY-TWO

MY EARLY YEARS

I have pictured in my memory those happy days I knew...

In the 1930's the houses in Clifton Street, Greenbank, Plymouth, nestling in the East of the City were three storeys high and most were converted into tenement rooms for families, some families having only have two rooms, others three or four. They were strong well-built houses in a nice residential area with plenty of shops in Clifton Street, Clifton Place and Armada Street. Nearby was the South Devon and East Cornwall Hospital known to most people as the Prince of Wales Hospital at Greenbank, and the Freedom Fields Hospital known locally as the City Hospital. Close to the two hospitals were the newly opened (1935) Police Station, Fire Station and Ambulance Station.

From 1936 I lived in number 13 Clifton Street. Standing on the westside of the street it had been tenanted since 1893 and was now home to my Aunt Muriel, Uncle Bert, and my first cousin Ernest Foster. (They obviously did not suffer from Triskaidekaphobia-fear of number thirteen) (I shall refer to Aunt Muriel and Uncle Bert as Mum and Dad in the rest of my story, and my cousin Ern as my brother, as that is what I was taught to call them from the very beginning). We were on the ground floor and the kitchen had a very big white earthenware sink with a wooden draining board. The room held a gleaming black-leaded grate with well brushed hobs, which would be lit in the evenings as it had a back boiler which heated the water to use the following day. I would be fascinated watching Mum cleaning the black leaded grate with Reckitt and Sons Dome Blacklead and grate polish, as an alternative she would use the Zebra Grate Polish.

Facing the main street, was the front room or parlour as some called it, which was only used on very special occasions, or if there were visitors. I remember vividly the heavy green chenille curtains, which hung from the window, and the piano that stood as a centrepiece, and was considered a luxury in those days. We did not have a bathroom. My bedroom was at the back and I would have to go through the kitchen to get there. I remember

Mum had a small wardrobe with my clothes stored inside and she would use Camphor mothballs to keep out the moths. They smelled awful. Outside was a long courtyard with a double clothes line on a pulley. The outside toilet, the outhouse and outbuildings, which were utilised as a washhouse and coal store right at the end of the court, were shared by all the tenants. Each tenant was allocated their own day to hang out their washing on the clothes line and they would have to take their turn at cleaning and polishing the passageway which all tenants used. When it was Mum's turn to clean the passageway, she would take out a large round tin of Mansion Floor Polish and the linoleum would shine so brightly one could see their face in it. One had to be careful when treading on the little runner mat as often anyone not treading gingerly would skid along because of the shiny surface. I remember that Monday was wash day for Mum, Tuesday and Wednesday for the other tenants. Three days of the week the house would smell of the various washing powders used on wash day. Rinso (popular since the 1920's) Persil (The housewives choice) Omo (launched in 1908) Oxydol and Dreft, which were launched in 1937. Lux Flakes were another favourite bought for tuppence a packet and Hudson's soap powder for one penny.

On the top floor there was a family called Lavers and on the first floor of our house was a lady called Mrs Pedrick; I used to call her Ped. She was a little Irish lady who had been widowed for many years, and she would call me Nicky instead of Vicky, because she could not pronounce the letter V, I can not explain why I was called Vicky as my name is Veronica, so I thought! However, on obtaining my birth certificate I noted I was actually christened Ida Mary Veronica Norman. Many children went through life christened one name but called another. I remember the landlord was called Mr Marks and he would call weekly for the rent, and it would be marked down in a little book to confirm that it had been paid. We had a coalbunker and cupboard in the outhouse, and in warm weather we would bathe there. A large copper would be filled with hot water that had been heated by the coal fire as there were no electric kettles or electric fires for the poorer housewives then. The water would be carried from the tenement in bowls or buckets to a large zinc bath, often the bath water would be shared by the next person, so if you drew the short straw and was last, hard luck! It was that or nothing. Out would come the Puritan soap, Fairy soap, Palmolive soap, or on the odd occasion depending on the funds available, a bar of Lifebuoy Toilet Soap which came on the market in 1933 at the princely sum of threepence. Other popular soaps were the Sunlight Soap also made by the Lever Brothers, the Pears "Golden Glory" transparent soap, which was quite expensive, and the white olive toilet soap sold by the Co-op. Mum had a bar of soap called Simpson Iodine Soap which was made from seaweed found on the coast of Scotland, it was considered a beauty treatment. It was quite expensive at sixpence per bar. Mum had received it as a present and no one else would be allowed to touch it! In colder weather we would bath in front of the fire in the kitchen, a lovely coal fire would be stoked up in the fireplace so the room would be nice and warm. I remember once when I was in the bath the gas lamp went out and Mum was feeling around in the dark for a shilling to put into the Gas Meter. After the bath the water was not wasted, often clothes or items would be washed and even the pet dog was bathed!

1930's. Simpson Iodine Soap made from seaweed considered a beauty treatment.

We had a dog called Judy, she was a dear mongrel terrier, and a tabby cat called Punch. I was being taught the rights and wrongs of life and was very happy. Home life was orderly and discipline was strict, but scrupulously fair. My education began at home and their teachings coupled with that of my teachers at school laid the early character foundation of my life. Mum had her own methods of punishment she never used her hands. How I loved tinned fruit and if allowed would have eaten it on any occasion. My favourites were the tins of Del Monte. We had a large old fashioned glass fronted dresser in the kitchen where the best china was displayed, and when I had been naughty my dish of lovely tinned fruit was placed on the top out of reach but where I could still see it. Believe me that was very effective! For extremely bad behaviour I was sent to bed early, I am sure this is familiar to many readers! I loved my second Mum so much, she was omnipresent and there was no doubt that we had a rapport which she was able to develop. The ambience her presence gave to me was the key factor in my upbringing and she was slow to chide. I idolised her and I would do anything for her. She had a magic way of persuading me to her way of thinking. She could obtain immediate reaction from me because she gently encouraged me in her teaching and I soon learnt what was considered to be the right socially accepted behaviour. There is no doubt that in my eyes she was the perfect teacher. My Uncle Bert was very abrupt and was not slow in using his hand if I stepped out of line. He was not so tolerant of my childhood misgivings. He was very much a rough diamond and men in those days were known to be strict guardians. He would often admonish me by saying "You are just like your mother (or father)" depending on my crime, and because we were pure blood kin, he was my mother's brother, we would often bicker. Mum would take control of the situation by being the mediator; sometimes he would upset me by saying "I am not your Dad" on those occasions I was not sure what to call him. His ambivalence toward me was obvious, yet at the same time he and my Aunt had given me a home where others did not want me, but how that remark would hurt, as I was only a child.

When I was still little, I can remember Mum taking me out in a pushchair during the summer months to Beaumont Park. I would wear a lovely floral printed bonnet to protect me from the sun as I had very fair skin, and copper coloured hair. If I caught the sun my face would be as red as a lobster. It always seemed that I was being washed or bathed, adults had an obsession for washing! I used to hate having my hair washed as it hurt when she squeezed the water out of my hair and every week there would be a performance and I would insist that it was not necessary to wash my hair so regularly! One can laugh now at the silly antics. When I went to bed I would always be tucked in and I would give Mum a kiss and she would say "Night-Night, Sleep Tight!" that memory is still with me to this day, I know I felt safe and would think to myself I am loved and somebody cares!

On Sundays I went to the Salvation Army Hall in Shaftbury Cottages for Sunday school. It was only around the corner, and I belonged to the sunbeams. We would wear grey and yellow uniforms with a funny little hat. I would melodiously sing to my Mum when I went home, "Jesus wants me for a Sunbeam, to shine for Him each day," "Some Sunbeam!" she would say, with a wry smile on her face. On Mothering Sunday I would come home from the Salvation Army with one daffodil. Although I only lived one hundred yards away, by the time I got home my daffodil would look rather limp and the stem would be broken. Dad said nothing, one look was enough! Mum took the daffodil from me and I would look at her wistfully and say, "For you, mum," trying to think of an excuse for its pitiful state. On taking the daffodil she would say "Lovely, dear," the stem would be shortened and it was placed in a jam jar of water and there it stayed until the flower died. She made no statement of reproach, and to me that was very re-assuring because that was tenderness at its best. She was indeed a very special lady. Easter was another very special time. On Good Friday if the weather was fine the whole family, would participate in the annual bun pilgrimage to Ridgeway, Plympton. It was an event that was eagerly waited for and we would walk all the way out and back to obtain our Hot Cross Buns. It was quite a distance from Clifton Street but it was lovely seeing the families together all making the same pilgrimage. Sadly the annual walk finished with the onset of war in 1939.

I was so happy at Mount Street School. I was enrolled in January 1936 at the age of 3 years six months in the infant class, and my teacher was called Miss Alma Geatches. She was a very good teacher. I remember vividly as an infant, playing with the large raised sandbox and the fun I had playing with the sand. There was different coloured plasticine, which we would make into little shapes, and various sizes of coloured wooden blocks, which we would have to stack into a pyramid, or build a design. It became quite apparent very early on that I was not going to have the qualities of an architect, my little pile was always falling down. One teacher would let us play bubbles. A shaped round wire dipped in a little dish full of soapy water was used to blow the bubbles. Each child tried to blow the biggest one, of course, mine were always little puny ones but how I loved playing with the water. Often there would be tears when we were eventually told to stop. For the first time I learnt the art of drawing shapes with a piece of white chalk on a slate. I did not use a pencil until I started in the junior class, where later we would be issued with powdered ink, which we would put in the inkwells.

Each day we had to drink a third of a pint of milk and the bottles were shaped to take that exact amount. My first Christmas at the school was to me a real thrill. On the 21st of December all the infants performed in a concert in the afternoon which parents or guardians attended, also in attendance were two councillors. We had been given packets of sweets and oranges presented by a Councillor called Mister A. Strachan, and there was a large Christmas tree lavishly decorated with toys displayed in a prominent position and my heart missed a beat, would I have a toy? Names were called and I waited and worried as the pile began to get smaller as I thought I would miss out, "Be patient, my dear," Mum said gently, as the names were being called in alphabetical order. Disappointed, and ready to sulk, I looked longingly at the teacher as she read the names on the tags. Suddenly my name was shouted out and I ran for my precious gift. It is so true- that little things mean a lot! Then followed the most exciting visit to the Santa Claus Grotto at the Plymouth Co-op Society shop. Oh! Happy Days!

Later, when I became a junior, I made my mum a lovely peg bag with fancy stitching around it called blanket stitch with different coloured silks. The sewing mistress was called Miss Green and she guided me through the making of this article. I was so proud as I presented it to my mum, and she kept and used that peg bag for many years. Each week when I went to school, on my hair would be a lovely new coloured satin hair ribbon, and I would feel so proud. With my ginger hair, freckles and blue eyes, the royal blue or bright green ribbon would look nice. I was often tormented when school closed as we headed for home, the boys used to pinch my ribbon, and I would cry and beg for it back but they would run away laughing. This went on for quite a few weeks and I tearfully told mum that I had not lost my ribbon but that the boys were taking it. "If you can't look after your ribbon" she would say, "I will send you in rags!" Well, it happened. Next day I came home minus my ribbon, so she tied my hair in a strip of white rag and I kept that for a whole week, the boys would not touch it! As luck would have it one of the boys told my brother Ern and he in turn informed mum, so she relented and sent me to school again with another new ribbon tied and secured with a hairgrip. My brother Ern told the boys to leave it alone or he would sort them out, and I would often use that in my defence saying "I will tell my brother!" knowing that he would look out for me. My brother Ern went to Mount Street Boys Senior School where he loved his Physical Training classes that were taken by an instructor called Captain F Carter. This stood him in good stead as later, when Ern was the right age; he was called up into the Army.

Home life was orderly and in the 1930's each day meals were programmed. They would be served on certain days and kept to a regular weekly menu. My favourite breakfast was on Sunday morning and that was a lovely boiled egg into which I could dip my bread and butter soldiers. Sunday mornings mum would cook in her gas cooker, I remember the model in our home was called Main, another popular model for the home which most housewives dreamed of owning was the new expensive Vulcan Stove with automatic oven-heat control. Most housewives would take advantage of making good use of the fuel being used, every shelf in the oven had food to be cooked to avoid wasting the empty space, cakes and buns would be made to last most of the week. There were no electric cookers, microwaves or fridges for the housewife then. Mum would make currant or desiccated coconut buns and place them on a wire stand to cool, occasionally she would make 'Maids of Honour' a little bun with icing and a glace cherry on top, sometimes she would make home made jam tarts and the pastry would just melt in your mouth. She always rested the pastry overnight and this made the texture so much better. Home made mince pies were another favourite of mine and I would often have one while it was still hot. Most housewives made their own mincemeat, however, on occasion Mum would treat herself to a jar of the Robertsons Mincemeat and as I collected the Golliwog figures that suited me just fine.

Housewives in the 1930's strived to save for this luxury Vulcan Gas Stove.

On occasion she would make a lattice apple tart for tea, and if there was any pastry left over she would let me practice making it into a jam pasty and cooking it myself, under her guidance of course. Mum would use her old wooden rolling pin and I would have a milk bottle as my rolling pin, and the scene would be hilarious as I made my attempt at crimping the pasty edges.

Another favourite of mine was when Mum made Welsh Cakes. These were cooked on a griddle but they took a long time to make so we would only have them on occasion. Sunday lunch would mean a lovely roast beef dinner with bisto or oxo gravy, vegetables and Yorkshire pudding. My mother would buy a fore rib and she would bone it herself, it was a lovely tasty joint and it would serve several meals. I used to love going to the meat market late afternoons on Saturdays with her as after four o'clock the meat would be auctioned off and everyone could buy at a cheaper price. Afterwards we would go to Dilleighs, situated at the back of the market, where seven-pound square tins of biscuits were on display. A variety of biscuits were laid in layers separated by sheets of opaque white paper and the broken biscuits would be set aside in a separate tin on the end of the counter, and these were sold at a cheaper price. Sometimes we would go to the Mutley Plain branch or to Bedford's Bakers shop on Mutley Plain where she would buy one pound of Huntley and Palmer's broken biscuits. Huntley and Palmer had

Goodbodys Café, a popular meeting place for a meal or cup of tea for the ordinary folk during the 1930's era. Look at those prices! Courtesy Western Independent & the Plymouth Reference Library. File 0003 CD. The Goodbodys café is still open at Mutley Plain Plymouth today but under different management.

their depot at the Great Western Railway Good's Yard at Valletort Road. Occasionally we would have a very special treat if I had been good and Mum had a couple of coppers to spare. She would take me to the Mutley Plain branch of Goodbodys Café for a pot of tea and I thought that I was quite the madam. Of course good behaviour was a must.

Another very special shopping trip was when Mum took me to the Woolworth's shop where "Nothing over Sixpence" counters were full of wonderful nick-knacks for children with sixpence to spend on anything they liked, what fun I had in choosing my little purchase. Another shopping adventure I loved was when she took me to the market; the stalls would be buzzing with activity. The smell of sticky toffee apples would mean a gentle enquiry for a penny from Mum to buy one for me, which usually resulted in success, 'Weekes' sweet stall was very popular with the children. The warmth permeating from the brazier coke fire with the smeech of the hot roasted chestnuts, the fish stall with the owner shouting out cod and hake going cheap! The household goods stalls, which Mum used to like and sometimes she would make a small purchase, and the farmers' stalls where Mum bought home made black pudding fresh from the farm, all these stalls brought a little colour into our lives. Twice a year I could earn another penny as 'watcher' for the Chimney Sweep who came to sweep the chimneys on Saturdays. I was detailed to wait outside the front of our home and shout when the brush came out of the chimney pot, and he would pay me a penny, nowadays not many coal fires exist and chimney sweeping is a dying trade.

Sunday dinner time, I can remember Dad sharpening the knife on a whetstone, or he would take it out to the stone step at the back door and scrape it forward and backward at rapid pace to hone the blade so it would be sharp enough to cut the meat, how I hated the sound of that! After our main meal we would have a sweet. Often mum would make a lovely suet fruit pudding with raisins and sultanas. She would cut off slices to have with our dinner, or she would make a plain one and we would have golden syrup spread on a slice for sweet, sometimes it would be home made creamy rice pudding with nutmeg sprinkled on top. On Sunday evening my Dad would have a beef sandwich for his supper, at teatime we would have some tinned salmon followed by home made trifle, fruit salad, or apple tart with custard. When mum made the custard she would put the custard back in the saucepan 'to turn' and I always had the saucepan to finish off the custard left in the pan. Often she would make a junket and that could be tricky if it did not set correctly. One of my favourites was Lyons Swiss Roll filled with jam and I would unwind the roll and then I would eat the strips, another favourite was the small round tuppenny Lyons Ice Cream block. How I loved a round of bread covered in Tate and Lyle Golden Syrup or Golden Shred marmalade. On occasion there would be a black treacle tart with strips of pastry criss-crossed along the top. My dislike was Caraway seed cake and if I had a slice given to me I would pick out all the seed, meanwhile mum and Dad had ate their portion while I was still working hard removing the seed one by one. "Eat that or you will have it tomorrow!" said Dad, "There is to be no waste in this house, cake is not cheap!" I struggled to eat it but it made feel sick and Mum could see that I did not like it and could sense my anguish, she waited until Dad went out of the kitchen and she scooped it up, put it in a paper bag and hid it in her apron pocket to throw away another time so as Dad would not notice. From then on Mum always bought the beautiful yellow Madeira cake and I enjoyed that, I shall never forget that little act for that is love and kindness at its best. Sometimes I could have toast and butter, but this would take time as the bread would be placed on a long toasting fork in front of the fire and we would have to wait for the bread to toast. Although the gas ring in the oven grill could be lit to toast bread it meant burning extra fuel and housewives were very economical in their use of fuel. In the 1930's electric toasters were not available to everyday working households. Everyone had to wait until the kettle slowly boiled for tea as only those who could afford it bought the new three pint polished aluminium Creda Electric Kettle which took seven minutes to boil and costing twenty-eight shillings that came on to the market in 1939.

Monday would be cold beef served with bubble and squeak, (mashed potato and cabbage mixed together and pan-fried) and if any was left over, a slice of fruit suet pudding also pan-fried. On Tuesday if there were any meat remaining, it would be made into a cottage pie and served with greens. If there were no meat left Mum would make a hot pot with root vegetables using a neck-end of mutton of course, as we could not afford Lamb. Wednesday she would make a lovely 'Baby's Head' which was a steak and kidney pudding enclosed in suet pastry and wrapped in a cloth and boiled, or sometimes it would be put in a basin. Thursday was home-made pasty day, my mother's pasties were beautiful and the aroma of those lovely pasties permeated the home. She would use beef skirt for cooking as it had a lovely flavour. When she made the pasties they would be placed on the butter or margarine papers that had been saved for them to be baked in the oven. Fridays we usually had fish, but because I did not like fish as a child, mum would coax me into having fish cakes, which I did not mind. Occasionally mum would bake a tray of home made cinder toffee for my brother and I. Mum would buy a tin of Golden Syrup, tip some of the contents into a saucepan with a knob of butter and a spoonful of vinegar. It would be brought to a boil and tested by dropping a little into cold water to see if it was set. The toffee was poured into a greased dish to cool and the smell of that toffee wafting through the home was mouth watering!

Mondays was always wash day and if I was home from school on holiday I would help mum with the washing, I loved playing with the water and would revel at the chance to help. She had a large boiler made of zinc, which was known, as a "Dolly Tub," with a dumper to pound away at the clothes. Washing machines did not feature in those days, I would try to help by pounding the dumper but failed miserably, she also had a washboard made of wood and metal, to scrub Dad's dirty overalls, and I would try to help out. When the clothes were washed I would help with a dipper to remove the water from the boiler until sufficient was removed to tip the rest out. We would tip the last of the water into the courtyard and use it to scrub the court with a large bass broom. Then she would rinse all the 'whites' with Reckitt's Blue Dollies and I was sure all the clothes would come out as the colour blue. I would help her to guide the clothes through the wooden rollers of the mangle, and I would want to try to turn the handle but my puny little frame could not find the strength, so Mum would smile and take over the task. When we finished I had to have a complete change of clothing, as I would be soaking wet, she would tease me by saying "Do one job and make another". Ironing was very hard work for the housewife in the nineteen thirties. Mum would have a small iron placed on the hob of the grate, or on a ring of the gas cooker to heat. Then using a protective cloth in her hand to place over the handle of the hot iron, she would pick it up to iron the clothes, it was a long job and I was not allowed to help on these occasions. Wednesday was my favourite day, as children would have the half-day off from school, and I knew she would take me to the picture house called the Cinedrome in Ebrington Street. One year she took me to see Bambi and when Bambi's mother was killed I cried and could not be consoled. To help me cope with the sadness I was promised an ice cream during the interval. Sure enough during the interval I had my ice cream, when another sad incident occurred later I cried again, "Hard luck!" said Mum, "You are not getting another ice cream" I soon learned that I could not outwit her.

Lido Bathing Pool Plymouth Hoe circa 1930's. From a private collection.

In the summer months if the weather was fine, mum would take me up on the Hoe to Shackey Pool and Tinside to learn to swim with my brother (cousin) Ernest. Later when I could swim, I would be allowed into the Lido pool, which had been opened in June 1933, and the Tinside extension proved to be very popular. My mum had great difficulty in getting me out of the water, my lips would be blue with cold and I would shiver but still refused to come out, I wanted to swim the channel and nothing would stop me, so I thought. "Well if you don't come out you can't have an ice cream," she would say. My goodness! You should have seen me move; suddenly it didn't seem important anymore to swim the channel! Sometimes on the Hoe Mum would let me watch the "Punch and Judy" show and as our cat and dog was called Punch and Judy I would imagine it was them playing the part. In winter months between adverse weather conditions I would play in the courtyard, Punch and Judy would be in the courtyard with me and if I was jumping "Bumps" with my skipping rope, Judy the dog would try to jump too! Skipping incessantly and at the same time chanting away with the verses of the day with my new skipping rope which had strong wooden handles, it was funny seeing the cat trying to catch the rope. Punch and I would sometimes play "Johnny Noddy" together which involved having a piece of mirror to reflect the round

"Johnny Noddy" in the bright sunlight on the house walls or the windows and even on the stone court yard ground. He would try to catch the fast moving reflection and we spent many a happy hour playing together. Sometimes I would have my wooden spinning top chalked with different colours and I would whip the top vigorously to produce a kaleidoscope of colours. Another game I had where I would bounce the ball on the ground singing "One-two-three alera, I saw my sister Sarah, sitting on a bumbalera, outside a penny bazaar" and on the third bounce would cock my leg over the ball as it bounced high in the air, and nearly all the children of my age played double ball against the wall.

I was not allowed out in the street alone very often, I would have to be content with the courtyard and as it was a tenement house it was made quite clear that neighbours or other tenants were not to be annoyed. Occasionally I would walk up to Clifton Place to post a letter for Mum or Dad, the 1937 Post Box was around the corner facing opposite the Greenbank Hospital. I remember the letter opening was so high up I could not reach and I would have to rely on someone walking by who would lift me up to post the letter. That post box is still there to this day. If I had time and the weather was nice the large doors of the Greenbank Fire Station would be opened and I would see the firemen busy at work, I dallied a while to watch the firemen cleaning the fire engines, they were kept immaculately clean. Great Western Railway workers worked long and unsociable hours and it often meant that on occasion Dad did all sorts of different shift hours, and as he had been promoted from Fireman to Engine Driver his shifts became longer as the trains were not allowed to exceed sixty miles an hour which meant he would be gone for two days and nights. They used to call it 'Double Home' duty. During bad winter days if Dad was working, Mum and I would play with a pack of picture cards called Snap! Sometimes I would get so excited that she had to calm me down, it certainly passed away the hours. When the Radio was switched on I would cavort around the kitchen dancing to that catchy little tune "All I do the whole day through is dream of you" and saying to Mum "Look at me!" trying to impress as a dancer. Then the inevitable happened, crash, bang, wallop, I had collided with the kitchen table. "I don't think I will be a dancer Mum I said," "Perhaps its for the best she murmured." If Mum and Dad were both home and busy I would play with a large button tin which had hundreds of different shapes, sizes and colours of buttons. I would draw designs with the buttons, or Mum would ask me to sort them out in sizes. It took quite some time to do this, and when finished they would all go back mixed together in the tin, a crafty way to keep me occupied!

Running errands was always a pleasure as it meant two things, a cash reward and freedom to roam without supervision. One errand that stands out in my mind was taking a large empty bottle to the little general shop to have it filled with malt vinegar. The smell was so strong and the vinegar was kept in a wooden cask and sold by the pint. Sometimes I would buy a little pack of mantles for Mum (Incandescent gauze round a gas jet) for the gas lamp in the kitchen. Most times running the errand would be for my Mum or sometimes for a neighbour, and I would receive a halfpenny or a penny, which I would quickly spend at the sweet shop or I would go to an Ice Cream shop in Clifton Place, called Pipers. I would take my little basin and they would fill it up with ice cream for threepence.

Looking back to those years reminded me of the number of small shops in and around Clifton Street, Clifton Place and Armada Street. On the corner of Clifton Street and Deptford Place was a Fish and Chip shop called Hingston and they sold lovely fish and chips, now it is a Launderette. Just around the corner in Deptford Place was a little watchmaker repair shop and the gentleman who owned it was called Basil Hocking. At number one Clifton Street was Mr Fuge who had a General Store and at number Four lived the Chimney Sweep Mister Wallis, and at number seven was a shop owned by Mister Frank Trueman. Number eleven (right next door to where I lived) was Mr Alex Robins a gents Hairdresser but in 1938 it became a clothes shop run by a lady called Mrs C. Williams, after the war her daughter took over the shop and sold baby linen. In number twelve was a gentleman called W. Lee and he was an umbrella maker. In number fifteen (next door to our home) lived the families Tait and Cook. At number thirty-four in 1939 was a gentleman called Noel Skelly, but in 1940 the shop was passed to Mister William Bond. At number Forty was the Pawnbrokers Shop owned by Herbert Moule and at number forty-one was Mister M. Baker who later passed the shop over to Mr Samuel Husband. Clifton Place was well supported by shops considering the size of the area. At number eleven was Miss Hilda Coles and at number twenty-eight was Pipers Grocery Shop. At number fifty-three Mrs Heather had a little shop and at number fifty-nine was Mrs Carter's Confectionery Shop, we children would make a bee line for her shop after school if we had a spare penny. There was a cold meat and dairy shop at number nine Armada Street, I think it was called Rockeys, and I would gaze in amazement at the huge baron of beef on display in the window. There was a little draper's shop at number eleven, which was owned by Mrs Annie Mew and next door was another sweet shop.

Mum would often take me down to the Co-op shop, number 10 Armada Street, which had been built in 1888 to buy her weekly goods, this would teach me about shopping and the importance of money. She always had a list and every item was marked down with the price beside it, the prices of goods did not vary very much in those days, housewives knew their bill down to the last farthing. Price increases would only be perhaps a ha'penny or even a farthing, not like today when increases are sometimes almost doubled. The shop was a hive of activity and on one side would be the dry goods and in the other section cold meat and provisions. Those were the days when tea was sold in packets, soda, flour, sugar and cereals arrived at the shop packed in sacks, and the contents would be weighed into one pound quantities and issued in little blue bags. Brown and Polson's corn flour was sold in little packets, and the shop assistant operated a bacon slicing machine to cut off slices of bacon in various sizes requested by the customer and cold meat was carved by hand. Cooking salt came in large blocks and a saw was used to cut off the amount required. Later Cerebos table salt in tins came on the market and pepper was weighed and sold into 1oz-paper cup bags. Lard and butter came in fifty-six pound blocks and small quantities were cut off as and when needed, and it was fascinating watching the assistant using the butter paddles to pat into shape a small quantity of butter on the marble slab.

Household Soap such as the red Lifebuoy and the green Puritan came in long bars and pieces would have to be cut off for the customer. Sometimes Mum would buy a packet of Robin Starch for the shirt collars belonging to Ern and Dad. One of my treats would be the Lemonade Crystals that were sold loose in a little packet which Mum would buy for me, put in a bottle it made a lovely fizzy drink, or if funds were available some chocolate biscuits. I would feel so proud that I could rattle off my mum's dividend number, seven treble six nought! I would shout gleefully, pleased as punch.

The Co-operative dividend was an extra source of income for the hard saving housewife.

I would be absolutely fascinated watching the method of paying the bill; the shop assistant would take the money and insert it into a brass canister, screwing the top firmly on. Then she would despatch it on a cable to the cashier, whose glass-fronted cabin was set high above the shop floor, no doubt for security reasons. She could only reach it by climbing the wooden steps specially made for access, in those days only one person was responsible for the money, so the cashier would be most important. The shop assistant would pull a handle attached to the cable and the canister would whiz up the cable where it would be detached, and the change dispensed and returned in the same manner down on another cable. I would stand there open-mouthed wondering how it was done, "Come along dear," mother would say and I would question her all the way home. It was many years later that I found out it was called the Lampson Paragon system. Mum stayed with the Co-op throughout the war years, as every housewife had to register for rationing.

It is so strange how little things are still remembered after so many years! On the corner of Mount Street there was a Fruit and Greengrocers shop (it is a Post Office now) and I think the lady who served there was called Miss Steele and they sold bruised fruit cheaply after 4 0'clock. Often I could buy an apple, orange, pear, or a banana, little did I know when war was declared that it was to be seven years before I tasted a banana or a grapefruit again. My real favourite was a toffee apple bought for one penny, sometimes the apple was really sour but the sweetness of the toffee would cover that up. On the corner of Wellington Street was the Wellington Public House and on the opposite corner was a baker's shop called Sambells (previously owned by the Martin family), the smell wafting from his little shop was lovely and it made me feel warm and safe. The aroma from the hot rolls he baked would entice anyone passing his shop to go in and purchase. His customers could buy bakery items cheaply after a certain time; one could buy four tufts for a penny. How my Mum and I loved those tufts with jam and cream, she would scald the milk and let it set over night and skim off the cream in the morning. Sadly in recent years the old shop was destroyed by fire and it has now been converted into flats.

Be sure you shampoo— whatever you do!

However busy you are—always make time for your regular Amami shampoo. It is very important to keep your hair scrupulously clean — and isn't it equally necessary to see that your hair is looking really attractive?

AMAMI SHAMPOOS.... 4d. & 7½d. (Prices inclusive of Purchase Tax.)

AMAMI

FRIDAY NIGHT IS AMAMI NIGHT

Friday night was Amami night!

Every Friday (I would only see him on school holidays) there was a fishmonger who called with his cart. He would push his handcart up to the Greenbank area to sell his fish door to door; it was no mean feat, as there were quite a few hills. I think he was called Samuel Seccombe, my mum called him Sam, and he had a fish shop in 43 Ebrington Street, in later years he had a stall in the fish market. He was a hard working man and my Aunt would buy two lovely gurnards for Punch the cat at one shilling and also a lovely fresh ray for my dad's tea, for me perhaps, some monk or whiting which she would make into fish cakes. Friday was the day Mum would buy her favourite weekly magazine called "Woman's Own" which cost three pennies, often there would be a useful knitting pattern included. Mum washed her hair on Fridays and she used the Amami hair shampoo and their logo used to be "Friday night is Amami night." Friday was also the day Dad would repair all shoes needing attention, he had a three-footed last and he would put a new leather sole on the worn out shoes. I always made an effort to be on the front doorstep when the old lamplighter came around to light the street lamps. He was an elderly gentleman who wore a flat cap and carried a long pole and he always smiled and spoke to the children who watch him fascinated.

On Saturday's my pal Douglas Tait who lived next door at number fifteen, and was five years older than me, would push a handcart down through Gibbon Street to the barbican where there was a coal merchant and customers could load their own cart with coal at a cheaper price, or to Chubb's Coal Merchant at the Great Western Railway Depot in Sutton Road. I would sit on the handcart on the way down but coming back I had to walk. One Saturday I kicked up a fuss, as I did not want to walk back, I wanted to ride back, Douglas said no! I continued to badger him, so he finally relented and let me ride, when I got home my dress was black with coal dust and poor Douglas was blamed. "I am fed up with girls" he would say but vowed never to take me again, the following Saturday we both tripped down again. It is true you know-girls always win!

Douglas lived with his widowed mother and had two brothers, Jim Tait who was called up into the Army, and Charlie Tait who joined the Royal Navy.

The Tait family remained my friends all through life and now they are all gone too, Douglas died in 1994 and I still miss him. I remember some of my other playmates in Clifton Street apart from the Tait's. The Cook family also lived in number fifteen, where the Tait's lived, and they had a boy called Billy. Then there was a girl called Jean Hassett who with her two sisters lived in number five. Jean had beautiful copper coloured hair and we played together throughout our early childhood years we also went to the same school. There was the Shaw family in number four, and the Lovell family who lived in number sixteen. On the East Side of Clifton street at number twenty-two my friend Shirley Liddicoat lived, we liked each other and found that we had much in common, she was a nice girl and we became firm friends and had many happy hours playing together. We would go to Freedom Park, a nice little park where children could play safely. Sometimes we went to Beaumont Park. One evening a week the Salvation Army had an evening called "Pea Night" where you could buy a bowl of cooked mushy peas for tuppence and watch the magic lantern film show which Shirley and I enjoyed. It was a way to encourage the people to eat vegetables to maintain their health. These were the years when life was orderly and any disruption would be frowned upon. However, my life was to change, as the next trauma to befall me was to spoil my paradise world.

Lifebuoy Toilet Soap Advert circa 1933. By kind permission Unilever Historical Archives Merseyside.

Dilleighs Mutley Plain circa 1930's /1940's. Photo from the Archives of the Plymouth City Museum.

Dilleighs near the old Plymouth Market circa 1930'/1940's. Photo from the Archives of the Plymouth City Museum.

CHAPTER THIRTY-THREE

MY MIDDLE YEARS

Tender moments that we treasure are in our hearts to last forever.

In 1937 my little sister Valerie was killed in a road accident outside Sherwell Church in Tavistock Road, Plymouth, she was seven years old. What I do not understand to this day is why she was on her own at a main traffic area without adult supervision. What was the volume of traffic in those days that a child could be so easily knocked down? I was five years old when she was killed and I was never told. Her death was hidden away, unspoken, as if the loss of someone so poor was of little consequence. It was only in 1998 that I found out the real truth, as often over the years I would ask what happened to my other two sisters that I never saw again. I did not receive an answer to my letter from the present day Social Services when I asked for information about my sister Valerie. I obtained her death certificate from the Register Office, which quoted her inquest number. When I visited the Record Office to ask to see the Coroner's Report for the year 1937 it was missing but eventually I scrutinised the microfiche of the local newspapers in the Library, and there I found the report of her inquest. In fairness the driver, who came from Tavistock, had been exonerated, as my little sister had run out in front of the car.

What angered me most is when I researched the information, I found out she had been going to Charles Infant School while I was in Mount Street Infants School. We were only three hundred yards away from each other yet never allowed to communicate. In the thirties children were seen and not heard and were not allowed to grieve or share their loss. Thankfully today's society is more aware of the child's need to understand and come to terms with the loss of a loved one. I do not even hold a photograph of her and that really hurts! There is a photograph in existence held in the family album belonging to my Aunt Muriel. She had wanted to adopt Valerie but was again thwarted by my Grandparents. When she passed away I never saw the album again as the immediate family as their right claimed it. My older sister Violet will be featured in a later chapter.

I was a little older now and graduated from the infant class to the junior class in Mount Street School and so began my real education. There was quite a frightening time on one occasion when the medical school nurse reported an outbreak of chicken pox, which was then followed by diphtheria, mumps and influenza. Immunisations followed, and there were regular medical inspections of children at the school. Of course I was not going to be left out so I caught the dreaded chicken pox and was ill for some time.

The teaching methods were excellent and I was taught very early how to respect our teachers, and it was made quite clear at home that I would reap the consequences if I were to offend them. We called our teachers by their correct name and no first names or familiarity was allowed. Teachers, like our guardians, were equally the back bone of our character training for the future, and I think sadly that this is where it has all gone wrong in the modern world, a lot of parents over rule the teachers' methods of discipline. In the 1930's courtesy to others, chivalry towards women, respect for elders and the knowledge that one could leave their back door unlocked in safety was considered normal behaviour. Children were innocent of the dreaded word sex and they were not taught this subject at school, nor was it mentioned.

I would get up to the usual mischievous tricks that all children did in time. I remember one day I had an awful toothache and the teacher sent me home. Mum took me to see the dentist and on the following day I stayed at home being rather spoiled and allowed out to play in the courtyard, I liked that! My little mind raced with ideas. The following week I complained again about my toothache, and once more the teacher sent me home. I had only been home one hour, and was enjoying myself jumping and cavorting around in the courtyard and playing with my toys when a voice boomed out, "In you come young lady - you are pulling a fast one" well that was that! I was marched back to school post haste! I would stay in for dinner as from 1936 free dinners were allowed at school especially if you were a child who had lost both parents.

I remember Mum would regularly save some shillings each week, one shilling would be toward her next kitchen item. Mum bought pot menders to repair her kettle or a favourite saucepan for housewives could ill afford to

Lawson's shop 1941-1952. Situated on the corner of Compton Street and Saltash Street facing Pound Street (now Cobourg Street). The shop moved to new premises in the heart of the city in 1952 at New George Street next to the former Western Evening Herald building. Photo courtesy of Lawson's Limited.

buy new each time a fault occurred. Lawsons is where she would shop to buy her kitchenware. They were Ironmongers and they dealt in cutlery, pots and pans, and even sold Meccano and Balsa Kits, toys and Hornby Model Trains which my brother Ern liked to collect. During the terrible bombing Lawsons (who came from Newcastle) were to lose the premises they had rented from Winnicott's since 1904 at 13 Frankfort Street. So they set up other shops at 1 Pound Street (Tool shop) & 34 Old Town Street (Ironmonger). Lawson shop now is in New George Street. One shilling would be kept aside for the Providence Insurance to ensure she could pay for the Doctor, as they would charge five shillings for a visit, and another purse held the money put away for the rent. One shilling would be saved each week for Christmas fare and the capon for Christmas dinner.

I suffered dreadfully during the fruit season or in the hot summer heat as my body became covered in heat-bumps, Oh! How they would itch! Mum would paint my naked body with calamine lotion from head to toe with a small new paintbrush, and tie old mittens on my hands at night to stop me from scratching them. In the winter months for my persistent cough Mum would rub my chest with 'Vick' or 'Camphorated Oil' which was meant to help my breathing but it had a very strong smell and sometimes she would give me a spoon of Ipecacuanha wine to ease my cough. Most children of the nineteen thirties will remember their regular weekly teaspoonful of the laxative 'California Syrup of Figs.' I liked the very tasty fruity flavour. By now my Mum and Dad began to worry, as it was clear I was undeveloped. I was just like a doll and the welfare kept a watchful eye to monitor my physical progress. I was constantly being weighed, yet I had a very healthy appetite and I was always first when food was around! I can remember my foster mother always knitting. She would make me pretty jumpers in royal blue, and turquoise and green. Knitting was a cheaper way to keep growing children clothed, and I also wore a flannelette liberty bodice to help keep me warm.

My foster Mum and Dad must have been frustrated sometimes with my ways, as like all children I had my likes and dislikes. I was a very highly-strung child and of course with my red hair chances were that my temper would be easily aroused. My folks were to learn very early in my life that I adored animals and when I saw them I would spend time cuddling, smoothing and talking to them, unfortunately, it didn't end there. Mount Street School was only five minutes away from where I lived but sometimes it would take me an hour to get home. They would be worried, as my tea would be waiting for me. When I did arrive I would have cats and dogs in tow and Mum and Dad would have to go around to the homes in the area to return them. I always had a special empathy with animals. Eventually it was arranged for my brother to bring me home or mum would come down and collect me. After a while I was allowed to go home on my own again with a strict rule that I was to be home in fifteen minutes but I found this was alright as I could still have my game of marbles on the way home, or have a conker fight (which I always lost as the boys' conkers were always bigger than mine) or a game of cocky fivers.

Sometimes we would play hopscotch, by chalking numbered squares on the pavement and hopping from square to square. Nearly all children had their "Flickers," cigarette cards that we use to play. A card would be standing against the wall, and then we would chose the same picture and try to flick the thrown card on to the one stood against the wall. If you achieved it, you won that card and the one who got most cards or tops was the winner. Remember the Churchman's, Players and Wills Cigarette Cards? So many subjects to chose from such as Greyhounds, Cricket Players, Radio Personalities and Film Stars. In the long winter evenings after I had done my homework, we would play snakes and ladders, or perhaps Ludo. Another favourite game was Draughts, also Tidley-Winks. We also had an old bagatelle board with nails set in small socketed circles with a plunger to pull and release, sending the small steel balls whizzing into the numbered sockets, the highest number receiving a ball would be the winner. I would spend hours cutting out paper shapes making paper dolls or aeroplanes. Some times we would listen to the bakelite wireless, (no televisions, stereos or videos in those days) and what pleasures the wireless would bring. How I loved the Saturday serial "Told by the Brownie." The dulcet tones of the forces sweetheart Vera Lynn, the beautiful sweet tones of Deanna Durbin singing "I can see the lights of home," and her lovely rendering of "Ave Maria." The British Broadcasting Corporation had two stations which the working class favoured, the Home Service and the Light Programme.

Children in the right environment were never bored and my dear foster parents ensured that I was kept fully occupied and they were always there for me when I needed them. Christmas was very exciting and we would count down the days until Santa Claus would hopefully pay a visit. The visit to Santa's Grotto in the Plymouth Co-op would be very special as I thrilled at the decorations and anticipated a little gift. Often if mum had the time and could afford the extra sixpence for the entrance fee she would take me to Spooner's caves which was even more special. The corridor was decorated with bright silver and coloured paper, a Fairy and a Christmas tree gave further delight and always Father Christmas would have a little toy or boxed game as a present. On Christmas Eve Mum and Dad were grateful that at least for one night, they could get me to bed early without any fuss, but they lost out in the morning as at 6 am I was up and opening my pillowslip looking for my Christmas goodies. They knew it was a lost cause so everyone turned out of bed for an early breakfast. It had to be so! As I had a lot to do sorting out my goodies and playing with my toys, and I wanted an early start on my sweets! Although times were difficult I know that my dear second Mum and Dad had struggled and strived to get me various little presents to make my Christmas worthwhile, and they did! There would be three newly minted pennies, a tin of quality street sweets, some mixed nuts, a cracker, a pretty coloured spinning top, which the handle could be pressed up and down to make it spin, and a variety of fruit and chocolate. One year I had a wooden yo-yo and the fun I had with that gave me many a happy hour. There would be the usual socks and clothes, which would be left to the last to investigate, and a new exercise book with my very own pencil! I still think that to this day it was a gentle reminder to complete my homework, which was always done under protest. I would have a nice new skipping rope with handles and I would spend hours in the courtyard skipping.

My early aspirations of being a ballet dancer were quickly suppressed, as I was more interested in being a tomboy! The present I remember the most was when I had my first little push two wheeled scooter, which I would stand on with one foot and push on the pavement with the other foot and speed along merrily. Of course traffic was not like it is today, one could play outside with reasonable safety. My one disappointment was that I never had a Teddy Bear and I really longed for one but they were just too expensive for my folks to afford. On Christmas Day the fire would be lit early, Dad would stoke it so we could have a roaring fire to sit around later. Tongs were used during the day to select lumps of coal to place on the fire to keep the flame burning bright and a log was put on top followed by a shovel full of coal slack. Christmas dinner was very special, as on Christmas Day we would

have a roast chicken with stuffing and all the trimmings. When the four of us sat at the table there would be the usual bantering as to who would get the drum stick, of course Ern or myself never won, neither did Mum, as it was recognised that the bread winner always received the leg. Despite our suggestions to encourage our folks to toss a coin for the other leg, it did not achieve any success. However, Mum bless her, would make sure that Ern and I each had the wing and ensured we had the wishbone portion to pull to make our

My one wish was to have a Teddy Bear as a child. Children of the poor rarely had one. Photo from a private collection.

secret wish. I could not get to my Christmas Pudding quick enough, as I knew there would be either some silver sixpences, known as 'Tanners,' or silver threepenny pieces inside. We called them 'Joeys' but by 1937 the silver thru'pence had been superseded by the new nickel brass piece, eventually the 'Joeys' were withdrawn in 1944. The race was on to see who got the most, but the fairness was plain to see as both my brother (cousin) Ern and I obtained the same amount each! Ern and I would have a very small glass of shandy, which made me feel quite grown up.

Teatime was special with servings of peaches and cream or fruit salad, jellies and blancmange, and home made Christmas cake. I also enjoyed a thick slice of bread with Golden Syrup or Robertson Bramble seedless jelly. In the evening we would sit around the lovely warm coal fire and the men would have their special drink and the women had their box of cocktails, six bottles bought in a box comprising of Late Night Final, Egg Flip and Green Goddess, I would have my lemonade. Boxing Day 1939 we went to see the Christmas Pantomime Dick Whittington. We sat upstairs in the gods; children and adults alike roared with laughter at the stage antics. I became aware as I got older that families shared and cared for each other, family values were paramount and people were more tolerant, and neighbours were always there to help out when troubles loomed. There was a recognised order of discipline, respect and good manners.

My health was causing some concern as the dust in the streets from bombed out buildings and raging fires aggravated my persistent cough, which would not go away, and my lungs were becoming clogged with fluid. My growth development had slowed, and I was smaller than some of the younger children at the school. Panic was setting in with mothers as the dreaded scourge of childhood polio reared its ugly head. The doctor and nurses were constantly weighing me and there was a deep disquiet at my physical progress. At school I was allocated two thirds of a pint of milk each day while most children only had one third of a pint each. I remember one summer being sent to Maker Camp in July for two weeks to "Get plenty of fresh in your lungs" mind you, it was fun! All the children could run freely about in a wide-open space near the sea and it was a real adventure.

Ern was now sixteen and wanted a room of his own, having left school he started in his first job as a van boy at Leggo Wilson Laundry Company and Jim Tait, Douglas's brother, was in charge of him. Later Ern was called up into the Army. I came home from school one day most upset as my pals had told me a lot of animals were being destroyed, pets who had been abandoned after the March 1941 bombing or whose owners had been left homeless. I dashed into the kitchen looking for Punch and Judy our cat and dog to find them both curled up in front of the fireplace, I begged Mum not to put them down and she promised she would not, "While we can manage we will keep them" true to her word Punch and Judy survived the war and lived out their normal life span.

On April 4th 1941 my sister Connie died in Mount Gold Hospital of pulmonary tuberculosis, she was fourteen years old. I was not told of her death and we had not seen each other since we came under the care of the

Public Assistance Board, I was not allowed to go to her funeral so another family tragedy was kept secret from me. Then came the catastrophic events that were to change my childhood forever. On the night of 22 & 23 April 1941 five houses which were situated near the top of the hill, near Clifton Place blew up caused by the delayed action land mines. They had received a direct hit and some of the tenants were killed. Audrey Blatchford and her son Derek Blatchford, who was taken to the Clifton Inn and laid out on the bar whilst all the men helped in digging out the victims. John Cuthbert was also killed and Mrs Laura Staple a housewife aged fifty was severely injured and later died of her wounds in the City Hospital. It seemed strange that so much destruction was taking place, yet one incident occurred from the damage that revealed a link to history. That was when number seventeen Waterloo Street had their windows and facia board blown off to show that the house had once been a dairy shop and still had the old board showing the shop as "Purdy's Dairy"

When the explosion took place my Dad was at work, he had been promoted from a Fireman to an Engine Driver with the Great Western Railway. Mother and I, and my pal next door Douglas Tait, were in the kitchen of 13 Clifton Street when the explosion went off, and it was terrifying! The whole house shook and staggered like a stacked pack of cards about to fall, Aunt Muriel was shocked and her face was etched in fear. She ushered Douglas and I into a corner, held us tight to the wall and threw her arms out to protect us. There had been no warning as it was a delayed action bomb and no one was in the shelters. "God in Heaven!" she cried, "That is Aunt Ethel's house next door", which was number fifteen where Douglas lived with his widowed mother. Douglas and I were scared stiff, this was no game, this was real and I began to cry. Little was I to know that this incident was to seal my fate, losing forever the home security that I had thought was mine, believing I was special to my foster parents. I did not know that I would forever lose the security of a loving family environment, a situation that was to lead to years of heartache and loneliness.

In the withdrawal register of Mount Street School it is noted that I left school on the 25 April 1941 and was transferred to Stoke House Orphanage on the 26 April 1941. I am still trying to get this missing piece of information from the Social Services as to whether it was a direct order for

| 26·4·41 | Entered Stoke House |
| 30·4·41 | Evacuated, with Home, to New Inn, Clovelly |

The record of my entrance into Stoke House Orphanage and my evacuation to Clovelly. How incomplete the welfare records in the 1940's. In these four days I had been wrenched from loving foster parents, put in an institution with 50 children, lost all my school friends and buried alive for many hours when Montpelier School received heavy damage from parachute land mines in April 1941 and evacuated against my will to Clovelly North Devon and lost forever my loving childhood.

all fostered children to be returned to the Institution with a view to evacuation, or the decision of my beloved foster parents. The evacuation approval order issued by Winston Churchill was purely on a voluntary basis and did not occur until May 1941. My entrance into Stoke House care was fraught with heartache, I remember Mum taking me to the Emergency Rest School on Saturday the 26 April 1941, I see her now, clutching my hand, in her other hand my little case filled with some of my clothes. She was grim faced and quiet and my questions were not answered that day. Looking back I remember Mum sewing my name on labels a couple of days before I was put in the institution. When she said "Goodbye dear, be a good girl" my heart dropped as I clung to her hand and Miss Holden who was in attendance released my hand from hers saying "Come along dear, you will be alright" "But I want to go with Mum" I blurted out! Mum turned and walked away and I knew she was upset as I was. It was a day which altered the way I lived forever, my morale went from euphoric to ground zero in one moment, bringing cataclysmic changes which were to transform my way of life. Suddenly I was plunged into an alien environment, the first seeds of emotional turmoil had been sown and my loving childhood was gone forever. Now I had lost two mothers, two fathers and two sisters and in addition, torn from my school friends and all the things I loved. I was eight years and nine months old. Lost too was my confidence, self-esteem and the security that had enfolded me in those precious years. For the rest of my childhood I was to have a very traumatic life.

MARCH, 18, 1941.

WAR WORK FOR WOMEN

No Exceptions To Registration

CHOICE OF JOBS NEAR HOME

All women not in the services or munitions had to register for war work irrespective of their domestic duties and age.

The distress at being separated from family and friends was in itself enough to deal with; it must have been a government order as other fostered

Women had to register for work during the war years whatever their domestic position. On my evacuation in April 1941 Mum was allocated work as a Carriage Cleaner (1941-1945) on the Great Western Railway. Mum is second from the left back row next to the two men.

children were being brought in to join the Stoke House group. An instruction had been announced that because of government policy all women had to register for war work either by entering the services or to work in munitions factories or on the railway. In 1941 women between the ages of 35 and 45 had to register, as older women were now to find work even though they had domestic and family duties. However, it was only the beginning of my troubles as I was to feel the full savagery of Hitler's bombers.

The next day was spent adjusting to the turmoil as the staff assembled and registered all the names of the children. The Stoke House children had been at Montpelier since the 24th April and had occupied the best rooms. Those children who had lost their clothes were being fitted with garments, which had been received from the war relief parcels; I had my own clothes that Mum had put in my little suitcase. There was much activity, I was bewildered and did not understand why I was there. Night fell, and we went to sleep in a mixture of beds. Some children slept on the floor in the Assembly Hall. I cried myself to sleep on the first night. The second day was a little better organised as the adults sat us down to our meals and children were being sorted into age groups. There was a flurry of activity and the plan to send us out of the city was delayed because the institution children did not have anywhere to go. This meant another day and night at Montpelier School and once again we took to our beds. There were those who did not sleep that night – the German Luftwaffe being one. They decided to continue with their bombing raids, the night of the 28th April 1941 was when they struck and Montpelier School now being used as an emergency rest home was their target!

This time our defences were caught out, as there was no air raid warning, but no one could possibly have any doubt. We heard the bombers and the thuds of bombs falling in the distance, each thud came closer and I was now wide awake. Mum had always organised my trip to the shelter or to the washhouse at the bottom of the courtyard at the back of our tenements, but

I had no idea where to go this time as I was in a very strange environment. Just for a few moments – time was suspended and there was a deathly hush. Had the bombers gone? Then came a thunderous crash! Four delayed action time bombs had exploded. I froze in fear; my ears rung and my nose began to bleed. I watched the walls crack and split open, heard the splintering of glass and saw huge lumps of ceiling come crashing down followed by the crunching of the stone walls which began to crumble. I jumped out of bed and crawled underneath whimpering at the same time, "Oh Mum! Oh Mum!" I cried out, but no one heard. Now there was the darkness, the dust, the silence and the smell. I sobbed in my enclosed tomb and wondered if someone would come for me. Four parachute land mines with delayed action had been my nemesis. Frightened and unhappy there was nothing I could do but wait. I wondered about the other girls, as I could not hear anyone. Being buried alive was a terrifying experience. Hours past and I had stopped weeping, I listened, just listened, listening for any sound of rescue. Terrified and alone with my thoughts I began to think of the things I would miss. One thought that went through my mind was when would I eat again, how will I get my next meal? I felt a pang of hunger course through my body and suddenly I felt very thirsty, strange what children think. Time could not be measured, as it seemed an eternity.

Suddenly, I heard scratching noises and someone shouting. "Help! Help!" I cried out, and I heard a voice shout out "Quiet everyone!" so I cried out again, "Help! Help!" "Alright darling, we are coming," was the reply. Oh those magical words! I waited with bated breath as the sounds drew nearer and I could hear the broken stones being removed. A hand pushed away the rubble from my neck and shoulders and he pulled me clear saying, "Come on darling-you are alright!" His dirty, lean and weathered face, showing signs of exhaustion, with a tin helmet on his head, was the most wonderful sight to behold. He was one of the many unsung heroes of the time. I clung to him reluctant to let go and when we burst out into the street I was passed on to a nurse. Many willing hands had rallied to our rescue, the ARP wardens, NFS, AFS, police, servicemen on leave, off duty nurses, the WVS, the Salvation Army and civilians. Quite a few children and one staff member had been buried that night and Nurse Penna sustained an injury to her leg. I had escaped unhurt physically, but the mental scars remain. I still wake at night in a cold sweat if I hear the drone of a plane's engine and I cannot sit facing a blank wall, if I do I experience a claustrophobic sensation.

We slept on the assembly hall floor the following evening, as that part of the school was undamaged. That night of 29th April 1941 Devonport High School for girls where the Fire Brigade had a reception base received a direct hit from a high explosive bomb and had to relocate to another area. On the 30th April 1941 two buses were requisitioned by the Plymouth City Council to take us to Clovelly, North Devon. The boys were put in one bus and the girls in the second and we were driven away from the war torn city leaving behind the savagery of bombing and the destruction. Ahead would be a new chapter in our lives in the little fishing village of Clovelly in North Devon, where they had never experienced bombs and still lived their peaceful way of life.

CHAPTER THIRTY-FOUR

MY LINK WITH CLOVELLY

On the 30 April 1941 I arrived at Clovelly with fifty other children, presumably under the Government Evacuation Scheme, having come by bus from Plymouth, tired, exhausted, and totally bewildered, I was eight years and nine months old and could not understand why I had been taken away from my foster Mum and Dad. We were taken to the New Inn to be settled in. The boys were put in the annexe and the girls in the hotel, and what a motley little group we were, dressed in old second hand clothes, hungry, and wondering what on earth was going to happen to us. I clung to Gwen Tyrell (who had been told to keep an eye on me) Crying, "I want my Mum!" not liking being so far away from my home and confused at my predicament. "You can't have your Mum, she not here!" said Gwen, and I remember the panic I felt and the feeling of utter rejection. The next day was Mayday and the villagers always celebrated this day as it was the first day of Celtic Summer and was considered an important festival in England.

The children of the village were participating in the Maypole dancing at Clovelly Court, swirling around performing the dances known as the spider's web, the twist, and the plait, which we were allowed to watch. The villagers gave a party for the New Inn group and we wore paper hats for the occasion and Nurse Penna took a photograph of us outside. It is one of two photographs I have of myself whilst in the care of Stoke House welfare, when you look at the photograph take a look at our grey socks, Nora Batty had nothing on us! We were still so shocked and tired that we did not fully appreciate the kindness and effort that had been put into making us welcome. As you see from the photograph none of us is smiling, having come from war-torn Plymouth we were still in a state of shock. The strangest thing happened to us that first night at the New Inn. We had been packed three in a bed until things were sorted out but very few of us, including the staff, could sleep. We had been conditioned to be ready to hop out of bed and run for shelter when the bombers came. Now we found we could not cope with the silence! Many children wet the bed that night; they had suffered so much. I cried on and off for two days longing and hoping that Mum and Dad would come down and collect me and take me home but they never came.

Taken at the New Inn Clovelly North Devon May 1941. The Stoke House children had been evacuated from Plymouth on 30th April 1941. All rows read from the left. Front Row. 1. Betty Bennett. 2. Veronica (Vicky) Norman. 3. Dorothy Sabine. 4. Margaret Bailey (Head turned). 5. Violet Ray. 6. Margaret Ray. 7. Pat Richards. (Slightly behind). Middle Row. 1. Miss Holly Penna. (RIP) 2. Gwendoline Tyrell. 3. Barbara Baker. 4. Sheila Hanson. 5. Pat Roberts. (RIP) 6. Ellen Saul. 7. Margaret Pester (Tall girl). (RIP) Back Row. 1. Betty Newham. 2. Dorothy Saul. (RIP) 3. Rosemary Buckingham. 4. Ethel Gerry. Photo (taken by Nurse Penna RIP) courtesy of Mrs Gwendoline Collihole (nee Tyrell) Plymouth.

However, we soon settled and most of us were registered at the Clovelly School and the villagers would be fascinated by the way the children were assembled at the New Inn to go to school. We would be marched to school in crocodile formation of twos from the New Inn right through the village and up Wrinkleberry Lane. The villagers were utterly amused by the rigidity of this rule and it was their comments that gently persuaded the powers to be to ease the restriction. From then on, we were allowed to go on our own but with a ruling that the older girls were to look out for the younger ones and there were to be no detours from reaching school on time. Although we played a little on the way back from school we were never late returning to the New Inn as we would miss our tea and not many children missed a meal during the war years.

I do not think that the school had any problems with the New Inn children, indeed, we revelled in the freedom, for the first time the original children of Stoke House realised that they had come from hell into paradise. I had been more fortunate than they had because I not lived in "The Big House" as Stoke House was called. The home had been destroyed on Saint George's day 23rd April 1941 and I had joined the orphanage five days later.

It is strange how fate can sometimes change a way of life or even a moment of time. For the children of the New Inn our destined moment came one sunny afternoon in early summer shortly after our arrival from Plymouth. Lady Astor had decided to spend a quiet few days with her friend the Honourable Mrs Betty Asquith at Clovelly Court, where she would often come to play tennis or to write some of her Parliamentary notes. She was a childrens' champion and when she was about to visit Clovelly she would inform the staff at the New Inn, however, on this particular occasion she did not announce her visit. On impulse she called in and was flabbergasted at what she saw. All the girls had had their dinner and were sitting in the lounge knitting, sewing or doing puzzles whilst two older girls were cleaning shoes in the back lane. Miss Holden the Matron was in her office. Never one to mince words Lady Astor called Miss Holden out and angrily said, "What are these children doing here?" "What do you mean Lady Astor?" she replied. "Get these children out into the fresh air, they are not to be imprisoned like this!" Miss Holden's face was like thunder, but she held her peace. Lady Astor turned and said to us "Children go down to the beach and play" We did not hesitate! We all dashed out and tore down the cobbled street to the beach with the instruction ringing in ours ears to be back by four thirty. Of course we can only speculate what conversation took place between Miss Holden and Lady Astor after our departure but we were never again restricted with such severity.

We settled into an ordered system and later when Red Cross parcels arrived and new clothes from the British War Relief Society of America were received, which included school uniforms, we began to look much better dressed. I experienced my first shock of institution rules when my hair was cut to be in line with all the other girls. I had lost my ribbon and received in its place a basin cut all around my head with a fringe in the front. All the boys had their hair shorn. The girls all had a velour hat in wintertime and I can still remember that mine was always slipping down over my forehead because I had such a small face and head. Eventually one of the older girls Dolly Saul sewed an elastic strap on my hat so I could keep it under control. We wore practical navy blue knickers with a pocket in the leg to keep our handkerchief in. I often wondered why the boys were always asking us "Can we borrow your hanky?" We wore navy blue gymslips and white blouses, our socks were grey and my shoes were buttoned and I would struggle on using the hook in an effort to engage the button in the eye. However, one of the older girls would do it for me, it was their camaraderie that kept me going.

Later I received some new hand made knitted jumpers from my foster mum in Plymouth and they were lovely colours, bright green and royal blue, and some of my pals envied me and I remember feeling secretly pleased that there was someone out there who cared. I wondered if they would come to Clovelly to see me but they never did. Was it because I was "out of sight-out of mind?" or was it because they were not allowed to? I wish I knew, because it is so hard to even think that my foster parents or my grandparents did not want to see me. There is one thing every foster child quickly learns and that is, they are always "on the outside-looking in!"

Miss Holly Penna doing the thing she liked most-walking! Taken at Clovelly circa 1941-1945. Note the smiling face, the children at the New Inn rarely saw her smile. Photo courtesy Mrs Audrey Ray (nee Stacey) Uxbridge Middlesex. (Holly's niece).

Each morning every child had to make their own bed, (additional beds had by now been supplied by the Red Cross and Plymouth City Council) it took me some while to do mine, as at home it had always been done for me. The sheets had to be tucked in correctly. The corners had to be shaped as an envelope and the blanket and bedspread had to fit tightly across the top. Miss Holly Penna, the assistant, would inspect the bed and she would drop a penny on the bed and if the penny did not bounce I would have to make the bed again. I hated this task, as I never could get it quite right and it became a daily challenge, Holly Penna seemed to react with great delight at her power to make a child feel inferior. Holly's imperious nature toward the children often caused discord where there was none. She would sometimes shout at us "Come on you little Tykes!"

We knew we were there under sufferance. One morning my luck changed as Holly Penna was poorly, so Nurse Audrey Penna did the rounds and as usual I was last. When she came into our bedroom all the other girls from our room were already downstairs waiting for breakfast. She looked at me and she must have sensed my despair and saw the bewilderment in my face. She said to me "Leave that little one, and go down for your breakfast" my heart lifted as she said "I will make that later, or perhaps one of the older girls will do it" we all liked Nurse Penna, she loved children. I will never know the truth but I suspect she must have said something to Holly because from then on my bed was never inspected again with such draconian measures.

Once at the New Inn I was starved of affection and there were no more hugs or kisses. I was so homesick and found myself always trying to please everyone and trying to prove myself as being worthwhile; I could not understand why I was there, the anger and frustration of pitting myself against impossible odds made me feel totally rejected and it still hurts today. Was I so worthless that I could be discarded and placed somewhere "out of sight-out of mind"? The children appeared hard and bore the character of being institutionalised and I had great difficulty coming to terms with it, as I had come from a sheltered environment and I had been brought down to earth with a bump. My first minder Gwen Tyrell called me "Miss Prim", as I had not yet fallen into the ways and lifestyle of the orphanage. As I still had living relatives I was much luckier than other girls living in the institution as the girls who had no relatives already bore the ignominy of an institutional bearing. My health was not good as my lungs were constantly making life difficult with a persistent cough, as I had inhaled so much dust from the dreadful bombing at Plymouth and I was so tiny for my age. From being a self-assured little girl I became a lost soul, however, the girls soon rallied around me and adopted me as one of the gang and I quickly learned what was expected of me, and because we were all in the same boat a common bond quickly formed. Amid the bonhomie was the inner feeling of self-preservation and it was then that the first lesson of sharing was imprinted on my mind. Because some of the girls had no relatives living or who just did not care about them, meant that the institution children had a very special bond together and if I was in any difficulty the girls would immediately rally to my defence. It was not all doom and gloom. It was good to be brought up during the war, there were many shortages but we learnt to manage and make do. Furthermore, we were taught to share, there was a wonderful spirit of helping each other, alas, the same does not apply today.

Beatrice Thompson Cook at the New Inn 1941-1943 taken in the Peace Park Clovelly 1942. Photo courtesy Mrs Muriel Ellison (nee Gray niece to Cook).

When it was mealtimes we used to sit at a long wooden table one for the girls, and one for the boys, and we sat on long wooden benches. Children sat at the table in age range, little ones at one end, older ones in graduated age until you got to the oldest and tallest. We never started eating until we had said our grace, "For what we are about to receive, may the Lord make us truly thankful" and then we would grab our knives, forks and spoons, and eat as if there was no tomorrow. If you did not clear your plate there was always one of the other children who would!

In the early years the food in the New Inn was just eatable, and memories linger still of the thick lumpy porridge made with water and served with salt for breakfast, Ugh! Sometimes on occasion porridge would be served with molasses. Now and again we would have Quaker Puffed Wheat or bread and margarine, (The bread used to be a dirty grey colour and it was many years before we saw the lovely white flour bread). On occasion if we had stewed apple for tea it would be covered with thick lumpy custard; puddings consisted of watery semolina, stodgy tapioca, glue thick sago, baked rice or swimming macaroni. Main meals would be Spam or Corn Beef hash, mashed potatoes and greens; all the vegetables were grown in small plots in the village and surrounding fields and in Clovelly Court. For the first time many acres of land were ploughed up as British farmers struggled to feed the country. Everything that could be grown on the land was produced to keep the nation fed, how hard they worked.

Sometimes we had liver, or toad in the hole (sausages in batter) we did however, have a roast dinner on Sundays and how we looked forward to that. Other days for dinner we would be served with rabbit stew (including the head) and dumplings, and we would have to "hunt for the meat" or alternatively, we would have tripe and onions boiled in water served with boiled potatoes, and we would have to eat it or go without. As a change "Cookie" would make cottage pies with onions and peas, there was one meal that was really dreadful and that was boiled cheese and rice, whoever gave that recipe to cook ought to have been made to eat it. There were always loads of haricot beans, which were tasteless and bland as there was no tomato sauce to give it extra taste. One could not forget the smell of the cabbage and if a child did not eat their greens which was supposed to be good for us as it was considered as 'roughage' we were not allowed any pudding, and believe me that roughage was rough! In between meals if one of us was really hungry and we could catch cook in one of her good moods we could occasionally scrounge a round of bread and dripping or a Marmite or Bovril sandwich. When the meals were served Cook would bring the food out in cast iron saucepans and cauldrons and they must have been very difficult to clean. I am not quite sure but I think the cooking was done on an "Aga" or "Esse" cooker and the fuel used would be anthracite or wood. Staff would have the scalded milk simmered slowly in a stainless steel pot on the black cooker to make cream, which they had, for their tea. Because children could be careless with china we always ate our food off tin plates and drank our tea from enamel mugs.

Looking at those rations allowed, makes one realise the difficult task the staff at The New Inn, Clovelly, had in feeding the always hungry children in their care and they must have worked extremely hard to maintain some order. The cooking done en masse meant that good food would be spoiled by sheer volume and cooked without flavour. The staff received parcels sometimes, for the children, from Australia containing large tins of golden plums and red plums but they were very sour, although we really enjoyed them. Staff went home each month on a free rail, or bus pass, with their parcels of food as their rations were incorporated into their monthly allowance. The children were supplemented with extra food on occasion by the kindness of the villagers, fishermen and farmers, who often gave fish, vegetables, rabbits, apples and plums. Mr Cruse the butcher who had a shop on the Hartland Road near to the Providence Methodist Chapel had the contract for supplying meat to the New Inn, which was paid for by the Plymouth City Council, often, he would slip in some extra sausages. The butcher shop had been in the Cruse family care for one hundred years, and sadly the last family member to take the business on, Christopher Cruse finally had to close in 1999. He had lost trade to the big business combines, sadly many small businesses have gone to the wall unable to compete with the price war.

Every night each child joined two queues, one side would be to have our hair combed for nits or fleas. The child would kneel down in front of either Nurse Penna or Miss Holly Penna and they would have a cloth on their lap and a steel comb, any livestock found was promptly drowned in a saucer of water and vinegar. Each child uttered a silent wish that they got Nurse Penna and not Holly Penna as she really hurt by gripping the jaw and combing vigorously. She was very heavy handed, whereas, Nurse Penna was more gentle with the children. The other queue was for the delicate children who would be given their dessert spoon of Cod Liver Oil and Malt, or Virol, and once a month each child would be given a dose of Epson Salt in a cup of tea. When that task was completed it was off to the bathroom to be bathed and we would be lathered in Lifebuoy Household soap or Carbolic soap and our hair was washed in black Derbac coal tar Soap, which would kill all known germs! We cleaned our teeth with salt and water, as there was no toothpaste available because of the rationing. Then, scrubbed and clean, we would have a hot drink and off to bed. Sometimes a child would rebel against having Cod Liver Oil and if Miss Holly Penna were in one of her bad moods that child would be punished. At Clovelly if children were naughty we would be put in one of the dark cupboards and told if we did not behave the "Bogey man would come and get us." There is a very dark side to life when a child is placed in an institution, thankfully they did not assert this punishment too often, as the villagers would have quickly taken note.

In July 1942 I remember receiving, through the post, a parcel for my birthday. It contained a small cardboard box full of brass threepenny pieces. My sister Violet who was serving in the ATS had sent the parcel to me as she had been saving the coins for quite some time. She was a pastry cook by day and in the evenings she helped to man the guns and take her turn at guard duty. It made me feel so happy to think someone still remembered me. I never had a visit from any of my family whilst I was at Clovelly, it was not allowed, for what reason I will never know. All the younger girls were in the sitting room either knitting or doing French knitting (cotton reel with four nails on top then threading the wool over the nails to make long strips of knitted wool.) I hated being made to constantly knit when really all I wanted was to go out and play. Suddenly, Miss Holden the Matron came into the room shouting "Norman" (we were called by our surname) there is another parcel for you. "Oh Boy!" I thought. I held out my hands in gleeful anticipation, pleased that I had a parcel of fruit. I could see apples, pears, plums and two oranges! It must have come from my Foster Mother; or perhaps it came from my Grandmother and Grandfather. I heard the murmur coming from my pals as they had already made up their minds that they were going to be my friends while I had the parcel. I ogled the fruit basket as Miss Holden advanced toward me and I held out my hands to receive the parcel longing to taste the fruit. Then came a moment of horror as she lifted it high into the air stating, "You will of course expect this to be shared Norman!" "Yes Miss Holden" I replied meekly, secretly furious at not being allowed even to hold the parcel, after all it was mine! I would have shared with my friends anyway. However, she retreated taking my parcel with her and I could see the look of disappointment on my friends faces, goodness knows what my face looked like. Half an hour later back she came with an apple, a pear, and one whole small plum for each girl, but no orange! To this day I wonder who had them. Surely it was the incumbents responsibility to ensure that I received what was rightfully mine.

We rarely got special treats in the early days at Clovelly. Just on occasion Miss Holden would let the children listen to childrens' hour on the radio. On birthdays or Christmas the girls would each be given a doll and for a day we were in paradise until the evening when they were taken away and we never saw them again. I remember mine was dressed like a French sailor with a little bobble on its hat, I wonder what happened to that doll? It was a cruel thing to do to take it away because for the girls a doll was a precious passport to comfort. Every week each child would have their pocket money to spend and I would have five pennies, and we would be given one penny to put in the collection tray when we went to Church on Sundays. I have since found that each child was entitled to one shilling each.

As soon as I had my pocket money it was over to the Tuck Shop to see Auntie Glad, (Mrs Gladys Ellis) whose shop was just opposite the New Inn and I would select the sweets that I wanted. I only spent three pence on my sweets, as I would keep two pence for other things. I often found I was over the limit and I would have to readjust my order to make the best of my three pence. Furthermore, when I came out of the shop although I had only spent three pence the sweets I had came to more than that, Auntie Glad had put a few extra sweets in my paper bag. My favourite selection was the Barratts sherbet dip with a liquorice stick, a one-penny Milky Way candy bar, liquorice comfits, some pear drops and a blackjack chew. I would have loved a bar of chocolate but I was quick to learn that hard boiled sweets and liquorice lasted longer than chocolate, besides it took a huge chunk from the ration coupons whereas a conservative selection went further. We did not realise then, that we had more than our two ounces of sweet ration, but later, when we had a reunion in Clovelly, it came to light that many villagers gave up their sweet ration to Mrs Ellis for the New Inn children. Many of those dear villagers and Mrs Gladys Ellis have long departed from this earth but it does not stop me from saying now. Thank you and God bless you for what you did!

I vividly remember the three miles long Hobby Drive, a rich mosaic of colours whatever the season. Hundreds of trees of every type planted by Clovelly folk who treasured the countryside and treated it with the utmost respect. I had never seen so many trees in one area like the Hobby Drive and some were so tall it looked to me, being so little, as if some of them touched the sky. There were oak, ash, birch, pine, beech, maple and London plane, many covered in ivy, mosses, navelwort and polypody ferns. In some areas little streams of water ran down to the valley and how we children would love playing with the water. In the spring would be seen glorious groups of flowers such as the deep blue bluebells, crocuses, tulips, snowdrops, thistle, primroses, and the creeping jenny another member of the primrose family. The buttercups, which we would put under our chins, and if the yellow colour was reflected it would mean we liked butter, so we believed. Then there were the cowslips so pretty with their apricot yellow and orange umbels affectionately known to Devon folk as the tisty-tosty plant, the prolific violets, cyclamen, small groups of wild garlic and clumps of pink purslane and not forgetting the honey scented wild honeysuckle and the strong green ferns. Wafting in the breeze the London pride and golden hawkweed and on the banks yellow fragrant gorse and heath and heather, and in secluded corners the neat purple wild orchid. Here and there dotted around were hawthorn bushes and the may blossom exuded a nutty scent. In the long grass would be long stemmed ox-eye daisies, and white and yellow

spring daffodils, in overgrown areas growing wild the bright yellow of the corn marigold. Even the weeds brought colour such as the little blue forget-me-nots, yellow groundsel, chickweed, and the dandelions, which we were not allowed to pick as they made you wet the bed! In the summer the beautiful purple and white foxgloves swayed gently in the breeze as the bees worked tirelessly to collect their nectar.

The beautiful Hobby Drive where the children of the New Inn and other evacuees played happily during the war years.

Our world in Plymouth had been the grey of destruction. Hobby Drive brought colour back into our lives. I would play there with some of the girls,

281

Rosemary Buckingham (Topsy) who was detailed to "Keep an eye on me," she had a beautiful mop of black curly hair and had been nominated as Gwen Tyrell, who originally looked after me, had been detailed to other work. Another girl who mixed with us was called Bernice Waight; she was an evacuee from Plymouth but not from the orphanage. Barbara Baker, Margaret Bailey, Sheila Hanson and Betty Bennett were other names I remember. There are more I know of but they would not wish me to mention their names. Sometimes we would be in trouble as most of the girls would go scrumping, but I had the uncanny knack of being caught. Of course, like all children we always tried to blame someone else but no amount of remorse would prevent our punishment, somehow breaking the rules gave us a little thrill, hands up readers! How many of you went scrumping?

I remember the nice lady called Miss Ruby Jennings, who lived in one of the two cottages near the fountain, at the top of High Street. I think it was either number six or seven, Miss Jennings would let us girls use her garden path as a short cut to the Hobby Drive, where we would pick flowers and gather wood for one penny a bunch or batch. When we walked up through Wrinlkleberry Lane we would pick anything and everything that could be eaten from the hedgerows. Sloes, mulberries, blackberries, damsons, strawberries from the wild strawberry clover, blue-black berries of the common bilberry, sour-sabs, hips and haws and the dog rose which today are eaten in salads. Close to the hedges scattered here and there would be a perennial dog's mercury plant, (unfortunately not edible-highly toxic if eaten) a very rare plant not seen in this day and age. We had to be careful of the ragwort with its yellow daisy like flower and bright green leaves, as it was deadly for humans and livestock. We would occasionally forage for anything edible in the fields and often would select a mangold (mangle-wurzel) to eat if we were still hungry on our way to or from school.

The hedges would be a profusion of wild flowers with ragged robin; hollyhock, forget-me-not, pink campion, wild garlic, and the dainty sky blue speedwell. The pretty white Dog Rose and the ruby red Rose Hips. In the summer, here and there, odd clumps of Sweet William where seeds had freely blown in the wind from gardens and naturalised in many areas, and in the crevices of the hedges, clumps of Saxifrage. If we were quiet (which was not very often) in the hedges we would glimpse just briefly a shrew or a vole scurrying to and fro, they were shy and timid creatures and in the fields we would see rabbits bolting away to their burrows and see the lightening movement of squirrels as they dashed to their nearest cover, or scampered back to their dreys. How we would chase the common speckled wood butterflies as we tried so hard to catch them in our hands. We never did manage to catch one; they were too quick for us as they soared into the air on their delicate wings. But most of all I remember the beautiful birds and that was really something to see them and hear them singing. In war-torn Plymouth singing birds were a thing of the past. My time in Clovelly was to be my very first awakening to real nature and what a wonderful experience it was. Of course, I did not know the names of all the flowers and birds then but I have imprinted in my mind the shapes, smells and colours that have enabled me to match the names to each of the species.

Butterflies skip in skirls of wind.
Flit to and fro with pretty wings.
Daintily landing like a feather-
Anchoring to the fern and heather.

Hearing lilting song birds sing-
With melodious trill.
Softened my ascetic heart-
To accept the offered thrill.

The lovely village bird life,
Living wild and free,
Sent tugs of envy to my soul-
Wishing it was me.

Veronica (Vicky) Norman.

Various birds could be seen and heard, the blackbirds with their bright yellow beaks and the spotted song thrushes, the little blue and yellow blue tit which mates for life and the finch family, bullfinch, chaffinch, greenfinch, and the delightful tiny yellow and green siskin with its black markings on the wings and head. The little plump dunnock and the beautiful yellow hammer with its distinctive song "A little bit of bread and no cheese!" Flocks of multi coloured starlings with their glossy plumage and the pied wagtail wagging its tail and skeeting along on its little legs. The pheasant or gamebird as it was sometimes called and the common hedge sparrow, the cooing of the ring collared dove and the call of the wood pigeon. Magpies swooping down from the trees, their black and white feathers flashing in the daylight, their wings a profusion of glorious multi colours. The raucous cawing of the carrion crow and rook, and the dainty little ruddock (robin redbreast) with its pretty red breast, a shy bird and always alone, the darting redstart with its red tail and white patch on its head and not forgetting the call of the cuckoo. They made me wish I could fly with them and maybe I could fly home to mum. Funny what children can imagine.

Sometimes when we left school and made our way back down Wrinkleberry Lane we would on occasion see a farm hand working on the hedges replacing the gaps in the hedge to keep in the farm stock and trespassers out. It is something I have always remembered, as I had never seen it done in Plymouth so it was a novelty to me. Certainly it was an art in itself and I was not to know that I was seeing a dying craft and I dallied to watch him fascinated. He had a razor sharp curved tool called a billhook and would be slicing the branches of hawthorn, hazel and field maple. He would have upright stakes planted in the soil and then he would take the strips of cut hedging and thrust it through like a woven basket interchanging from front to back, what craftsmen these men were, the love of the land showed in his hard calloused hands, I never knew his name but he turned and saw me watching and he smiled, in the distance I heard a voice calling me "Come on Vicky-We will be late for tea!" I said to him "Goodbye" and he turned and answered "Cheerio young un!" and I ran down to join my pals. In the summer months on the way to school we would see the cornfield coloured golden yellow and the whole field would have patches of bright red field poppies known as the corn rose, what a beautiful sight.

Clovelly Donkeys coming up Wrinkleberry Lane circa 1998. Photo courtesy of Miss Genie Bolduc. Houston. Texas. USA.

The girls and I would sometimes be lucky enough to see the donkeys being brought up Wrinkleberry Lane to be taken to stables for a rub down and their feed, or in the village especially during the weekends. The men who brought the donkeys loaded with goods would ensure deliberately that every now and again the donkeys would have nothing on their backs and that was our signal to have a ride on the donkey, Oh! How I loved those rides! Two donkey's names I recall were 'Malachi' and 'Jenny' most of the children at the New Inn had their favourite donkey. I remember one occasion when I could not reach up to get on the donkey and my pals were up and away on theirs, "Wait for me!" I shouted, "Well hurry up then!" they replied. Mr Scott our gentlemen gardener and odd job man was standing outside the New Inn and on seeing my predicament lifted me on to the donkey, laughing at the performance. His hands were so strong and gentle and he often gave us little treats we were not officially allowed, he was indeed a very nice man.

The fun we had with the lifeboat men will never be forgotten, these were a special breed of men, to us they were Kings dressed as fishermen. They had the patience of Job as we swarmed over their lifeboat in the station with our grubby hands, and the thrill we had when they would do a practice run with six children at a time. The salt sea air blowing into our cheeks and the swaying of the boat would make our tummies turn. When we returned to the shore, they would lift us out on to the beach with their strong kind hands, their rugged faces showing a look of content on having given the orphan kids a treat. Many times the lifeboat crew would come to the New Inn with sacks of fruit or other 'goodies' rescued from the sea when ships were sunk in the Bristol Channel. Sometimes George Lamey the Coxswain of the Lifeboat would go out in the boat called the "Saucy Lass" that was owned by himself and his friend Bill Braund (who was in the Navy) to gather in the harvest from the sea. Thank you George Lamey and the Lifeboatmen of 1941-1942 the time I spent in Clovelly. The RAF at Hartland Point had their own fishing boat moored at Clovelly and they would often pass in some fish to the New Inn to help feed the hungry children. Many a Saturday I played on the beach, turning over pebbles, looking for crabs with Margaret Bailey, and Muriel Gray, the Cook's niece who would visit her Aunt at the weekend. If the water was calm we would collect flat stones and hurl them skimming along the surface of the water to see how many times we could make the stone bounce. What fun we had!

During the summer when the lighter evenings came the older girls were allowed to stay out a little longer, a marked contrast to the first months of summer the Stoke House girls were at the New Inn. It was lovely playing with other evacuees and village children. One very special day in lent which the villagers called "Lanshard Day" was spent playing in the Hobby Drive kicking empty tin cans around. It was a custom, which goes back to the middle ages, and was supposed to drive the Devil away. Afterwards we had to collect all the cans we had kicked about to return them for recycling for the war effort.

Nurse Audrey Penna and her niece Audrey Stacey taken 1938 whilst at home in Saltash Cornwall. Nurse Penna was still at Stoke House then but this is how I remember her at Clovelly. A kind person who loved children and it is she we would run to if in trouble. Look at that Doll & Doll's pram, how the Stoke House girls would have liked that!

Of course, we Stoke House children were not angels! We would get up to mischief at times and when we did we would laugh with some measure of satisfaction. One mischief I remember particularly being involved with along with three other girls, was the occasion when Nurse Penna had left her bedroom door unlocked and as the door was ajar we peered inside out of curiosity. Her bed was neatly made but it was the first of April and April Fools day was just the tonic we needed. Stripping the bed the girls hurriedly remade it into an "Apple Pie" bed, interlacing the sheets into one another so when she got into the bed she would not be able to put her legs down. I stood guard to watch for any sign of Nurse returning to her room as the dastardly deed was done, and we giggled hilariously. We dashed down to get our breakfast and saw Nurse Penna talking to Matron in her office and as we passed we had a secret smirk on our faces. Next morning we were a little apprehensive, as we all knew this would be the day of reckoning. For a few moments of glory we spent hours wondering what repercussions there would be – and would retribution be quick? As we meekly marched down to our breakfast we were very quiet, and most of us achieved a look of innocence. As Cook was serving our porridge Nurse Penna spoke saying, "I see someone was busy in my bedroom yesterday!" None of us would look her in the face so without speaking a word we had given ourselves away. She smiled and said; "I will forget it this time-do not let it happen again." Thankful we had been forgiven and grateful that nothing was said to Matron, we heaved a sigh of relief. We had been careful not to treat Holly Penna the same way as she had a Parti'Pris nature and would not have taken it so lightly. I shall always remember that little incident.

My first and only Christmas in Clovelly was very pleasant; the villagers had given a Tree to the children of the New Inn, it was kept in Matron's room. We were most content making the paper chains with various coloured crepe papers and helping to decorate the Christmas Tree with white cotton wool (courtesy of the Red Cross) to mimic miniature snowballs. Villagers, staff and teachers, had organised parties and we had some lovely teas. Scrumptious jellies, sandwiches, bread and jam, sweets, cakes, chocolate, tins of fruit, paper hats, balloons and a small present, I opened my present gleefully and found I had a new comb. The adults had done us proud as everything was rationed, how did they manage to save so much for the parties? Among the suppliers were the soldiers in the convalescent home who had given their chocolate rations to the children in the New Inn and the Red Cross nurses had supplied tins of fruit. Some of the children went carol singing under the auspices of an adult in control and I was lucky to be one of them. We worked our way up through the village singing a medley of carols and when we got to Clovelly Court the adult carol singers were welcomed with hot hop beer laced with nutmeg and rum, or mulled wine, we children had mince pies and a hot cup of Cocoa. Lovely! I was well looked after in the care of Stoke House at the New Inn, Clovelly, and have no complaints about my treatment. If I was punished for any misdemeanour, it was fairly given; I had not experienced (thankfully) the rigid treatment that the girls and boys had suffered in the 1930's institution of Stoke House in Plymouth.

My only inner anger, which I still feel today, was the indifference by the authorities in not telling me why I was taken away from my foster parents and the restriction placed on them to prevent them telling me. My Grandparents also were very angry at not being told I was placed in the orphanage, they had been evacuated to Buckingham after the March 1941 bombing in Plymouth. From that time on I always had the feeling of guilt that I had done something wrong and that I was put into the home for punishment and I have borne that punishment for all of my life. That memory of being taken away without ever asking me for my viewpoint will never fade, for without question it was to change the course of my life forever.

In July 1942 I was taken to Bideford by one of the staff of the home to a clothing shop to be measured for a new coat, I was so excited. The one finally chosen was green with a velvet collar and I thought it lovely; I could not wait to tell my pals at the New Inn. However, upon returning to Clovelly neither I nor the staff member, had the coat, so I was unable to boast about it to my friends. I asked if the coat was to be mine and was told "Children should be seen and not heard!"

My sister Violet who was in the Army was married at the Congregational Church in Buckingham, Buckinghamshire, to a sailor called Ronald (Bob) Grant (who came from Parkstone in Dorset) on the 2nd August 1942. I did not go to the wedding nor was I informed of the event. Because two of her grandchildren had died and Little Vi (my sister) was not living at home Grandmother pressurised the Welfare to release me into her care.

On the morning of 27 August 1942 I was awakened from my bed at six thirty, told to wash and dress and go down for my breakfast immediately. "What is happening?" I asked. "Come along!" said Matron. "Wash your hands, comb your hair, and eat your breakfast." Apprehensive, I began to wonder what was happening and then Miss Holden the matron came out with the new green coat with the velvet collar and as she put it on me, I asked "For Me?" she nodded and I thought I was special. My big ideas were short lived as she ushered me along to her office where Miss Male a social out worker was waiting, she had come from Plymouth to collect me and escort me to Buckingham a small market town in Buckinghamshire. Miss Male lived at Chapel Street, Devonport. "You are going to your Grandparents today, and Miss Male will be going with you," My views had not been considered, I wanted to go back to Mum and Dad in Plymouth, but it was not to be. So began my odyssey and with it the loss of all my friends and the sadness of leaving Clovelly. We had to travel to Bideford for the early morning train which meant leaving right away, so I never had the chance to say goodbye to my pals, when they came down in the morning I was gone, just like that! I was now ten years old and I had spent one year and four months at Clovelly, but it is an experience in my life that I will always remember.

When Gwen Terrell was detailed to other tasks Rosemary Buckingham was detailed to keep an eye on me and she was a regular playmate. A big girl with beautiful jet-black hair pictured here in 1943. I have not been successful in tracing dear Rosemary. I would like to know what happened to her. Photo courtesy of Ethel Finnerty (nee Gerry) Benfleet Essex.

High Street Clovelly 1939 picture taken by Mr Paul Ellis. The donkeys were a source of pleasure for the children in the New Inn. Photo courtesy of Miss Sheila Ellis Clovelly.

Clovelly 1942-1943. On the Donkey Miss Holly Penna (smiling again!) Right standing with flowers Miss Mabel Coombes (Cook's sister) Left Rosemary Buckingham (New Inn). Staff at the New Inn was issued with travel tickets to and from Plymouth once a month. Photo courtesy Mrs Audrey Ray (nee Stacey) Middlesex.

The Junior Girls July 1942 top of High Street Clovelly. From the Left. 1. Irene Ayson. 2. Violet Ray 3. Margaret Bailey. 4. Dorothy Sabine. 5. Veronica (Vicky) Norman. (10 years old). 6. Barbara Goldstein. 7. Betty Bennett. 8. Margaret Ray. Copyright by kind permission Mrs Audrey Ray (Nurse Penna's niece). Special thanks for copy of photo to lady at Plympton who wishes to remain anonymous.

CHAPTER THIRTY-FIVE

THE BUCKINGHAM EXPERIENCE

When I arrived in Buckingham in late August 1942 my Grandparents met me at the railway station; they were so thrilled to see me. In those days one could catch the train at Bletchley for Buckingham, I looked well and they were pleased, I was ten years old. We lived in a cottage at 6 Victoria Row Buckingham and the garden at the back of the cottage led to the river that flowed through the land. Next door lived a family called Gunthorpe and I remember three names as Violet, Pearl and Kitty. My Grandmother had fought a one year, four month battle with the authorities to remove me from Stoke House care. I believe my Grandparents did not know that I had been put into the home, as their home in 12A Buckwell Street Flats, Plymouth, had been destroyed in March 1941. They had been evacuated to Buckingham before 28th April 1941 so they thought I was still in Plymouth living with my Foster Parents. When they found out that I had been transferred to Clovelly and taken away from my folks they were angry and it would appear they were not even told by my foster parents or the welfare of my secret removal to an alien environment. I have still not found out the real truth about the missing days from 26-4-41 to 30-4-41. Social Services say they cannot find them, yet they have found my records starting from August 1936 to May 1952, strange how four crucial days of records which would tell me the truth as to how I was taken into Stoke House care should be so elusive? Taken away from my loving home in April 1941, my heart still ached to be back home in Plymouth. My time spent in Clovelly gave me a healthier outlook and I must admit I had enjoyed my time with all the girls to play and go to school with.

The life styles were so different in Buckingham than that of Clovelly. Whereas the evacuated children had been accepted and integrated with the North Devon villagers, in Buckingham the rigid class barriers were still in force. As the war continued it became clear that the Buckingham residents had not experienced the dreadful bombing that the evacuee children had endured and as such they were too far removed from the harsh realities of war. Sadly some evacuees were treated with contempt, as there seemed to be a hidden animosity that now and again surfaced when some villagers considered the evacuees as intruders into their controlled village life. Buckingham Town never knew the terrible consequences of a bombing raid and could not envisage the effect it had on the children from the cities who had gone through the shocking trauma. The local children laughed at my quaint Devon accent; my erudition did not meet their standards. In Buckingham I found myself isolated and lonely, I did not mix with other children, they looked on me as a rank outsider and they would taunt me with remarks such as "I am not to play with you because you are an evacuee and you talk funny." My Devon accent was different from the Buckingham dialect as they would address people as "Me Duck" and they would round off with another unacceptable remark as "Besides you are an Orphan!" as though it was a disease, or "My mother said I am not to play with you!" another hurtful remark was "Go home where you came from we do not want you here!" I had hoped that the London evacuees would embrace me in their playgroups, alas, they too kept to their own kind. I yearned to mix with them but Granny and Granddad said "Keep yourself to yourself" but Granny did not understand that I needed to mix with children of my own age.

How I missed my Clovelly pals and I was so angry at being taken away from Clovelly for good and never seeing my little pals again. Another thought constantly in my mind was that I was so far away from Plymouth. Because I was a loner the village children bullied me and I became more isolated. I know I went to Buckingham Junior and Infant School in Well Street in Buckingham, but I cannot remember a teacher or the school, with affection. It was a very old building with five classrooms for the juniors and a timber building with two classrooms for the infants and all the windows had been made shatterproof. The Infant teacher was a long serving employee called Miss Alice Palmer, school lessons for the junior pupils were part time as another school, Marylebone Central School, was sharing the premises. Often local children would attend for lessons in the morning and evacuees in the afternoon, the classrooms were overcrowded with as many as 40-45 pupils, so individual teaching was limited. School lessons were often out of sequence and the curriculum was haphazard, a far cry from the good teaching curriculum at Mount Street School Plymouth and the Clovelly School in North Devon, the best lessons were the nature and history programmes broadcast on the school radio.

Teachers were coming and going midway through a school term and I cannot remember any names of the teachers who taught me although the Headmaster was called Mister Thomas Ramsden. In the playground two Air Raid shelters had been built and I was bemused by the fact that the teachers did not hold practice runs to the shelter in the event of a German bombing raid. They had indeed been lured into a false sense of security and there were times I did not take my gas mask to school, however, the shelters were never needed and only served as an adventure playground for the pupils. The toilets were outside and we used cut out pieces of newspaper for hygienic purposes as real toilet paper was rationed and not many pupils could get toilet paper from the teachers. School meals were cooked in the Oddfellows Hall and eaten at the Secondary School Canteen. I blanked most of the three years that I attended at that school out of my mind. I do know my education was spasmodic and as there are no records to help me ascertain my standard I wrote to the Education Authorities in Buckinghamshire but they were unable to help. Strange that they did not even have the Admission or Withdrawal Register yet they never experienced a bomb, so they cannot say the records were destroyed in the war. On return to Plymouth my school report showed me as being two years behind the standard of education, yet when I left Clovelly my standard was on a par with all the other pupils.

Angry and resentful I lost my sense of identity and began to question relationships previously taken for granted as a feeling of guilt ascended on me, and I was beginning to feel heartaches. I realised I was a burden to my Grandparents and did not belong anywhere. To offset the loneliness I would spend hours in the garden feeding the chickens or down by the river playing with the water and feeding the ducks, or fishing for tiddlers and minnows near the bridge in Well Street. I loved going blackberry picking as Granny would make blackberry jam no sugar of course, but I enjoyed it.

I did not attend any Sunday school in Buckingham; granny was a strict non conformist. The religion I had been taught was the Salvation Army at Shaftbury Cottages Plymouth, where I had lived with my beloved foster parents in my early years. In Clovelly on Sunday the children, and myself, were made to attend All Saints Church that was a Church of England denomination. When the weather was nice I would sometimes play on my own behind the Buckingham Church known as St Peter & St Paul situated at the top of Church Hill. On one side of the church the sun would shine strongly, and I would wrap my arms around the shaft of sunlight and hug it close to me determined to keep it for myself. This way I could always have sunshine in my life, but when I opened my arms the sunshine had gone, it was hopeless, who can hold the sunlight or catch the wind? I hung on awhile hoping a playmate would turn up, and when they did not, I played alone, until I got tired of my own company and headed for home. On good days I would go swimming in the Buckingham swimming pool or sometimes in the river. Saturday morning I would go to the Chandos Cinema to see the films for children. I missed all my pals at Clovelly and I wondered if they ever thought of me, there I had lived with children, played with children and went to school with children, now I was alone. How I longed to see my sister Violet who was in the ATS. My Aunt Violet who lived with us was courting and if she took me out when accompanied by her gentleman friend she would make me walk fifty yards behind them so as they could talk privately. This was alright for them but terribly lonely for me. Have you ever wished that you could step back in time and change an event that was not of your making? Change it - to how you would want it to be? I did! Oh! How I wished that I could have stopped whoever made the decision to take me away from my foster Mum and Dad on that heartache day of 26 April 1941 with those three dreaded words: Entered Stoke House! It is said that there is a price to pay for love, but I never could come to terms with being the one to pay the price.

However, it was not all bad in Buckingham, on one or two occasions I was lucky enough to be invited to a tea party at the American Base or the Town Hall where the Americans put on a party for orphan children. That was lovely, the food and goodies were smashing, tinned fruit, ice cream, jellies, sweets, chocolates, and the fancy cakes were really scrumptious! We had to take a plate, a spoon and a mug with us to the tea party, and Granny gave me a large paper bag for me to bring home what I could not eat there. Games were played and each soldier had a child to look after, and we were really given a wonderful time and a present. Just before we left the party the servicemen set up two tables and two queues were formed for each child to share any goodies left over. I took out my paper bag to obtain my goodies and was most surprised as the girl in front of me had a seven pound biscuit tin and I thought there would not be any left for me. However, the Staff

293

Sergeant made sure every child had an equal amount no matter what size container it had. I had become aware of the importance of claiming food or sweets whenever or wherever. "Be sure to bring home what you can," Granny said. Bearing this instruction in mind on receiving my bag of goodies from one sergeant at the white table, I quickly nipped over to the blue table for a refill from his stock. His face was a picture as it appeared most of us had the same idea and with raucous laughter they filled up another bag of goodies. I can especially remember the big blocks of chocolate they had, almost like cooking chocolate, ecstasy to us kids. Food was still rationed and it must have been very difficult for my Grandparents to keep a growing girl, who was always hungry, fed, especially as they were so poor. Sometimes my sister Violet would send some money from her ATS pay to help out and my Aunt Violet helped to supplement the income as she worked in the E. & F. Richardson's Paint Factory (formerly a flour mill), however, it was difficult for her as she was saving to get married.

The recipes my Granny would concoct would make one smile or shudder today, but remember during the war you ate anything going because you were never sure where your next meal would come from. Rabbit stews were filling; sometimes there would only be a round of bread cut up in a cup of Bovril or kettle broth when money was short and times were desperate. Udders and riddies were boiled, chitterlings fried, and alternatively tripe with onions or home-made brawn would be served. There were times when I had a bad attack of bronchitis that Granny would give me a cup of hot tea, which included segments of a crushed marsh marigold flower (herb of the sun), which was considered an ideal remedy, Ugh! Older people believed that this beautiful wild flower was one of nature's great treasures, the use of natural herbs was not uncommon by the older generation in those days. Three lonely years passed and in August 1945 with war hostilities ended my Grandparents decided to return to Plymouth.

CHAPTER THIRTY-SIX

RETURN TO PLYMOUTH

Oh for the touch of a vanished hand and sound of a voice
that is still....

We returned to Plymouth from Buckingham in early 1945, the war was coming to an end and with no further risk of bombing many evacuees were returning to their former homes. However, families had to obtain permission

My National Identity Card shows some addresses during the 1940's/1950's.

to move throughout the country and every man, woman and child was issued with another new National Identity Card which recorded their known addresses for national security. We moved to a small rented house at 8 Green Park Avenue, near Mutley Plain, Plymouth. My sister Violet had left the ATS so she moved in with Grandma, Granfer, and me, as her husband Bob (Robert Grant-my brother-in-law) was still in the Royal Navy and had not yet been demobbed. My Aunt Violet remained in Buckingham as she had now married and apart from visiting on holiday she was never to return to Plymouth. I was much happier now having my sister living with me; it was the first time we had

been reunited as a real family. "When Bob is released from the Navy we will get our own place and you can come and live with us" my sister said. I was so thrilled because she was so much younger in her ideas and more on my wavelength, I was now thirteen years old.

On the 16th May 1945 my sister Violet had a baby girl and she was named Constance Valerie after my other two sisters who had died. I was so thrilled being an Aunt at thirteen, having my own niece; it made me feel quite proud. Now at last there would be family unity and for the first time since I was wrenched from my loving foster parents so heartlessly in April 1941 I felt more secure and content. However, once more fate was to strike a cruel blow! My lovely niece died on the 16th June 1945 of gastric enteritis, she

My sister Violet who I loved dearly in her ATS uniform 1942-1943.

had lived for exactly one month. We were all so upset and it deeply saddened the household that it was decided we would move away from that house and start anew elsewhere away from the unhappy memory of a little baby lost.

We moved to a three-bedroom house in an area known as the White City at 31 Holmes Avenue, Efford, Plymouth, and my sister Violet came too. I was so excited at having my own bedroom although there was hardly any furniture as we were so poor. My dear Grandparents Albert and Harriet (Nell) Foster had been bombed and burnt out of Buckwell Street Flats in Plymouth in 1941 and when they moved to Buckingham they had lost everything. Naturally when we did return to Plymouth apart from ourselves, there was nothing to bring back and as they were now in their seventies they could not afford to buy new furniture. My sister Violet bought some second hand furniture from her army pay, which she had saved, and the Salvation Army helped with an old hospital bed for me. There was an old dressing table sadly in need of repair and varnishing; however, to me it was sheer luxury, my very own dressing table. For my bedside table I had an old orange packing box which had two shelves and with the box stood on end and covered with an old curtain I then had my own bedside cabinet. My Gran

The wedding of my Aunt Violet to Arnold Pargeter, Buckingham. Back Row. Uncle Bert (Dad) Aunt Muriel (Mum) Gran & Grandfather (Pop) the Foster family.

and Granfer had decided to keep some chickens down in the garden so we could have a fresh egg and poultry for Christmas and I was very happy to help Gran and Granfer with mixing the food for the birds and cleaning the chicken run. Living next door to us was a very nice friendly family called the Damerells and I often wondered what happened to them.

Sometimes I felt down and out, as I could not have a new dress or spending money because we were so poor and I know how frustrated I was with constantly living in old second hand clothes, and if I went out I had no money to spend. All the other girls who had parents would show me the things that had been bought for them and I must be honest and admit I envied their luck. I loved the water and swimming, but in those days it cost six-pence to enter Tinside pool and although I could swim out to the rafts it meant dressing and undressing on the foreshore. As a young growing girl I wanted a little privacy, so I would collect all the empty pop bottles and return them to the kiosk. I received a penny for each one I returned and in this way I paid for my entrance into the pool which allowed me to use the dressing rooms, and I also earned enough to buy an ice cream and a bottle of pop. Looking back now I remember seeing some adults deliberately leaving their empty bottles for the children to pick up, I think they knew some of the children were poor and this was their way of helping us. On one occasion I remember earning a little extra as one of the visiting American warships had called into Plymouth for refuelling and the Yankee sailors had left many empty bottles lying around. I did something very daring, I went into Williams Savoy Café in Union Street and bought a cooked tea, I ordered steak, mushrooms, peas and chips! I thought I was quite the little madam eating out in style.

At home sometimes food was scarce especially if the folks were short of money; Granny would come up with all sorts of cheap food to make ends meet. In very cold weather we would have tripe and onions, there was quite a variety such as dark, plain, honeycombed and bible tripe, and it would be cooked in milk with the onions and served with potatoes. On occasion perhaps chitterlings were bought cheap from the meat market and these would be pan-fried, another delicacy the older people loved was boiled udder, riddies or pigs trotters. Granny would frequently make brawn from a pig's head, on another occasion we would have faggots made from scraps of meat served with chips or home made stew with oxtails. The one thing I did not like was when the greens had been cooked, as Gran would make me drink a cup of the cabbage water that the greens had been boiled in. "Ugh! I would say-it is horrible!" "You must drink it, as it is good for you! All the iron is in the boiled water and will give you strength!" was her reply. Sometimes when my Grandparents pension had run out and they were waiting for the next payment of money we would improvise to make the food stretch further. To stem the hunger occasionally I would have a thick round of bread spread with dripping, or watercress sandwiches and when

Lady Nancy Astor on a visit to Efford Community Centre in 1948. First left Front is my Grandmother Harriet (Nell) Foster who lived at 31 Holmes Ave. Second left back row is her friend Sarah Reid. Lady in middle back row (behind baby) Mrs Northcott. Second from right (front row adults) and person just behind are the Drake Sisters. Lady holding baby middle row Mrs Hexter. Third from the left back row holding little girl is Mrs Gregory. Rest unknown.

Gran ran out of money we would often have a basin of sop (bread & milk) or kettle broth!

Granfer was a dear man and he would now and then go to the Bluebird Public House for a pint and when he came home he always had some sweets for me, I never knew how he got them because sweets were still rationed. My Grandmother had some wise sayings and old-fashioned remedies, I can remember when the road was being tarred in Holmes Avenue she made me go outside to breathe in the air to try and clear my lungs. Grandmother would take me to the Efford Community Centre on occasion but I did not like it as the people were all too old or too young, I wanted to be with girls of my own age. My dear Grandparents had loved my sisters, and I know they loved me, it was just that the age barrier was so wide that I could not be old and they could not be young so I was caught in a time trap. I feel very sad now that I gave them so much heartache, but we can all look back and think of the things we should or could have done.

On my return to Plymouth I had a persistent cough and I was underweight, I was immediately sent to the Little Efford Open Air Council School on instruction from the Medical Officer as my lungs were once again cause for concern and I had become a delicate child. Run by the Plymouth City Council, which overlooked the Plym Estuary, its high altitude location ensured that pupils received maximum fresh air and sunlight. Mount Tamar Open Air School also shared the premises. Here was an eclectic mix of old and new school lessons, some school lessons were taken outdoors in the fresh air, and once again I had to try and pick up my schooling in yet another strange new environment. The Headteacher was called Mr. Frost and I remember a teacher called Miss Williams and Assistant Teachers Miss Holland and Miss Swann. The lessons were varied and quite different to

Buckingham School. Physical training classes, nature study, handicraft, were mingled with the normal educational classes. Each day the nurse would inspect the children, careful examination of the hands, nails and shoes took place and woe betide anyone appearing with dirty nails. Any child caught with dirty shoes, hands or nails were made to stand in front of the class and the parents or guardians of the children were reminded by letter of the need to send the children clean to school. After dinner we had to go to bed for an hour and a half and we slept on an old army camp bed with wooden frames, with ex-government blankets and a heavy canvas cover. The walls of the prefabricated classrooms designed like chalets would be opened to allow plenty of fresh air to penetrate. Once a week we would be given a hot bath or shower to stimulate the circulation, and we had to attend school on Saturday mornings. Every day each child had two thirds of a pint of milk aside from the milk used for puddings.

A typical weekly menu for the children of Little Efford Open Air School Plymouth circa 1930's/1940's. Copy courtesy of Mrs MA Vatcher former Headteacher Woodlands School Plymouth.

The food was reasonable as all the children who attended the school were delicate and had medical problems, which meant we had to have special foods and diets. Each day a select menu was earmarked with a variety of foods, every child had to be at school early to ensure that they had a cooked breakfast. It was always a cooked meal and their obsession with fried bread every day made me so curious that I asked "Why do I have to eat fried bread every day?" "It will grease your lungs." was the reply. If we had porridge it was made with milk and treacle. Another pleasure was real butter.

The grounds had their own vegetable plots and all the vegetables were grown there with the exception of potatoes which were delivered each week by a trader. The garden also had its own fruit trees; each day every child had an apple or some plums. Some of the meals were sheer luxury for the children, Stew with vegetables and dumplings, baked stuffed hearts or meat pie. For sweet, date pudding and custard, tapioca pudding, fruit salad (my favourite) rice and fruit pudding and suet pudding with Tate and Lyle syrup! For Tea we would have fruit salad or bread and jam. I must admit I tucked into every meal I could and I had a healthy appetite. I stayed there for six months and on showing a healthier improvement I was transferred to Charles Secondary Modern School near Shaftbury Cottages, North Hill.

I stayed in for school dinners as orphans with no parents got their dinners free while other children with parents paid threepence. I went to five schools in nine years, Mount Street Infants school, Plymouth, Clovelly School, North Devon, Well Street School, Buckingham, Efford Open Air School, Plymouth, and Charles Secondary Modern School, Plymouth. My schooling had been disrupted so much that I was two years behind in my education. This was a lovely school and I enjoyed every minute I spent there and what was most pleasing was the wonderful contact I had just around the corner in Clifton Street! My paradigms, Aunt Muriel and Uncle Bert (Mum and Dad) who I had not seen since I had been taken away from them in April 1941. It was on visiting them that I found out Mum had registered with the Great Western Railway as a cleaner for her war work in 1941. With Dad being an engine driver and Ern having been in the Army, it could explain why I had been returned into welfare care. I had asked my former foster parents many times the reason for my removal into the children's home. They never would say, despite my constant questioning over the years, it was in their opinion best forgotten.

Being so close to where they lived, every Monday afternoon when school was over I would go there for tea. My ex-foster mum would give me a threepenny piece for my bus fare home to Efford. The three pence Gran and Granfer had given me had been spent on sweets at the school tuck shop during the lunch hour; I was lucky to have free school dinners, which helped tremendously. I was now much happier as my sister Violet and I were at last reunited as a family, she was ten years older than I, but it was still wonderful to know her and to have a sister was to me very special. We did not go out very much as she was always very tired and had to rest regularly.

School leaving age had been raised to fifteen years after a government ruling in 1936, but exceptions were made if the child's guardians were poor as my grandparents were, they could take you away if they needed help of wages. Unfortunately this happened to me! In 1945 the Old age pension was £2 per week and it was difficult to keep me fed and clothed on such a meagre pension. As they were my legal guardians my grandparents did not have an allowance for me only the 7/6 orphan's state pension. I was not deemed, as "in care" so there was no boarding out allowance or welfare support for them. On my fourteenth birthday the orphans pension was stopped.

I was taken away from school in August 1945 at the age of fourteen and put into my very first mundane job as a domestic servant, which I immediately hated. I left there and became a baker's assistant at Hill's Bakery. Here I had a nasty accident trying to carry the large hot trays of pasties from the oven, I dropped one on my big toe and it was very painful. Next I started a job as a junior helper in Beechwood's Meat Factory in Alexandra Road, Mutley, Plymouth. They made pies and pasties and my job was to clean and be a general dogs-body.

My world was once again turned upside-down as after work one day on my return home as I approached our front door I was met outside by another teenager. On greeting her, I was surprised when she turned toward me and taunted me with words that I could not believe. "Your sister is dying then" she smirked! "What do you mean?" I asked! "Everyone knows!" she retorted! But I did not know - and I ran indoors and said to Granny, "It is true what they are saying?" She saw my anguish and she knew it was no use lying. "Yes dear" she said! "Why? Why? Why?" I cried! Angry, I asked why I had not been told, it was not fair for me to hear from complete strangers and not to be told by my own family was wrong. "We wanted to keep it from you, as you would not understand" Grandmother said. My sister had consumption or tuberculosis (TB) as it was known then, and only had a short time to live; she was only twenty-three years old.

My anger was ready to explode-but there was no one to diffuse it! No one could put my family back together, so what then was life all about? Who would help me to mend my broken heart and restore my confidence in a frightening world, my life felt wasted and I was sure I was being singled out as a unwanted reject, perhaps God was punishing me for all the mortal past sins of the Norman dynasty. Sometimes I would hide away and cry thinking it was me that was wrong and that I should not have been born to bring my family so much bad luck. This was the final straw that led to a downward turn in my emotional characteristics as I lost control. I did not get into any trouble with boys and I did not destroy or become a vandal. I became emotionally out of control as I vented my anger toward anyone who came near me, and I hated that girl who had taunted me. Children can be very cruel and I remember that I felt incomplete and inadequate like a pawn on a chessboard and it still rankles today, I lost trust with everyone, Who cared? Who would listen? I was not pretty, smart or rich, I was just an ordinary girl, yet it seem that as soon as I experienced some measure of happiness it was snatched away! I felt that I did not belong to this world and faced with a bewildering destiny I reacted strongly. I had to honestly take stock of my imperfections and accept that I did not have much to offer. Desolate, rejected, isolated and lonely, the thought of the approaching death of my loving sister made me realize that love was not for me and I considered the fate about to befall my sister was to be the ultimate punishment in life.

I became an angry teenager and at the age of fourteen in October 1946 while I was at work, I retreated to the toilets and there I tried to commit suicide by hanging. It is only because someone cut me down unconscious and rendered first aid that I am still here today. It is strange how one at such a tender age of fourteen, young and foolish, can find the courage to die but not the courage to live. There was no such thing as psychotherapy for young adolescents in the 1940's, the older child from an institution found life very complex, and as there was no family compassion to support them, it was difficult to relate to the expected sociability. Autonomy did not exist in the war years for children and indeed has only now been accepted as an important factor in giving children the right to have a say in their own future. I found myself constantly trying to please and succeed and indeed looked for praise and encouragement that I so badly needed. I was taken to a remand home at Woodside for three weeks and later I appeared before the court in 1946 and was sentenced to three years in an approved school in Leicestershire for my crime of attempted suicide. They allowed me to say goodbye to my sister and grandparents and the last words my sister ever spoke to me was "Be good dear or I will come back and haunt you" I managed a smile as I said I love you and I will be good. She has never haunted me and I miss her to this day. No one seemed to understand or care how I felt, the anger and frustration, the loneliness and grief, the embarrassment and confusion, the utter feeling of being worthless, and the loss of emotional control. I remember that awful feeling of having nowhere to run and of being trapped, there seemed to be no way out of the desperate situation I found myself in, perhaps I was being too narcissistic. As an adolescent on the brink of womanhood I found myself sinking into an abyss, devoid of controlled thoughts and in utter despair, and the pain still remains. Resentful and deeply depressed I asked myself, "What is life all about?" At some point in our lives all of us need help, a mentor to help stabilise the chaotic and emotional turmoil.

My dear Grandparents did not breach the generation gap in my emotional crisis. Seeking the right adult is important to young teenagers in the hope that they will find the right person to act with compassion and to expect them to understand young people who need a positive role model to relate to and who can communicate on their wavelength. To label a child as a failure at any age is disgraceful. Of course, we carry our past with us – we cannot escape it! I had a naivety that created nostalgia for days when the better things in life prevailed, I soon realised it was only an illusion wrapped in wishful thinking. It is easy to philosophize what should or could have been, all these years I have lived with the shame and now in my twilight years I hope that my God will forgive me and accept me into his home in heaven. Time they say is a great healer, but I still remember my feelings on my attempt at suicide as rage, bitterness, anger, and frustration. The emotional turmoil bubbled away underneath the surface for so long as I tried to come to terms with it and trying not to feel sorry for myself or to wallow in self-pity. But inside I was screaming, occasionally I would react with an emotional outburst or I would be just the opposite and shut myself off then no one could hurt me. I remembered feeling cheated of a normal childhood and happiness, seeing other children with parents having the things they had when I could not have them made me envious, we were so poor my grandparents could not afford the items I wanted.

There was no compassion at my attempted suicide, only punishment, and when confronted with the question why? I could not explain and merely answered "I was miserable" Who cared how I felt? Who would listen and understand? I kept the pain and sorrow locked away in my heart – yet my very being wanted to blurt it all out and talk about it to someone I could trust

St Mary's School Kibworth Hall, Kibworth, Leicestershire in the winter of 1947. We were snowed in and cut off from the outside world for a few days. I wonder if this mansion is still in existence today.

and who would be sensitive to my feelings. To be able to speak to someone who is kind and supportive and who would share sympathy is therapeutic. After spending two months at Woodside Remand Home in Plymouth I was transferred in January 1947 to St Mary's Home at Kibworth Hall, Leicestershire, to start my sentence of three years. It must have been a manor at some time in its history as it was enclosed in many acres of land. A welfare officer had accompanied me to the Hall from Plymouth and when we arrived after many hours on the train it was about seven o'clock in the evening. My thoughts were of cells and chains and brutal punishment and I was scared stiff, however, I refused to show this feeling and kept an outward look of calm. I know I was angry with myself for failing to commit suicide, as I could not even do that right! On our arrival it was a very pleasant surprise as all the girls and staff were all gathered around a huge log fire in a beautiful fireplace. It was a Girl Guide evening and at first I was suspicious, but my bad thoughts were soon overcome, as the staff were so friendly. We were given hot cocoa and sandwiches and I was introduced to two girls who were to become my friends during my time there. I later found out that is was run by a Church Children's Society and I was greatly relieved that I was not in a prison environment, during my stay there I was treated firmly, but fairly, and with respect.

In February 1947 I was called into Matron's office and told that my darling sister Violet had died, I could not respond as my heart froze and I walked away and made my way to the garden to contemplate how I would cope with this grief. They did not let me go to her funeral, so at the age of fifteen all my family had gone and I had not attended one funeral! Violet has a military grave in Ford Park Cemetery as she contracted the illness whilst serving in the ATS exposed to all winds and weather and long hours of day and night duties. For a while I became quite a misfit at the home as the staff struggled to correct my emotional crisis. Finally with patience and understanding I began to respond and in May 1948 after being held for one year and six months I was allowed home on licence and monitored by a very nice Probation Officer called Miss Latham. I was allowed out on licence with my Grandparents, they had requested my release from the authorities seeking began to respond and in May 1948 after being held for one year and six months I was allowed home on licence and monitored by a very nice Probation Officer called Miss Latham. I was allowed out on licence with my Grandparents, they had requested my release from the authorities seeking compassion on the loss of three of their grandchildren and as I was the only survivor they wanted me home with them. Also they had written many letters fighting for my release as they had considered my sentence as too severe, as I had done no wrong to any person, only myself.

On my return to Plymouth I quickly found work and I was visited frequently by the welfare officer at home and I tried to settle down into a normal life. It was difficult as my grandparents were old now and they did not allow me to live the normal life of a young teenager and my frustrations once again began to take hold. I drifted from job to job in an effort to improve myself; my dreams of becoming a Vet were long gone, as my education did not meet the standard required. I obtained a job as a junior shop assistant but I was always giving the wrong change so that was short lived. I tried to join all three services but the answer was "Sorry you are too short!" After the war the height was set to a certain level, during the war any height was acceptable! Grandmother was a non-conformist and she would not allow me to join in the activities of young people, but by the grace of God my welfare officer made a spot visit whilst I was home and she asked me what I would like to do. My goodness! It was the first time anyone had actually asked me what I would like!

When I was at the approved school they had a Girl Guide company, which I was allowed to join on good behaviour, and I remembered how I loved the Girl Guide meetings and being involved as a team. Every girl was taught to work and play with each other and to support each other and learn the sense and importance of team spirit, remembering this I said, "I would like to join a guide group" and as I was just over the girl guide age I was greeted into the Sea Rangers and I was quite pleased. My welfare officer had approached Miss Stella Johnson who was the Youth Officer appointed to oversee young teenagers and it was she who approached the Skipper Miss Margery Cross to invite me into the crew. Sea Rangers were the happiest days of my life; the camaraderie and adventure gave me a new outlook on life and I learnt the meaning of teamwork and helping others. I did not have time to think only of myself and this was good. My unit was SRS Devonshire and our

Sea Rangers with the launching of our new boat SRS Devonshire August 1952. The boat was built at Scantleberry's boat yard Pomphlett Plymouth replacing our old naval whaler that we formerly used at Sutton Pool. Starting from the left.

Commodore Bryant, Mrs Bryant, Pat Jenkins, Diane Creswell, Barbara Mills, Barbara Andrews, Margaret Casbourne, Margaret Harley, Veronica (Vicky) Norman, Sylvia Penny, Diane Burgess, Joyce Loram, Joyce Jeffery, Jean Mcmullen, Myra Green, Joyce Sweet, Margery Cross (Skipper) Janey Blatchford, Margaret Newcombe (Matey) Christine Smith & Margaret Honey. Oh! Happy Days!

skipper was called Miss Margery Cross and her brother Ben Cross was in charge of a Scout Group. The first mate Margaret Newcombe (affectionately known as Matey) was to become a life long contact; there were two other Sea Rangers units called SRS Musketeer and SRS Revenge. I struggled and scrimped to buy parts of my uniform each month and eventually succeeded in getting the full regalia. Each year we would participate in the Sutton Harbour Regatta or the Port of Plymouth Regatta, racing our boats against the Girls Nautical Training Corp, and most times we won! Not a mean feat as our boat then was an old twenty-seven foot navy whaler clinker built with fourteen-foot oars, and many happy hours had been spent on the "Pickle and Tar" work to the boat to keep her smart and shipshape. I was so proud when I won my Boating Permit to show I had qualified to take charge of Four Sea Rangers under oars for the River Plym, Arnold's Point and Hooe Lake.

Now life was more worth while and my morose feelings began to drift away. I remember one meeting when our skipper informed the company of a trip to London for a Sea Ranger gathering, and she informed everyone that we would be meeting Princess Elizabeth. My heart missed a beat as my Grandparents or myself could not finance that trip and I knew I would miss out again. However, what a thrill I had when six weeks later with only three weeks to go for the trip to London my skipper and first mate Margaret Newcombe informed me that the unit had been running raffles and jumble sales without my knowledge and they had saved enough money for me to go to London with the crew and even enough for additional spending money. I have never forgotten that wonderful and kind act which forced me to go to London with the crew and even enough for additional spending money. I have never forgotten that wonderful and kind act which forced me to acknowledge that there were good things in life, and what a trip to remember! Camping at Meavy in Dartmoor was very exciting, out would come the old army bell tents and equipment that had been kept stored through the winter. Kitbags, dixies and sleeping bags and blankets would receive there first airing and when we made camp each ranger had a task to complete after the tents had been assembled, mine was to collect punk and kindling (small twigs and dried leaves) to start the camp fire. Food would consist of baked beans and sausages, for bread we would have bags of flour, make a hole in the centre of the bag of flour, pour in cold water, stir with a stick then bake on a stone. We would sit around the campfire singing "Camp Fires Burning - Camp Fires Burning, Draw Nearer -Draw Nearer, In the Gloaming - In the Gloaming, Come sing and be Merry". Great fun! My next success was earning my Coxswain badge, which gave me the ability to take four sea rangers in a boat up the river with me as Coxswain, I felt so proud, and I know my dear Grandparents were thrilled.

Now there were so many things to do, to enjoy life, so much to look forward to, so many tomorrows. The shock and reality of life sometimes frighten teenagers as they suddenly become overawed at the loss of childhood and find themselves facing adolescence. In this modern age children are growing up too soon as they indulge in adult activities and consequently lose out on their childhood, but in the 1940's it was the other way, we were constantly restricted in growing up. I could not wait to grow up so I could make my own decisions and not have to knuckle down to institutional restrictions. In 1949 Aunt Violet came down to Plymouth on holiday from Maids Moreton, Buckingham, and it was decided that I should go back with her as she would find me a secure job and then I would live with her for a while as this would help Gran and Granfer. I readily agreed and on completion of her holiday I went back with her. Aunt Violet lived in a cottage in the village of Maids Moreton, in a small cul-de-sac called School Terrace. I stayed there for two weeks and then my Aunt Violet said "I have a job for you," excited at finding work so quickly, I reported to the National Heart Hospital in Maids Moreton in late May 1949. However, on arrival I was told it had been arranged for me to sleep in and that I was employed as a domestic servant! To honour my promise to my dear Grandparents I started work there in the kitchen as a cleaner but was very angry with my a job for you," excited at finding work so quickly, I reported to the National Heart Hospital in Maids Moreton in late May 1949. However, on arrival I was told it had been arranged for me to sleep in and that I was employed as a domestic servant! To honour my promise to my dear Grandparents I started work there in the kitchen as a cleaner but was very angry with my Aunt Violet as I felt I had been let down with false promises. Bewildered, I could not settle so in January 1950 I left and returned to my Grandparents in Plymouth. I quickly rejoined the Sea Ranger crew SRS Devonshire.

Then out of the blue came the next shock! Grandfather was taken ill and died. He was a gentle and dear man, and he loved us, as we loved him, he and my Grandmother had tried with all their hearts and meagre worldly goods to love their dead daughter's children. None of us were able to repay them, Valerie, Connie and Violet were also dead and I was just starting out on the threshold of womanhood so had not been in the position to do anything for them. On this occasion I was allowed to pay my last respects to my dear Granfer and this helped me tremendously to come to terms with the grief in a more natural way. In December 1951 Grandmother decided to go back to Maids Moreton in Buckinghamshire to be near her other daughter, my Aunt Violet who had married and settled there and never came back to Plymouth, other than to visit on holiday. I did not want to go with her as my work was here in Plymouth and there was nothing in Maids Moreton for me and I had made up my mind to improve my standard of education and seek better employment.

My two Aunts in the Orchard rear of School Terrace at Maids Moreton Buckingham during a holiday visit circa 1950's. Left Aunt Violet (my Godmother RIP) Right Aunt Muriel (Mum my Paradigm RIP)

I was determined this time to have a say in my future and I refused to go as my work was here and this was the city of my birth. The welfare was apprehensive, as I was not allowed to live alone at sixteen. What was I to do? I did the only thing I could do; I visited my Mum and Dad (Aunt Muriel and Uncle Bert) and asked them to take me. They did not hesitate, as my brother Ernest had returned from the Army and had married and obtained their own rented accommodation and was living at number 37 Clifton Street which meant there was a spare room at number thirteen. My foster parents stated that I would have to live to their rules, which I accepted without question, as I knew that I would be fairly treated. I moved back with my foster parents that I had been so happy with in my infant and early junior years. It was to be the best thing I ever did as I settled down right away and I decided to improve myself by going to night school determined to get away from mundane jobs. The welfare officer visited on occasion to check on my progress. The very last report made by the visiting welfare officer in May 1952, after a visit to my Aunt and Uncle in Clifton Street, was sent to the Children's Society Committee at St Mary's School, Leicestershire. They had insisted on periodical reports as I was still technically under licence. The report stated 'Quite happy with her Aunt and Uncle, thoroughly enjoying Sea Rangers and is now first class!' The two main factors that had put my life on the road to stability were my beloved Foster Parents and the Sea Rangers.

Bush Radio Factory Plymouth in the 1950's. Photo from City Museum Archives.

In the late 1940's and early 1950's many factories were opening and the wages were so much better, the day of the domestic servant was coming to an end and there were plenty of jobs with the rebuilding of the city after the terrible destruction of war. I applied for a job at the Tecalemit Factory and I was taught how to be a capstan operator and I was very happy and mixing with girls of my own age. I stayed there for a few years but soon found out that other new factories were opening and the employers were vying for workers tempting them with better wages.

The TR 82 Radio made at Bush Radio in the 1950's a very popular radio. My assembly line consisted of 22 very hard working young ladies and we were happy in our work until alas in the 1960's the Union was formed. Photo courtesy Mr Raymond Vittle Plymouth.

Lady Astor and J. Arthur Rank had opened a new Bush Radio factory in June 1949 at Ernesettle in Plymouth and rumour had it that the wages were far superior to what we were being paid at Tecalemit. In 1953 I took the plunge and applied for a post as an operator wiring and soldering radios. I did well and in two years I was made a key girl and in three years I had become a charge hand with twenty-two girls under my control. I organised every girl's operation on the radio sets to ensure they completed their hourly target so they would qualify for their bonus. The radio set made by my team was the TR 82, which was to prove a very popular radio in the 1950's, they were issued in two colours then, one in light grey and blue, the other in brown and tan. Meanwhile I continued to go to night school paying for my own courses and buying my student books. I would study some evenings at the reference library, as in those days the reference library was open until 9 o'clock in the evening. I would do this so as to avoid burning my Mums electricity at home. After night school which, I attended twice a week, I would call in at the El Sombrero cafe which was a homely and friendly coffee bar where young people could meet. In the 1950's it was located in Drake's Circus, because of its risqué setting most guardians did not like the young people frequenting the café, but it was harmless.

"Jessica" my little 1958 Island Blue four doors A35 saloon with 948-cc engine at Bush Radio in 1964 the year the car was bought. I still have her now in the year 2002.

I saved my spending money so that I could take driving lessons, as I wanted a car of my own. I saved for ten years then in 1964 I bought my own car. I was so proud as I did it all on my own and I bought a little second hand baby Austin, a 1958 Austin 35 four door saloon Island Blue in colour, which I named 'Jessica' and I was the second owner, and I still have that car today. Finally I left Bush Radio as the operators were earning more money than the Chargehands; the operators could earn bonus whereas the Chargehands had none. The workforce was now coming under a newly formed union and this led to a lot of discontent and many workers left the factory then. I wanted to enter the Civil Service where pensions would be paid on retirement so I continued to study hard and took my examinations to qualify from the industrial to the clerical side. Standards were high and open examinations restricted to a limited number, however, I succeeded in making the grade and having achieved what I had wanted to do I remained in the Civil Service until I resigned in 1993.

Now I am retired and I am still studying; I go to college twice a week for Computer Technology and thankfully have succeeded in passing most of my examinations. My next challenge is the Internet Course, as we the older generation must learn to become computer orientated or we will be left behind in the modern world.

Author's Footnote. To any young person who may read this book who is contemplating suicide, I can only say, think my dears, reach out and talk to someone you can trust. Talk to an independent person not connected with your family, as it may be a family incident that has put you inadvertently in that frame of mind. Remember that you would have to live with it and the shame for the rest of your life if you fail like I did, and furthermore, so will your loved ones! Life is for the living and love can only be gained by living.

In 1999 Age Concern made available and produced a booklet entitled, "A practical Guide to Coping with Bereavement" and this was issued free to the public. It is pleasing to note that they stress the importance that Children need to grieve their leaflet states "Children should be informed immediately by the person closest to them children are very quick to sense atmospheres and they should be told the truth in a simple and honest way. Identify personal items associated with the person they have lost. It is helpful for a child to look at a photograph or something that belonged to the deceased. Encourage children to attend the funeral: being excluded from the funeral may prevent children from coming to terms with the death, which could lead to problems later in life. Explain to children what happens at a funeral. It is always good that someone else close to them is beside them at a funeral to give them comfort and reassurance. Children have strong emotional feelings and they need to be attended to at this time. Bereavement is a difficult time for people especially when there are small children involved."

Myself Veronica (Vicky) Norman taken in 1951 proudly displaying my Sea Ranger Trefoil Badge.

A photograph of me taken in 1953 at the age of twenty-one and old enough now to vote. Living with my Foster Parents again smartened my outlook and I was happy earning my own keep.

Some of my working colleagues at Bush Radio circa 1950's /1960's. I am standing front right.

Left. My sister Violet Grant (nee Norman) Right. Aunt Violet Pargeter (nee Foster) with Judy our liver & white cocker spaniel. Circa 1946.

St Mary's School Kibworth Hall Kibworth Leicestershire 1947. Front row left is Miss Swann who gave me a bible for Christmas and I still have that bible today. Third right front row "The Matron Miss L Adams" firm but fair. Second right front row Miss Saunders. I am third from the right second row front. Note the dolls and the cats making life acceptable for wayward teenagers.

My sister Violet is fourth from the right front row. This photo was taken by S. Feather a portrait photographer from Anglesey year unknown. I do not know what regiment it is as movements were secret. I do know she was once at Grimsby with 484 battalion.

CHAPTER THIRTY-SEVEN

WHERE ARE THEY NOW?

The loss of those we love leaves gaping wounds, but we have the memory of a living love. Take Comfort. (Fra Giovanni AD 1513).

Raymond Blatchford. (RIP) (1931-1987)
Raymond Blatchford's mother was very ill after the birth of her last baby and was unable to take care of her children. Raymond's father had to work and with five children left to raise he realised he could not cope alone, he was advised by the NSPCC to have the children taken into care. With a heavy heart he placed four of his children into care in 1938. Raymond at the age of seven years old went to Stoke House, Gladys, thirteen, and Richard ten, went to Doctor Barnados; one son of working age stayed at home and the baby, John, was kept in the City Hospital. Children were allowed to stay on at the hospital until they were three years old if they did not have parents to look after them. However, when a child reached the age of three the welfare would approach relatives to see if any one would take the three year old, if not it would have to be put in a childrens' home. Raymond spent the rest of his childhood in the care of Stoke House and was evacuated to Clovelly in April 1941. Gladys and Richard spent their childhood at Doctor

(Raymond Centre)

Barnados; the baby John was one of the children killed in the hospital at Plymouth in the bombing of March 1941, he had just reached the age of three.

Father kept in touch with them all and it was always his intention to get them together again, but circumstances made it extremely difficult. Undaunted he never lost contact and when the war was over and all the children grown, the family reunited and promised that they would keep in touch. Raymond was seventeen before he saw Gladys again who was twenty-two. Raymond was a good-natured lad; but he would never talk of Stoke House or Clovelly. It would appear he just did not want to know and shut the unhappy experience away in his mind although his sister Glady asked many times. She and her brother Richard had a happy time at Doctor Barnados. When Raymond left the Scattered Homes he was apprenticed to a farm at Averton Giffard as a labourer. Whilst in his teens Raymond's father and a friend called Alfred Nix decided to bring him home to Pembroke Street, Devonport, Plymouth, in 1947 to have a family environment. Sadly Raymond's Father went blind but his brother Richard took care of him until his death.

Raymond never married, but did in later life find a lady friend who was to become his wife. But fate again dealt a cruel blow as he found out that he had an incurable disease and decided not to put his fiancée through the trauma of marriage to someone with a fatal illness. Raymond died on the 14 May 1987 at St Luke's Hospice in Plymouth and his sister Gladys Ward, who lives in York, was deeply saddened, at his loss. Gladys was thrilled when she received a photograph from the author of Raymond as a child as she never saw Raymond again after they were taken into care. She was so overcome at seeing her brother's childhood photograph and determined to see Raymond included in the book made the effort to supply the author with the information you have now read.

The Newham Family.

Betty Fleming (nee Newham) has vague memories of the Scattered Homes and Stoke House, but does remember running away once from Stoke House. Betty states that she was fortunate in having four brothers, who although separated in childhood, kept in touch all their lives. Having now reached the golden years, in her early seventies, her interest is in today and tomorrow rather than the past. Happily married for thirty years to John, her second marriage, she is enjoying her retirement. They live in Victoria, Canada. Leslie Newham her brother has only one or two memories of Clovelly and his life in Scattered Homes. He had no photographs of himself as a child and was thrilled to see the unearthed photographs researched by the author. He moved to Hertford in 1957 and married the love of his life Pat in 1961 and had one son and one daughter. A painter and decorator he is now enjoying his retirement. Larry Newham, another brother at Clovelly, sadly died in 1988.

Told to the Author by Muriel Ellison (nee Gray) niece to Beatrice Thompson (Cook)

Muriel Gray
Clovelly 1942.

My Aunt Beatrice Thompson was the Cook at Stoke House Childrens' Home, Plymouth, and at the New Inn Clovelly. My name is Muriel Ellison (nee Gray) and I was born on 30 January 1931. I used to visit Clovelly when my Aunt was employed there, as it would be a lovely day out down on the beach and exploring the cobbled streets. My cousin Jean McFadyen and I always went on a Saturday and we would play on the swings and slides with the orphan children, it was great fun! My cousin and I have a lovely photograph taken on the beach in 1942. My parents and Jean's parents would take us, so it was a real family gathering. We would go to the beach with Miss Penna and her sister, who were staff at the New Inn, and would go swimming and the Penna sisters would paddle their feet. We used to ride on the donkeys if we could; it was not always possible, as they had to carry their loads up through the village. I remember little Vicky (Veronica Norman) she was so well mannered, full of fun and always laughing, and I had often wondered what had happened to her and how she had got on in life. There were so many children who had lost their parents and I was secretly pleased that I still had mine! My Aunt tried in little ways to make up for the loss of love to the orphan children; she would slip them crusts of bread when the official matron was not watching.

My Aunt Beattie fell and broke her ankle in Clovelly and she was not able to return to her post after that. When I saw the cutting in the newspaper featuring Vicky and her search for the Stoke House children I was thrilled, as I had not seen her since she left Clovelly. When we had the first reunion in 1997 I met so many of the girls I used to play with, but I never knew the sadness they had experienced, and it was only through talking to them that I realised just how lucky I had been. Seeing photographs that we had never seen before gave me the opportunity to step back in time, and the reunion renewed many old friendships. My Aunt Beattie was very ill in 1943 and sadly she died in 1944, so she never knew how the children fared, she had a hard life and was a hard worker, it was not easy cooking for fifty children and staff with war rations. How Beattie would have loved the reunion!

Mrs Gwendoline M. Collihole (nee Terrell)

Gwen was born in 1927 and was abandoned as a baby at Woverton and spent the whole of her life in Scattered Homes and Stoke House never knowing who her parents were or from where they came. As a child in the Stoke House institution she never knew the meaning of love and as she grew into a young girl she suffered with a debilitating medical problem. This made her a vulnerable target and was often beaten; a stick kept on the wall for this purpose. She was made to wash her own sheets at times and her life at Stoke House was made unhappy and she was to endure constant beatings and would often appear with bruises all over her body. Alone and unwanted she could no longer bear the anguish and finally ran away from the institution. Children were always returned to the home when re-captured so life was made even more unpleasant. Transferred to Clovelly in 1941 she had hoped life would be more acceptable but her gypsy nature often conflicted with the staff members and she would once again endure a beating, her nose and mouth would bleed but she refused to cry. There was no one she could complain to and if she did know of someone she could not risk being a target again. Gwen remembered being unable to eat a meal that had been placed in front of her, so the staff placed the same meal in front of her at the table for a week until it went bad. The staff told her she would have no food until she ate that particular meal. Twice Gwen ran away from Clovelly. The first time she was caught near Clovelly and returned to the New Inn, on the second attempt she made it to Plymouth walking many hours, sleeping rough and scrounging food from the land, finally she managed to get a lift for the remainder of her journey to the City.

Gwen Terrell (Right) Miss Holly Penna (Left) Clovelly 1941.

On her return she realised there was nothing left of the town she had known. The city had been ravaged and burnt beyond recognition, she gave herself up and was placed in a home for unmarried mothers and for a while she worked for them to help supplement her keep. She never returned to Stoke House or Clovelly and she has stated that, "I have never forgotten and I shall never forgive them for what they did." Throughout her life she has had to bear distressing nightmares of those dreadful times. Gwen was started as a kennelmaid at Milehouse Plymouth and liked working there, but like many Scattered Homes children drifted into different jobs until her happy marriage and the birth of her sons. Now a Grand- Mother she showers her grandchildren with love, although suffering from ill health copes with courage and fortitude and she still lives in Plymouth.

There are many missing childhood friends that we wonder about: Where are the girls? Sheila Hanson, Betty Bennett, Betty was a nice quiet girl partially deaf. Rosemary and Iris Buckingham, Audrey and Margaret Pester, Margaret was last known to have worked at Milbay Laundry but a telephone call from a former working colleague has confirmed that Margaret had died, there is no information on Audrey. Barbara Goldstein, little blonde haired girl, one of the youngest in our band of orphans sent to Clovelly. (There are relatives looking for you, please get in touch). Joan Hodges was evacuated to Clovelly with her brother Dennis and remembers Miss Foster and Mr Hesketh the Headmaster of Clovelly School. Dennis and Joan now live in Plymouth. Found again were Ethel Finnerty (nee Gerry) happily married and living in Essex who, with her husband, attended the reunions at Plymouth and Clovelly. Ethel still resents the treatment she received as a child in the home. Patricia Maria Roberts was reluctant to talk about her days in Stoke House; the hurt was just too much. Pat lived in Devonport for most of her life until she was taken ill, her family decided to place her in a nursing home at Saltash for medical care. Sadly Pat passed away in November 2001 and her daughter is hoping to obtain her mother's records from the Authorities. Some past members of the childrens' homes do not wish to keep contact with the author and have asked to remain anonymous and their wishes have been respected. For those who recall the far off days united together in an unexpected adventure, kindled by the wartime spirit, and who remember our former childhood pals, time will never erase those memories etched deep in our minds. There will always be a place for them in my heart.

Close in the nest is folded every weary wing,
Hushed all the joyful voices; and we, who held you dear,
Eastward we turn and homeward, alone, remembering...
Day that I loved, day that I loved, the Night is here!

Rupert Brooke.

Dorothy, Ellen and Iris Saul were three sisters all placed in the home. Sadly Dorothy Saul has died and her daughter Susan stated that Dorothy would have loved the reunions and to be able to meet the girls again. Ellen Bryce (nee Saul) is married with children, she too did not want to remember those childhood days, and she still lives in Plymouth. No contact has been made with Iris Saul who was, in 1942, about to be adopted but it is not known if the adoption took place. Marlene Haddrell (nee Ayson) contacted the author after the reunion at Clovelly and was sorry she did not hear of the search in time, she now lives in Sussex. Marlene, sister Irene and brother Charles, were in the care of the Orphanage and they were at Clovelly. Barbara Hicks has been in touch, she was at the New Inn in 1944 and was one of the children boarded out with foster carers in 1945 when Plymouth City Council removed all the orphaned children from Clovelly.

Barbara Laurie (nee Baker) has been in touch and she attended the Plymouth reunion. She married her sailor husband in 1958 and raised five children. They still live in Plymouth. Barbara was separated from her sister whilst in care and never saw her again, it was sixty years before she found out that her sister still lived, but it is doubtful that they will ever meet. Sisters Beatrice, Lillian and Marion Lomax were all taken into care under the auspices of the Scattered Homes. Two of the sisters ran away from their foster family in 1940 unhappy and distressed at the treatment that they had received. Beatrice attended the reunion in Plymouth and she cried tears of bitterness as she recalled her childhood years.

Where are the boys? Leslie Travers, Fred Morgan, Micky Mare, David Stansbury, (your brother Ron is looking for you) George, Henry, William & Thomas Buckingham, John and Robert Lomax, Douglas Stribley, Fernley Dawson, Albert Pester, Donald Hamley & Bernard Prout. William and Derek Bartlett were both at Clovelly as their Mother was ill and Father in the Army. William was very unhappy at the family separation and states that he had a very bad time in the social care. The one thing he remembers vividly was the Mulberry Harbour moored in Clovelly Bay prior to the D-Day Landings. Information has been received on Victor Frood who loved to tease the girls and was always involved with high-spirited activities. His family has been in touch after hearing the appeal on Radio Devon for lost friends. They were so thrilled to hear his name mentioned. His wife Mary and daughter Shirley travelled to Plymouth to meet the author of this book, now they have a photograph of Victor as a child. He would never talk about his childhood to his family although he was happy at Clovelly. Many years later he took his wife and daughter to Clovelly but still did not tell them he had spent four years of his childhood there. Victor married Mary Jane in 1953 and they had one daughter Shirley. He worked for many years on various farms before finally settling with his family in Cullompton, Devon. In later years he worked for South West Water until his tragic death at the age of fifty-one in 1984 from a heart attack. Charles Ayson has been located and maintains regular contact with his sister Marlene. How has life treated you all? Wherever you are I hope that life as an adult has been kinder to you than your childhood. There are photographs that are available if required by contacting the author.

It was lovely making contact again with two of our former teachers Miss Williams and Miss Blann and receiving their memories for this book. Found again were Sybil Bond, Margaret Bailey, Pat Richards, and the boys, George Stuart, Ron Stansbury and David Dunbar who have graciously given their stories. Some former Scattered Homes children were still too traumatised to submit their stories, as the memories were so hurtful. Others have tried to keep it from their family as the stigma remains. Another two ladies had presented their stories but withdrew them later unsure of the consequences. There are thousands of citizens in the country who have experienced the same heartaches that we have. This book and our true stories will be a memorial to them and their sufferings.

AMERICA'S HEARTACHE.

It is fitting that we offer our condolences for loved ones lost to the citizens of the United States, and the British families, who on that dreadful day on 11th September 2001 experienced a cruel attack which killed many innocent victims. It has left a legacy of more orphaned children and many more broken hearted families. Across the Oceans and the Continents many people now grieve. Each generation has had its share of broken hearts. We offer our thoughts and prayers to the bereaved families of America as we, the generation of the 1940's suffered the terrible bombing of the Second World War, know the hurt that you will face with all its tragic humanitarian consequences.

This was an attack on the freedom of the western world, but adversity will always unite people in a common cause to stand firm against injustice and their spirit will not be broken. Many long years of heartaches will follow before peace of mind is fully restored. Here in Britain we extend the hand of friendship to you in the United States in the certain knowledge that you will keep your faith in God and his all-inclusive love, which embraces every race and creed. We know that through his strength you will endure.

> "My soul, there is a country where earthly conflicts cease,
> Where all thy ways are gentleness,
> And all thy paths are peace."

References and Acknowledgements.

Right Honourable Baron Sir John Francis Arthur St Aubyn & Lord St Levan. Fifth Baronet. DSC. DL. The Mount, Cornwall.

'A Short History of Higher Stoke & Milehouse' (1965) by David Ayers.

'A View of Plymouth Dock, Plymouth, and the Adjacent Country'. Published by A Granville & Son 1812. (Author not named)

A.S. Neill

Anne Morgan, Archivist.

Archive Library and Picture Editor Mr Peter Holdgate of Western Morning News. Plymouth.

Book of Knowledge Volume Two Waverley.

Brindley's Directories

Cadbury Limited. Bournville, Birmingham, England.

Centura Foods Limited Droylsden Manchester.

'Concerning Clovelly' by Antony Hippisley Coxe 1980.

Councillor Dennis Camp (Lab)

Councillor Vivian Pengelly (Con)

Deborah Watson, Archive Assistant.

Doctor Robert Crowte MBA PhD Barnt Green Worcestershire.

F.T.B. Lawson Limited. George Street Plymouth.

Fiona Pitt Human History Department Plymouth City Museum.

Flintoff's Directory 1844

HMSO "An Introduction to The Children Act 1989" A new framework for the care of children.

Honourable John Rous. Clovelly Court Estate.

Imperial Publishing Company Limited Hendon London

Imperial Tobacco Company Limited Southville Bristol

James Robertson & Sons Limited (incorporated with Centura Foods).

Kelly's Directories various.

Land Registry Office. Plymouth.

Lysons Magna Britannia 1822 History of Devonshire Volume Two.

Miss Ethel Mannin. Novelist.

Miss Jean Tozer Justice of the Peace Plymouth.

Miss M.A. Vatcher. Former Headteacher. Woodlands School. Plymouth.

Miss Sheila Ellis. Local Historian. Clovelly

Mount Street School Greenbank Plymouth.

Mr Dick Eva, War Memorabilia. Plymouth.

Mr F Cook Hornchurch Essex.

Mr F.S. Blight. (1951 notes) Stoke Library. Plymouth.

Mr Harry Clements B.E.M. (formally Clovelly) now Bideford, Devon.

Mr Ian Criddle Assistant Local & Naval Studies Librarian.

Mr Jim Graham Head of Plymouth Social Services and the Social Services Researchers.

Mr Keith A Russell. Former Head Plym Business College. Elburton. Plymouth. BA. PGCE. MED.

Mr Kenneth Seeby Perry Barr Birmingham.

Mr Paul Brough, Former Plymouth City Chief Archivist.

Mr Peter Wagland. Thornborough. Buckingham. Bucks.

Mr Richard Tuffin ASVA. Plymouth.

Mrs Ann Chiswell's notes. Stoke Library. Plymouth.

Mrs Christine Gardner Local History Enthusiast Plymouth.

Mrs Janet Pullan Social Services Secretary Plymouth.

Mrs Jean Richards (Nee Scott) Plymouth.

Mrs Joan Taskis Local History Enthusiast Southway Plymouth Devon

Mrs Mary Spann (nee Russan). Birkenhead. (Granddaughter of Mrs Emily Furzeman)

Mrs Maureen Selley Family History Group Plymouth.

Mrs Pamela (Trudie) Hodge Plymouth.

Ms Joy David Plymouth (Editor)

Naval Chronicle Volume 18 1807.

Nestle's Rowntree UK Ltd, York. England.

Nestles – Nestec SA. Avenue Nestle 55. Vevey. Switzerland.

Newspaper Devonport Telegraph (19 September 1829)

Novartis Nutrition UK Consumer Relations Office (Ovaltine).

Plymouth City Reference and Local History Library.

Plymouth Corporate Services Directorate. Civic Centre, Plymouth.

Plymouth Corporate Services. Department for Re-Generation. Plymouth City Council.

Plymouth Directory, Johns, 1823.

Plymouth Directory, Rowe, 1814.

Plymouth, Devonport and Stonehouse Guide by LLewellynn Jewitt. FSA.

Rachel Broomfield, Archive Assistant.

Sunday Western Independent Newspaper. Plymouth.

The Brodrick Collection, Devonport.

Trebor Bassett Limited, Research & Services Department, Hertfordshire, England.

Unilever Historical Archives. The Lyceum. Bridge Street. Port Sunlight. Merseyside.

Walkers' Nonsuch Limited, Stoke-on-Trent, Staffordshire.

West Devon Record Office Plymouth.

Western Evening Herald Newspaper. Plymouth.

Western Independent. (Sunday Independent) Extracted newspaper articles:

Western Morning News Newspaper. Plymouth

'Your right to know – Freedom of Information Act' published by The Stationery Office Limited.